LMS
LOCOMOTIVE PROFILES

No. 4 – THE 'PRINCESS ROYAL' PACIFICS

by
DAVID HUNT, BOB ESSERY and FRED JAMES

The new order could be seen waiting in the background as 46201, in clean Brunswick green livery, prepared to leave Carlisle Citadel station in the spring of 1961. Only two of the 'Lizzies' ended their days without AWS, both 6201 and 6210 being stationed in Scotland. They were also the only two that didn't spend much of 1961 in store. Just over a year after this photograph was taken, it was all over and Princess Elizabeth *was withdrawn. Happily, though, she was saved and only a few years later was being restored.* J. M. HAMMOND

WILD SWAN PUBLICATIONS

INTRODUCTION

For the fourth in our series on LMS locomotives we are considering the first true Stanier design, which appeared in 1933. According to several writers with first-hand experience, prior to 1932 the internecine squabbles within the various departments of the LMS to do with the design, provision and operation of locomotives had done little either to enhance the company's reputation or to optimise its locomotive stock. Whilst it is true to say that there had been some good post-Grouping designs produced, such as the Horwich moguls, 'Royal Scots' and 2–6–4 tank engines, there were also poor to mediocre ones like the 2–6–2Ts and 7F 0–8–0s. The introduction of the 'Scots' was also surrounded by circumstances that suggested lack of cohesion and co-operation between the various departments of the railway. It is also true that attempts were being made to standardise types and fittings as well as perpetuate those classes that proved most cost-effective. To that end, LMS versions of the Midland Class 2 superheated 4–4–0s, Class 4 superheated 0–6–0s and Compounds were being built in considerable numbers.[1] None of this, however, was evidence of any real common purpose or direction and much of it was reportedly bedevilled by ill feeling and parochialism within the company. When William Stanier was brought in from the GWR to take charge of LMS locomotive affairs, therefore, he was seen by many as its potential saviour and the shape of his designs was awaited with great interest. The first one turned out to be a big express passenger engine of a type not seen before on the LMS or its constituents – in fact, not seen to any great extent on most British railways – and was not immediately outstanding, although it adequately did the job for which it was designed. Some of its problems were caused by ideas that Stanier had brought with him from the Great Western but, fortunately, he was not a man hidebound by preconceived notions and so solutions were found. The result was a class of excellent machines that laid the foundation for what was arguably the best express passenger design ever to run on a British railway – the 'Coronation' Pacific – as well as the Stanier marque in general. Thus, we regard the 'Princess Royals' as an important class for inclusion in this series as well as, according to requests from readers, a popular choice.

It would seem a relatively simple task to relate the entire history of each of twelve locomotives in a book such as this. However, that does not take into account the fact that there cannot ever have been such a small class with more differences. Boilers and fittings, fireboxes, frames, pony trucks, cylinders, motion and tenders all exhibited wide variation, both as built and due to subsequent alterations. Collectors of our books will by now be used to our exhortations concerning the use of photographs by modellers and artists when trying to portray a particular engine at a particular period. Never was such advice more pertinent than for the 'Princess Royals', even though we have done our best to cover all the relevant details. Note that we are not going to include the 'Turbomotive', No. 6202, in our coverage as it was very different from the rest of the 6200–6212 series both in its turbine driven form and after rebuilding as a conventional reciprocating locomotive in 1952 named *Princess Anne*. We hope to include an article about it in a future issue of *LMS Journal*.

As with our previous volumes, there may well be statements in this work at odds with what has been written before about these engines. If we are aware of it, we bring attention to the fact and give our sources or reasons for disagreement. Otherwise, we can only state that we have done our best to be accurate and if any reader knows better we would welcome the input. As well as the usual sources of information, we have been fortunate enough to have had access to some correspondence to the late David Tee, A. F. Cook, and one of the authors from the late Eric Langridge, who worked at Derby Drawing Office when the engines were being designed. Indeed, Langridge was given the job of redesigning the type 1 boiler when it was found that its steaming qualities were poor as originally built.

As many will by now be aware, corrections and additions to our works are being published in *LMS Journal* and we want to encourage those readers with specialist knowledge or material to share it with us and the rest of our readership. To that end, please feel free to contact the series editor, David Hunt, either by post via Wild Swan Publications or by e-mail through our web site at *www.midlandrecord.com*. One plea we would make about criticism of these books is that it should be realistic. As an instance, there is little we can do about the type of comment that goes, 'Your table shows engines A, B and C at shed D in 19XX. I don't remember them, what work would there have been for them there?' Our only possible response is to point out that we merely go on the information we have available and that just because one person doesn't remember something doesn't mean it didn't happen (in this particular example, it must also be remembered that engines were often at particular locations only for a very short time). If, however, we are presented with additional facts or corrections based on documentary or photographic evidence or positive personal experience, we are only too pleased to publish them and admit that infallibility isn't among our attributes.

Although we try to use correct terminology in these works, we also believe it appropriate to use railwaymen's expressions. In this context, terms such as 'Black 5' rather than 'Class 5' and 'Lizzie' for 'Princess Royal' – both of which would have been familiar to those who worked with them – will be seen in our books. In our view, such expressions are not only valid, but also help to enliven the text.

Our thanks as usual go to Dieter Hopkin and Phil Atkins of the National Railway Museum for their help, not only in providing many of the drawings used in this book but also with other research material essential to accuracy. Our other 'team' member, Phil Chopping, has also been instrumental both in obtaining information and in collating what we already had and is proving to be a godsend. The late David Tee was also in the process of helping us at the time of his death and our good friend David Jenkinson has given us assistance with the livery section as well as some thoughts on boilers. We also owe thanks to Terry Essery and John Poole for helping us to obtain some of the enginemen's appreciation of the locomotives. Without all these gentlemen, our task would have been much more difficult. In particular, though, we must single out Bob Meanley for thanks. Bob was involved in the restoration of No.6201 and is now Chief Engineer at Tyseley and his assistance with all sorts of information, advice, proof reading and the loan of drawings has been invaluable.

David Hunt, Bob Essery and Fred James

ORIGINS

The first Pacific locomotive to run in this country, nearly fifteen years after the type's introduction in the United States, was the Great Western's No.111 *The Great Bear* in 1908. It was to all intents and purposes a 'Star' Class 4–6–0 with a huge boiler and trailing truck and was not a success, being a poor steamer and prone to hot trailing axleboxes. It also caused the operating department all sorts of trouble by fouling platforms, being banned from most of the GWR system and awkward to turn because its overall wheelbase of 60ft 3¼ in meant it couldn't use most turntables. Eventually it was broken up in 1924 and some parts were used in the construction of a 'Castle' Class engine. The next 4–6–2s on British metals were built by the North Eastern and Great Northern Railways in 1922 and ten years later the LNER had 75 of the GNR design. Designed to haul 600 ton trains over long distances, the Gresley Pacifics were successful machines that were steadily improved with long lap and long travel valves, higher pressure boilers and large superheaters.

Interest in Pacifics had been extant in drawing offices and CME's staffs of the LMS since before the Grouping, driven largely by the requirements of the West Coast Main Line (WCML). The first tentative proposal for a 4–6–2 from one of the constituents had been made by J. F. McIntosh in 1913, just before he retired as CME of the Caledonian. It was intended to reduce the need for double-heading expresses between Glasgow and Carlisle but nothing had come of it. After the First World War, the WCML expresses south of Carlisle were handled mainly by the L&NWR 'Claughtons' but they were suffering from a host of problems with deteriorating performances, cracked frames, failing axleboxes, broken springs etc. and double-heading was endemic. North of the border the situation was little better, the Pickersgill 4–6–0s having proved disappointing and the older Caledonian 4–4–0s and 4–6–0s still providing most of the motive power in pairs. George Hughes of the L&YR, who became CME of the combined L&NWR/L&YR system in 1922 and then the LMS in 1923, identified the need for stronger, more powerful locomotives for the WCML expresses. As well as putting his rebuilt 4–6–0s to work between Crewe and Carlisle, therefore, he instituted design

LMS express power. With the valves lifting and smoke-filled exhaust, No. 6209 is seen here pulling away from Rugby with a heavy train in April 1948. Even though they were to some extent eclipsed by the later and more numerous 'Coronations', only a few years after being introduced into service, the 'Lizzies' continued to haul the fastest and heaviest West Coast expresses until their eventual demise fourteen years after this picture was taken.   J. A. G. H. COLTAS

studies for a Pacific.[2] A diagram for one was produced in 1923 but was succeeded in June 1924 by another proposal that was to have shared a boiler and other components with a 2–8–2 freight engine. The boiler was to have been 19ft between tubeplates, 5ft 9in inside diameter and pressed to 180psi, which was the highest boiler pressure Hughes would tolerate. An 8ft long firebox with forward combustion chamber and 42 sq ft grate was proposed, together with a 600 sq ft superheater and 168 small tubes giving a total of 2,715 sq ft heating surface. Its four cylinders, arranged in the manner of the rebuilt Hughes 4–6–0, would have been 18½ in x 26in. Coupled wheels were to have been 6ft 9in diameter on a 7ft 3in + 7ft 3in wheelbase, total wheelbase 37ft and estimated weight in working order 95 tons. It would have been coupled to an eight-wheeled tender weighing a notional 54 tons, of which 8 tons was coal.

A few months later the design was amended to have three cylinders but the whole exercise was virtually negated, at least for a time, by the insistence of J. E. Anderson and J. H. Follows that the 'small engine policy' of the Midland's last years

would be applied to the whole LMS system. We won't go into the arguments about 'Midlandisation' and the tenets of Anderson, Follows and some other like-minded Derby men who ended up in high places within the LMS, as they are not really germane to this book. Suffice it to say that ex-Midland men seem not only to have held key positions, but to have persuaded the Board to adopt the structure developed for the Midland after 1909. In this arrangement, a Superintendent of Motive Power was jointly responsible to the CME for maintenance of locomotives and to the General Superintendent for running trains. Anderson, as Superintendent of Motive Power, could not himself override the CME but with the backing of Follows, who was Chief General Superintendent and in 1927 became one of two Vice Presidents in charge of operations, his opinions carried a lot of weight. These men were not ignorant of the realities of running a railway, nor were they organising some sort of conspiracy, but were advancing what they saw as the most cost-effective answers to the new company's requirements. The answer to the WCML problems proposed by Anderson and supported by Follows was to split the trains and run a 'little but often' service. Motive power was to be provided by the LMS version of the Midland Compound, which had performed well in comparative trials against various engines from the other constituent companies and was a proven economical and cost-effective machine. For a while, therefore, work on a Pacific was all but suspended, which at least enabled progress to be made with the Horwich mogul before Hughes' resignation. Whether the alteration of the Pacific scheme to three cylinders was in order to win the support of Anderson, who favoured such layouts, we don't know.

The operating conditions of the WCML, however, didn't suit the Follows/Anderson concept because the traffic density was already too great to allow more, smaller trains to be used. Hence, double-heading was still frequently employed and eventually even Follows and Anderson had to admit that something bigger was needed. The only locomotives that could reasonably be expected to take the trains single-handed, however, were the rebuilt L&YR 4–6–0s, whose performance and fuel consumption were disappointing to say the least.[3] Hughes resigned in July 1925, although he remained for a while effectively CME as described in *LMS Locomotive Profile 2*, while Sir Henry Fowler prepared to take over. Hughes' Chief Draughtsman and Technical Assistant, J. R. Billington, had died suddenly the previous May and Fowler's choice for his replacement was another Derby Drawing Office man in the person of Herbert Chambers. In September 1925, the Horwich Chief Draughtsman, G. M. Gass, went to Derby for an interview with Sir Henry during which the latter outlined proposals for alterations to the Pacific and 2–8–2 schemes. Gass reported back to Hughes who then wrote to Fowler that he had no objections to the changes, nor to design effort being transferred to Derby. These occurrences show that the big engine schemes, as far as the Drawing Offices were concerned, were not quite dead despite the opposition of Anderson and Follows. Fowler was an advocate of compound expansion and in October 1925 he toured France, talking to engineers from the major railways about their experiences with compounds. The outcome of his fact-finding was fairly indefinite with some claiming up to 15% saving in coal whilst others showed up to 9% more maintenance costs. Ideas on the best design

details for compounds were as numerous as their designers. Sir Henry's enthusiasm for the principle seems to have been undiminished, however, and the Pacific and 2–8–2 schemes became four-cylinder compounds. One of the Hughes 4–6–0s was altered to try out Derby Drawing Office's ideas on the subject, which proved to be sound, and detail design work proceeded at Derby, Crewe and Horwich until, in February 1926, five Pacifics were ordered to be built at Crewe. They were to have been nearly 71ft long, including a standard Fowler 3,500 gallon tender, and to have weighed 101 tons.[4] Frames and overall arrangement would have been substantially the same as the four-cylinder version of the Hughes 4–6–2. They would have had 26in stroke cylinders, outside high pressure ones 16¾ in diameter driving the intermediate coupled wheels and low pressure 23⅝ in ones connected to the leading axle. All four valves were to have been driven by two sets of outside Walschaerts valve gear and a Horwich type starting valve would have supplied high-pressure steam to the low-pressure cylinders whenever the cut-off was greater than 95% in either forward or reverse. The 7ft wheelbase bogie was to be a swing link type, coupled wheels were 6ft 9in diameter on a 7ft 3in + 7ft 3in wheelbase, and the trailing truck and rear framing were very similar to those eventually used on the Stanier Pacifics. The Belpaire firebox would have been 8ft long with a 43½ sq ft grate and, in order to achieve an acceptable tube length, would have included a 5ft long combustion chamber. The barrel was to have been 17ft between tubeplates and 5ft 9⅛ in diameter outside the front ring with a working pressure of 240 psi.

Whilst this activity was proceeding, however, events with far-reaching consequences for the LMS were taking place on the LNER and GWR. Exchange trials in 1925 between a 'Castle' Class 4–6–0 and a Gresley Pacific showed that performance of the smaller 4–6–0 was the equal of the east coast engine and that a locomotive the size of a 'Castle' could provide the power necessary to haul the WCML trains. To Anderson, this was the answer to the Operating Department's problems and convinced him that there was no need to build anything as big as a 4–6–2.[5] His opposition to the Fowler design was not, as some writers have claimed, simply because he didn't understand what was needed but was based on economic reasoning. Not only would a fourth cylinder and a trailing

truck increase construction and maintenance costs, but the need to provide longer turntables at key locations would require capital outlay. Obtaining clearance from the Civil Engineer's Department for the engines' use on major routes other than Euston to Glasgow Central without what was believed to be expensive reconstruction was also problematic (some of these objections have echoes of *The Great Bear* about them). With the backing of Follows, Anderson persuaded the LMS Board to negotiate with the Great Western for the loan of a 'Castle' in September 1926. Details of the ensuing trials and the subsequent machinations that led to the production of the 'Royal Scots' will be left to a volume on those engines. Suffice it to say that Anderson, sponsored as he was by Follows, seems effectively to have been deciding locomotive acquisition policy at the time and he wanted a three-cylinder 4–6–0. All work appears to have ceased on the Fowler Pacific in November 1926 in favour of what became the 'Royal Scot' and there things remained as regards motive power for the WCML expresses until Stanier's arrival.[6] The remainder of Fowler's time as CME and E. J. H. Lemon's tenure from 1929 produced nothing of any note as far as our present work is concerned.

Stanier's appointment in 1932 brought with it not only some excellent design precepts from Swindon but a direction and cohesion that had been lacking in LMS locomotive affairs since the Grouping. He also put the relationship between the CME and the Motive Power, Operating and Civil Engineer's Departments on a more logical footing. In doing so he ensured that once the Operating Department had defined the requirements for locomotives, the CME and his staff would be solely responsible for meeting them. Also, he insisted that the Civil Engineer make known the parameters by which schemes would be accepted or not and that proper surveys be taken to confirm or ease loading gauge restrictions. These surveys showed that many of the hitherto absolute restrictions were quite unnecessary and many more could be eased with minimal attention to structures. It is interesting to reflect that had Fowler insisted on such surveys, many of the arguments against his big engines would probably have been negated.[7]

Shortly after his arrival, Stanier instructed E. S. Cox to prepare proposals for a range of standard locomotives to meet future operating requirements and first on the list was a Pacific. On the face of it, this was somewhat surprising. The 'Royal Scots' had been successful when introduced and even though problems were developing with them, they weren't due to the engines' type or size. Even if more powerful locomotives were required, it would have been natural for Stanier, given his background, to stick with the 4–6–0 layout. The power outputs being attained by the Great Western's 'Kings', introduced by Collett in 1927, were unsurpassed in Britain and quite sufficient for any trains the Operating Department may have wanted to run on the LMS system. There were, however, two factors that militated against the development of an LMS 'King'. Firstly, the Operating Department wanted an engine that could run through from London to Glasgow, so that better use could be made of available assets, but the coal used on the LMS left more ash and clinker than did the Great Western's soft Welsh steam coal. The 'Royal Scots', even after their valve leakage had been sorted out, could only run from London to Carlisle, irrespective of tender coal capacity, simply because their grates and ashpans weren't big enough. Additionally, the continuous power output required over what was a longer and harder road than the Paddington–Plymouth route meant that a larger firebox and boiler were pretty much essential requirements. The adoption of a 4–6–2 layout would enable a wide firebox and large ashpan to be positioned behind the coupled wheels, with their overhang, as well as the cab, supported on a trailing truck. This thought process was evident in a note appended to the 1933 building programme that read, 'Whilst the Royal Scot loco has proved satisfactory in service and has met what was anticipated when this type was designed, it is considered desirable that we should have information as to the efficiency and costs of the Pacific type of loco on Royal Scot workings. It is further proposed to build three Pacific type locos of greater power and grate area than the Royal Scot'.

Two schemes were produced for Stanier's consideration. The first was for an engine using the 'Royal Scot' three-cylinder front end arrangement, motion and other chassis components. Its cylinders were 19in x 28in, coupled wheels 6ft 9in on a 7ft 3in + 7ft 3in wheelbase and estimated weight 94 tons. The boiler was 22ft between tubeplates, pressed to 250 psi and the firebox had a 45sq ft grate. Its tender was virtually the Fowler 4,000 gallon type originally intended for the 2–8–2 scheme

with an equally divided 15ft wheelbase carrying 4,000 gallons of water and 9 tons of coal. The second, which was the one selected for detail design work, had four cylinders arranged as in the GWR 'King' Class but with four independent sets of valve gear rather than two sets plus rockers to drive the other two valves. Originally it was to have had 6ft 9in coupled wheels on the same wheelbase as the three-cylinder version but, by the time the final drawings were prepared, the diameter had been reduced to 6ft 6in and the coupled wheelbase extended to 15ft 3in. Work proceeded quickly, no doubt significantly due to the new sense of purpose that Stanier engendered in his department, and in June 1933 the first of what were undeniably magnificent looking machines was turned out from Crewe.

CONSTRUCTION AND MODIFICATION

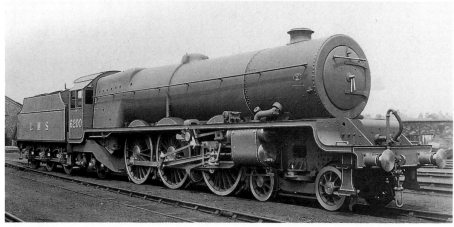

This study shows No. 6200 at Crewe when newly built with the vacuum stand pipe set high above the platform and standard buffer heads, but without smokebox door plates, nameplates or anti-vacuum valves — note the blanking plate on the front of the outside-cylinder steam pipe. The picture illustrates many of the features of the first two engines, such as the GWR-pattern slide bars, solid axles, and radius rod attached to the bottom of the expansion link rather than to an offset tail. The first type of motion bracket, with its distinctive casting projecting above the platform, can also be seen. Although the lack of combustion chamber is not particularly obvious in this view, the arrangement of washout plugs on the early firebox and boiler is obvious, as is the top feed pipe outside the clothing. The shape of the chimney, single mechanical lubricator on the right-hand platform and type of pony truck axlebox covers were peculiar to 6200 and 6201 as built. The tender was fitted with roller bearings, which can be discerned by close examination. The photographic grey finish shows the lining used with the crimson livery to good effect, but by the time 6200 entered traffic its makers' plates had been moved from the smokebox to the leading splashers. The protrusions from the shoulders of the steam chest were the sighting plugs referred to in the text and it can be noted that there was no access plate in the cylinder clothing. The angle and positioning of the sand pipes shows that gravity, or 'trickle' sanding was fitted.
                                                                        F. MOORE

The first two 'Princess Royals' entered traffic on 27th June and 3rd November 1933. The initial order, approved by the Mechanical and Electrical Engineering Committee on 27th July 1932, was actually for three engines but the third became the turbine-powered 6202. Estimated cost was £9,210 each but, in the event, Nos. 6200 and 6201 alone were reckoned between them to have cost £28,019 with their tenders, which was a very large sum to pay for two locomotives in 1933. Even though the cost included some patterns and tools that were later used for the 1935 production, it must have given the Board cause for thought. The fact that they were

found to be somewhat indifferent performers and relatively uneconomical in coal consumption can't have helped either. They did, however, satisfy their main design criterion, which was to enable trains to be run through from London to Glasgow without changing locomotives at Carlisle. For this reason alone, the production of a further ten engines was sanctioned by the M&EE Committee and they duly entered service in 1935 at a more modest outlay of £8,538 per locomotive and £1,154 per tender. Some of the savings were due to the re-use of patterns, etc and natural economies engendered by batch production. Others were because of the switch

When she first entered traffic, 6200 slowly accumulated name and number plates over a period of several weeks. By the time this photograph was taken, she had acquired nameplates and a white enamelled shed code plate but was still lacking a smokebox numberplate. Buffer heads were still round, which led to occasional problems with buffer locking on tight curves in depots or yards.
COLLECTION J. BRAITHWAITE

As well as trial runs and express passenger trains, the two 'Lizzies' were employed, when first built, on what are commonly called 'running in turns'. In this photograph, taken at Watford Junction, 6200 appears to have been in charge of a goods train, but the headlamp confirms that it was an express passenger train. The fact that the engine had its full complement of name and number plates as well as oval buffer heads, indicates that it had been in traffic for a couple of months.
AUTHORS' COLLECTION

from cast to fabricated components wherever possible, such as motion plates and bogie pivot supports, frame stretchers, pony truck stretchers, and platform supports. Fortunately, the problems encountered with 6200 and 6201 were largely solved by a fundamental change in boiler design, described in the next section.

When built, Nos. 6200 and 6201 were the longest non-articulated locomotives running in Britain, being 74ft 4¼ in over the buffers of engine and tender. Their estimated weight in working order was 104½ tons with 21 tons on the bogie, 22½ tons on each coupled axle and 16 tons on the trailing truck. No actual weights ever seem to have been recorded or, at least, to have survived, but the engines are known to have been substantially overweight and we believe that 6200 was nearer 112 tons.[8] Various measures, described in the relevant sections, were taken to reduce the weight of subsequent engines and we believe 6201 originally weighed about 108 tons. The main production batch were even lighter, but we have not discovered any reliable figure. Their tenders weighed 54 tons 2 cwt. Given the number of later alterations and additions to the frames, not to mention the swapping around of pony trucks that went on, the weight of any particular locomotive must have altered virtually every time it was repaired. It therefore probably made little difference what the official figure was. Tractive effort at 85% boiler pressure was 40,300 lb and they were given a power classification of 7P, the first LMS locomotives so annotated.

The first of the Class, No. 6200, was named *The Princess Royal* after the lady who was Colonel-in-Chief of the Royal Scots Regiment. This, it was felt, was appropriate for the first of a class of locomotives that was meant to replace the 'Royal Scots' on the WCML expresses. The second was named *Princess Elizabeth* and it was this engine that gave the class the nickname of 'Lizzies' by which railwaymen knew them.

The first two locomotives were allocated to Engine Diagram 175. After that, things got a little complex with several variations in the 175 series as well as the 257 series of diagrams. Because these additions depended on differences in the engines both as built and as later modified, we will leave further information until after their description. Full details will be found at Appendix A. Details of building dates, lot and order numbers are given in the accompanying table.

No. 6200 is seen in this view still in a slightly grubby photographic grey but with its makers' plates moved to the leading splashers and backing plates for the nameplates attached to the intermediate splashers. The shapes of the axlebox bearing covers on pony truck and tender are apparent, the former being peculiar to the plain bearings on the first two engines and the latter to the Hoffmann roller bearings on the straight-sided tenders. Details to note on the cab include the gangway door, stiffening angle and wing plate, sliding window, and absence of side screen on the fireman's side when the engine was first built. The boiler feed pipe from the exhaust steam injector can be seen behind the platform angle with the larger bore steam pipe from the smokebox to the injector behind it. The injector itself is seen in front of the tender footsteps.

C. L. TURNER

Number	Name	Lot No.	Crewe Order No.	Date into traffic
6200	*The Princess Royal*	99	371*	27 Jun 33
6201	*Princess Elizabeth*	99	371*	3 Nov 33
6203	*Princess Margaret Rose*	120	395	1 Jul 35
6204	*Princess Louise*	120	395	19 Jul 35
6205	*Princess Victoria*	120	395	24 Jul 35
6206	*Princess Marie Louise*	120	395	1 Aug 35
6207	*Princess Arthur of Connaught*	120	395	9 Aug 35
6208	*Princess Helena Victoria*	120	395	16 Aug 35
6209	*Princess Beatrice*	120	395	23 Aug 35
6210	*Lady Patricia*	120	395	6 Sep 35
6211	*Queen Maud*	120	395	18 Sep 35
6212	*Duchess of Kent*	120	395	21 Oct 35

*Derby O/8254 was also issued on 20th November 1932 to cover work carried out for these engines and O/8827 issued on 14th August 1934 for modifications.
We believe that names under consideration for Nos. 6213–6217 included *Queen Mary*, *Queen Elizabeth*, *Princess Alice* and *Princess Alexandra*.

Authority was actually given by the Board in July 1936 for the construction of five more 'Princesses' in 1937 but it was decided before construction began to redesign them. The new, improved, engines were the first of the 'Coronation' Pacifics and no more 'Princess Royals' were built.

BOILERS

Probably the most immediately obvious change made by Stanier was the introduction to the LMS of taper boilers. This was hardly surprising, coming as he did from a railway on which they had been standard for thirty years. The principle of the taper boiler was that it provided large water spaces around the firebox and outer rows of tubes at the firebox tubeplate, where evaporation rates were highest and good water circulation essential. At the front tubeplate, however, a reduced water space was permissible as the heat transfer, hence turbulence and evaporation, were less and circulation not as critical. It could be seen, therefore, that they were an excellent way of reducing the weight and volume of a boiler without impairing its ability to produce steam. They also permitted the firebox tubeplate to be of similar area to that at the smokebox, which allowed the tube area to be maximised, and minimised the

This view of The Princess Royal at Watford Junction in the autumn of 1933 shows to advantage some of the details of tender No. 9000. An interesting point raised by the photograph is that there is no shading discernible on the lettering or numbering, although it is apparent on other contemporary studies. This illustrates the difficulty sometimes of deciding on the livery in photographs taken on orthochromatic film. The tender's roller bearing axlebox end covers can just be seen above the platform edge. Note that the tank vents had been extended to the top of the side plates by the time the picture was taken.

effects on water level over the firebox crown due to surging. One of the main benefits of Stanier's boilers, however, was that they were reckoned greatly to have reduced maintenance costs on the LMS. The story of the type I boilers fitted to the 'Princess Royals' is complex and, therefore, we will cover it in three sections. We will. start by describing the design and construction of the first three boilers, then discuss the development and production of the remainder before finally covering subsequent modifications to all of them.

THE FIRST THREE BOILERS

The Type I taper boiler, or coned boiler as it was referred to in contemporary LMS documents, was designed by Jack Francis and, since it was the first Stanier boiler to enter service, we will try to describe it in some detail. According to Eric Langridge, its form was influenced by the boilers of the abortive Fowler Pacific and Gresley's Pacifics as well as the Great Western's No.I boiler.[9] The barrel was a full truncated cone, as opposed to other early Stanier boilers in which the front ring was parallel, and tapered from 6ft 3in external diameter at the Belpaire ring to 5ft 9in at the front tubeplate.[10] The bottom of the barrel was horizontal, so the shape was actually an oblique, rather than true, cone. This was sometimes said to have been so that the proportion of steam to water space could be maximised at the firebox. It is also likely that it had a lot to do with raising the bottom of the barrel at the throatplate so that the firebox depth above the trailing frames could be maximised. The first two boilers produced for Nos. 6200 and 6201 were made from mild steel plates, the front ring being $^{13}/_{16}$ in thick, the middle ring $^{27}/_{32}$ in and the rear one $^{7}/_{8}$ in. Longitudinal joints in the first and third rings were at the top whereas the middle ring had its joint offset 45 degrees to the left. Each joint was welded for one foot from each end and covered by butt straps riveted on inside and out. The telescopic lap joints between rings were cylindrical, i.e., the end $5^{3}/_{8}$ in of the rings were not coned, so that better joints could be achieved. The upper throat was a 15in wide, $^{7}/_{8}$ in thick steel plate with the Belpaire corners formed in it and was riveted over the rear ring. Because of its length, the boiler had cast-steel support saddles and gunmetal pads under the first and third rings that slid over corresponding frame stays as the boiler expanded and contracted. The front of the firebox foun-

No. 6201 Princess Elizabeth *was photographed shortly after being built, stil with round buffer heads, and coupled to a tender with roller bearing axleboxes. As stated in the text, the available records show the tender to have been built with plain bearings but we have come to the conclusion that it was actually turned out with roller bearings and then altered. Only the first two engines had the atomiser steam cock under the streamlined cover at the rear of the smokebox when built, as seen here, and the normal pattern of vacuum stand pipe was as shown. The prominent top feed pipes on the early boilers as built stand out in this view, as does the two-part reach rod with its transfer shaft at the rear of the trailing splasher and unsupported rear portion. Later engines had a different arrangement. Below the slidebars can be seen the crosshead vacuum pump fitted to all the engines when built. The sighting plugs on the steam chest with otherwise smooth cylinder clothing may be noted.* W. L. GOOD

When 6201 was first built, she was fitted with indicator shelters so that diagrams could be taken out on the road. As can be seen in this photograph taken at Camden, at the time there were no nameplates fitted and the tender had roller bearings.

AUTHOR'S COLLECTION

dation ring also rested on frame brackets and gunmetal pads and a vertical diaphragm plate connected the foundation ring to the drag box. This plate was flexible so that it could accommodate movement of the firebox with temperature variation but its fixing bolts were difficult to keep tight and sometimes sheared, which caused engines to be stopped on more than one occasion.

Water was fed to the boiler from a Gresham & Craven 13mm live steam injector on the left-hand side and a Davies & Metcalfe 12mm Class H exhaust steam injector on the right via top feed clacks on

the middle ring. From the clacks it entered the boiler and flowed over a forward facing scoop onto an inverted vee-shaped deflector, arranged fore and aft, thence into two longitudinal feed trays. The idea was that the feed water was pre-heated before mixing with that in the boiler and solid impurities were collected in the trays,

Continued on page 12

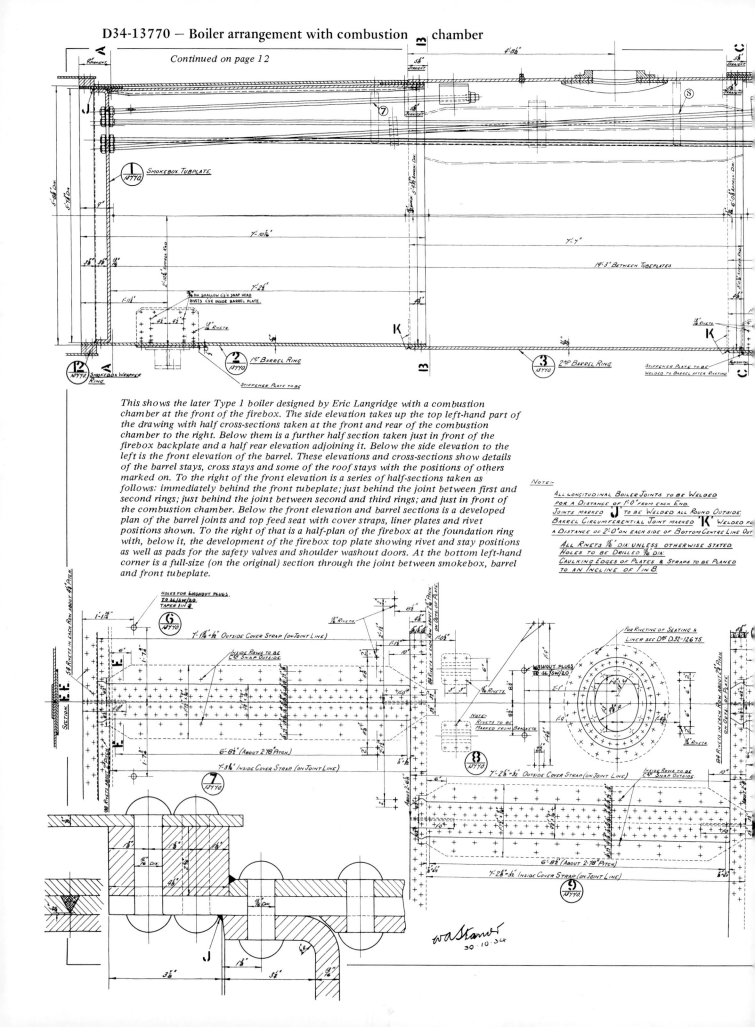

This shows the later Type 1 boiler designed by Eric Langridge with a combustion chamber at the front of the firebox. The side elevation takes up the top left-hand part of the drawing with half cross-sections taken at the front and rear of the combustion chamber to the right. Below them is a further half section taken just in front of the firebox backplate and a half rear elevation adjoining it. Below the side elevation to the left is the front elevation of the barrel. These elevations and cross-sections show details of the barrel stays, cross stays and some of the roof stays with the positions of others marked on. To the right of the front elevation is a series of half-sections taken as follows: immediately behind the front tubeplate; just behind the joint between first and second rings; just behind the joint between second and third rings; and just in front of the combustion chamber. Below the front elevation and barrel sections is a developed plan of the barrel joints and top feed seat with cover straps, liner plates and rivet positions shown. To the right of that is a half-plan of the firebox at the foundation ring with, below it, the development of the firebox top plate showing rivet and stay positions as well as pads for the safety valves and shoulder washout doors. At the bottom left-hand corner is a full-size (on the original) section through the joint between smokebox, barrel and front tubeplate.

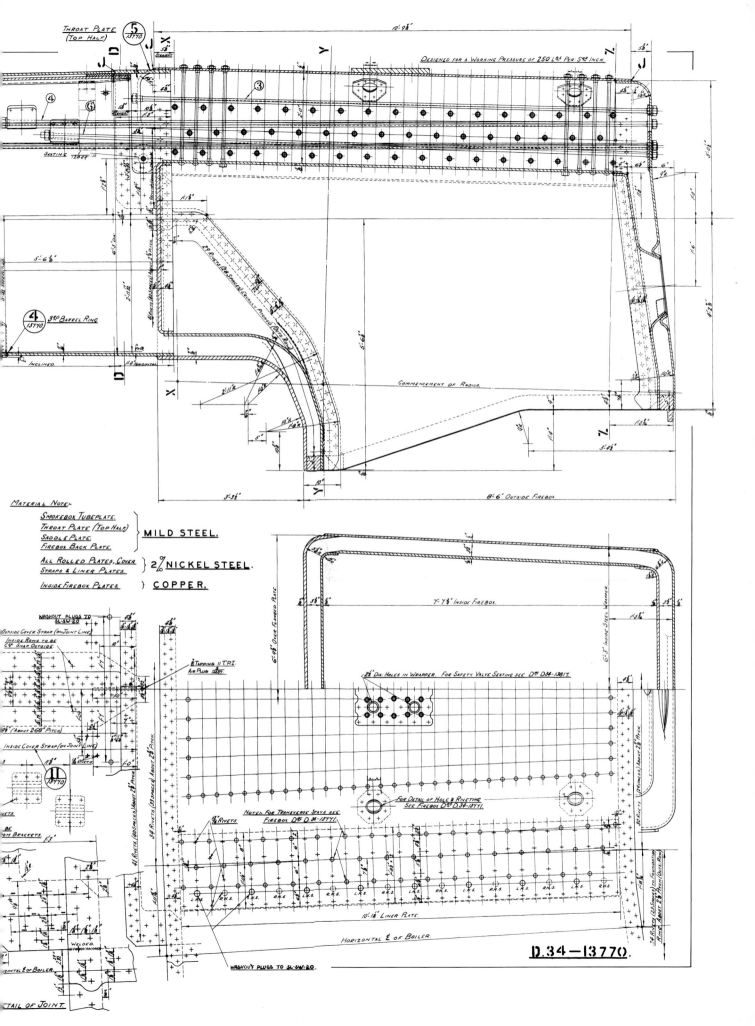

THROAT PLATE (TOP HALF)

DESIGNED FOR A WORKING PRESSURE OF 250 LBS PER SQ. INCH

MATERIAL NOTE:-

SMOKEBOX TUBEPLATE.	
THROAT PLATE (TOP HALF)	} MILD STEEL.
SADDLE PLATE.	
FIREBOX BACK PLATE.	
ALL ROLLED PLATES, COVER	} 2% NICKEL STEEL.
STRAPS & LINER PLATES.	
INSIDE FIREBOX PLATES.	} COPPER.

4/13770 3RD BARREL RING

D.34—13770.

These cross-sections are referred to on pages 10/11.

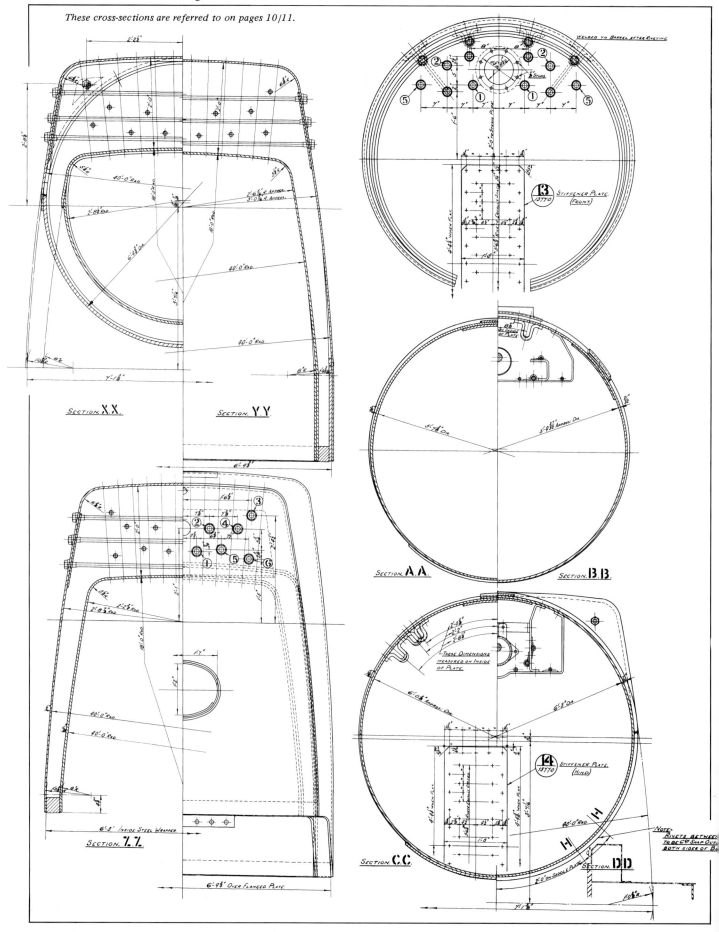

Section. X.X.

Section. Y.Y.

Section. Z.Z.

Section. A.A.

Section. B.B.

Section. C.C.

Section. D.D.

which could be accessed through the manhole cover and cleaned. It also provided some measure of de-aeration to remove entrained oxygen from the feed water. The feed pipes to the clacks were proud of the clothing.

In order to keep down the tube length and to provide more space for complete combustion, the Belpaire firebox had a sloping throatplate. The 45 sq ft grate was 7ft 1in wide at the front and tapered to 6ft 1in at the back, the rear third being horizontal but the remainder sloping. The wrapper was in three pieces, the longitudinal joints arranged to be halfway down the water space above the inner firebox, and was riveted over the Belpaire ring at the front. The lower part of the backplate, or doorplate, sloped outwards towards the bottom but the upper part was vertical to facilitate the attachment of stays. Six very long steel longitudinal stays from the top part of the front tubeplate were connected to the vertical part of the doorplate, as were shorter ones from the Belpaire corners and rear of the barrel. The longitudinal stays had intermediate supports and there were two further, short longitudinal steel stays from the front tubeplate to the second ring of the barrel plus a further two to the third ring. Previous Derby practice of having sling stays and palm stays at the front of the firebox was discontinued and all the firebox stays were direct.[11] There were seven washout plugs in a row along the left-hand side of the firebox and six on the right, all being level with the inner firebox crown. On each side there were two more plugs further down and one just ahead on the barrel. Four 2½ in Ross 'pop' type safety valves, set to 250psi, and a horizontal whistle, often described as a Caledonian-style hooter, were mounted on top of the firebox and a blow-off cock was fitted on the left-hand side near the front.

The copper inner firebox was made from ⅝ in thick plates with a one inch thick throatplate and the firebox stays in the end rows and the breaking zone were also copper. The exceptions were in the fire area above the grate, where steel ones were used, and at the bottom of the throatplate where they were made from a copper/nickel alloy — the first alloy stays used on the LMS. To help facilitate water circulation, the foundation ring was 3¼ in wide but the spacing between inner and outer firebox sides widened to 5½ in at the top. For the same reason, the minimum

distance between inner and outer throatplates was 4⅝ in. Spacing between the crown of the inner firebox and top of the outer shell was 2ft, which was a feature of Churchward boilers designed to give ample volume for steam above the water level.

Tubes were 20ft 9in long, which was to prove somewhat excessive, and the fitting of small tubes and superheater flues followed Swindon practice.[12] Flues were reduced in diameter for a short length at the firebox end and were threaded and screwed into the one-inch thick copper tubeplate. Both flues and small tubes were fitted using water side expanders and then beaded over. There were 170 small, 11swg steel tubes, each of 2¼ in outside diameter, and 16 steel, 7swg superheater flues of 5⅛ in outside diameter in two rows, the latter being in keeping with Swindon's principle of low degree superheat. Each flue contained two single return 1⅜ in diameter, 11swg superheater elements but the header was Derby rather than Swindon pattern.

The boiler was domeless, steam collection being via an upward-facing fishtail orifice at the back of the main steam pipe. It was placed in the top of the steam space immediately in front of the firebox and conveyed steam to the regulator, which was situated in the superheater header. The rod for the regulator had, therefore, to run the full length of the boiler and a balance weight was fitted to the regulator handle to assist the driver. A sight feed lubricator supplied oil to the regulator valves in the header.

The front tubeplate was the drumhead type flanged into the front ring and made from 13/16 in thick mild steel. The smokebox was attached to the boiler barrel extension in the same way as on the Horwich 2–6–0, i.e., with a 2³/₁₆ in thick forged steel distance ring fitted between their overlaps. This allowed the boiler clothing to remain flush with the smokebox. Rather than the built-up smokeboxes that had been the norm on the LMS, Stanier used a cylindrical smokebox that rested on two saddles — one part of the inside cylinders and one between the outside ones. At the rear of the smokebox were deflector plates designed for two purposes. Firstly, they were supposed to distribute the draught more evenly over the boiler tubes and secondly were meant to prevent any large cinders from being taken up the chimney by the blast. The idea was to break up the cin-

ders by impact with the plates and then deflect the pieces to below the level of the blast pipe. For tube cleaning they could be hinged out of the way and for maintenance could be removed altogether.

The steam pipe to the exhaust steam injector branched off the blast pipe, through the rear of the smokebox and aft to a grease separator between the frames. The purpose and action of the grease separator was as we have described before (see page 13 of *LMS Locomotive Profile No. 3 – The parallel boiler 2–6–4 tank engines*). From the separator, it passed through the right-hand frame ahead of the trailing coupled wheel and on to the injector.[13]

The smokebox door was another departure from what had become the LMS standard with a 45 degree bevelled edge that fitted onto a similarly bevelled front ring. It was held closed by a dart that located in a centre bar so that as the dart was tightened, the dished door was pulled into the ring seat. Under a domed cover near the top of the smokebox on the left-hand side was an atomiser steam cock, which provided steam to atomise the cylinder lubricant, and the regulator lubricator pipe.

The chimney, reportedly designed by T. F. Coleman, extended a foot above the smokebox, making the top a notional 13ft 2in above the rails. It had a single iron casting for rim, base and liner with the blower ring and petticoat pipe attached to its underside. For casting purposes, the portion between cap and saddle had a recess around the outside and this was filled by two ¼ in thick steel plates bent into half rings and welded together round the casting. Thus, there was a definite parallel section a few inches wide in the middle.[14] Boilers 6048–6050 retained these chimneys throughout their existence.

The ashpan was central to the design philosophy but its depth at the sides was limited because of the hind frames and there was a hump in the bottom to clear the truck centre casting. To help keep it clean and to ensure adequate air supply to the grate, it had several special design features. As well as front and rear dampers, there was a rearward facing one in the bottom of the ashpan. Water taken from the exhaust steam injector feed pipe could be directed via another 5mm injector and sprayed through the shallow side sections so that ash would be washed into the main, deep part of the ashpan and choking prevented. There were also doors on the upper sides of the pan immediately below

D32-12678 — Smokebox arrangement — non-combustion chamber boiler

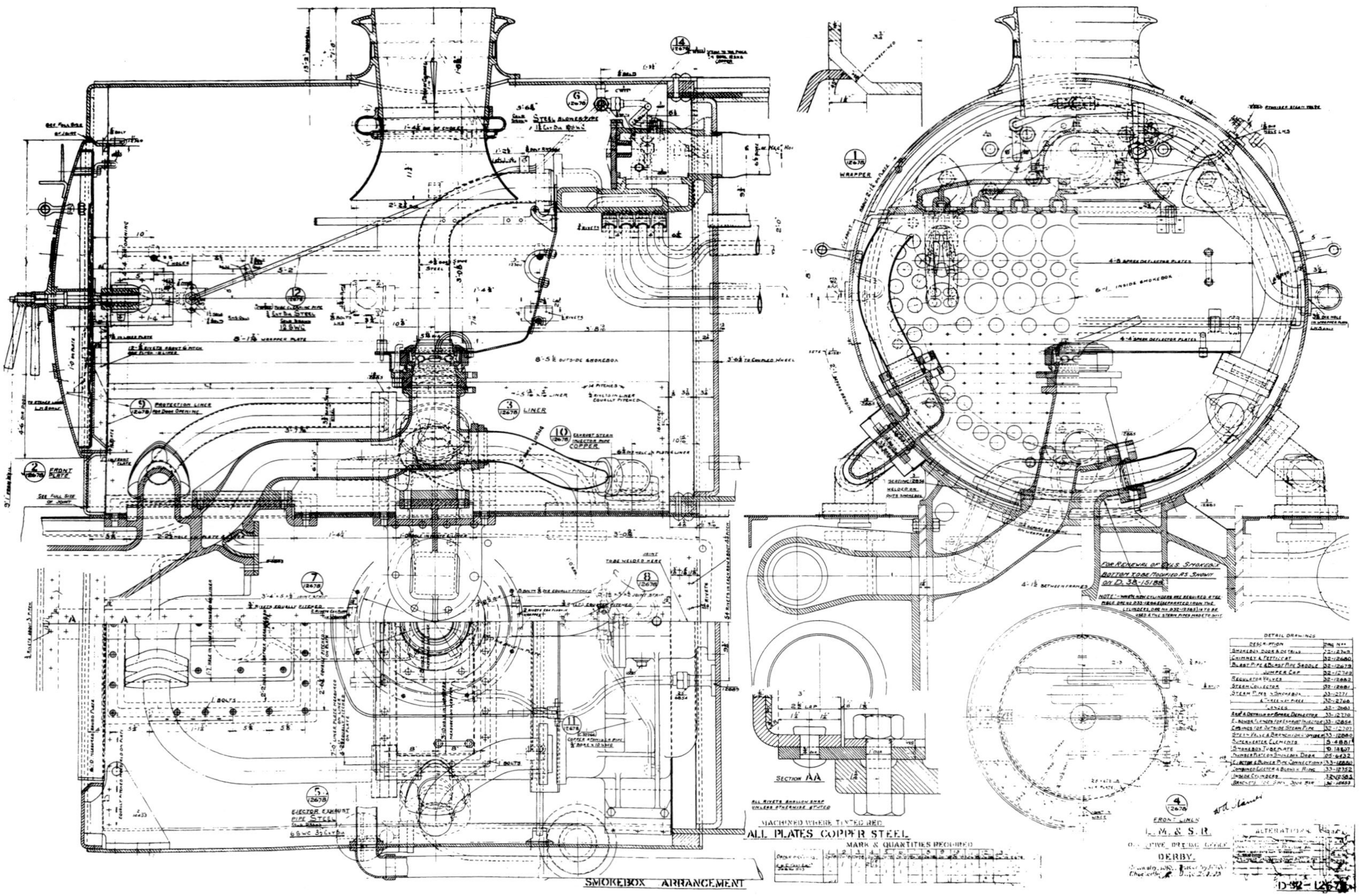

This drawing shows the smokebox arrangement of the first three boilers as built. At the top of the smokebox to the rear is the superheater header, from each side of which the steam pipes to the cylinders can be seen running round the inside of the wrapper. Alongside the blast pipe they split into two, one branch from each exiting the smokebox and leading to the outside cylinder with the other running forward to the inside one. The exhausts all join together at the base of the blast pipe. The ejector exhaust and blower ring are combined. The former can be seen entering the smokebox on the right-hand side of the split front elevation, which is the left-hand side of the locomotive, and curving up around the inside of the wrapper. On the plan view it enters at the bottom and goes across to the ejector exhaust ring around the base of the chimney, which is seen in section on the side elevation. The blower steam pipe comes from the tubeplate and runs across to the base of the chimney, ending at a perforated blower ring in the same casting as the ejector exhaust. The blast pipe has a Swindon-style jumper top, designed to lift under conditions of strong blast to reduce back-pressure. The superheater header casting projects further out into the smokebox than usual because it incorporates the regulator valve, although details of the mechanism are not shown. The deflector plates, designed to even the draught over the tubes and direct any live coals drawn through them into the bottom of the smokebox, can be seen in section on the side elevation coming down from the front of the superheater header to the top of the blast pipe. They are also shown on the right-hand half of the front elevation. Note that the drawing illustrates a boiler with just two rows of super-heater flues and that details of the single-piece chimney with steel ring between cap and saddle can be seen.

the firebox foundation ring for raking out ash from the shallow side areas when the locomotives were being disposed. All doors were operated independently from the cab but the operating mechanism was unreliable and they would sometimes fail to close properly with detrimental effects on steaming. Over the years, various modifications, both official and unofficial, were applied to overcome the problem.

Boiler and firebox were lagged with a compound called 'plastic magnesia', which was a paste containing asbestos fibres, applied whilst the boiler was hot. It was covered in 14swg steel clothing panels attached by stools, hoops and crinolines as described in previous volumes (see drawing on page 14 and caption on page 41 of *LMS Locomotive Profile No.2 – The Horwich moguls*). Each panel was made in two halves that overlapped by two inches top and bottom, the left-hand ones being on the outside at the top. The halves were joined by ⅜in screws at about 11in pitch and held in place by 2in wide 14swg steel bands, the ends of which were flanged and bolted together beneath the boiler. At the top, each band was attached to the clothing panels by two ⅜in screws. Outside diameter of the clothing at the smokebox was 6ft 2in and at the Belpaire ring 6ft 9⅜in. Maximum width over the firebox clothing at the throatplate was 7ft 4⅜in and at the backplate 6ft 5⅝in.

The third type 1 boiler was intended for use with the turbine-powered No.6202.

D32-12680 — Chimney and petticoat

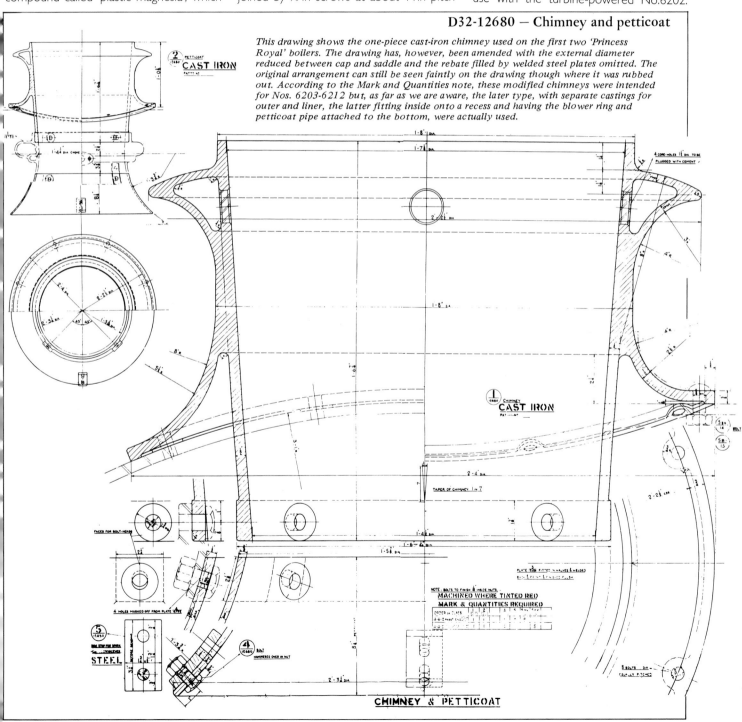

This drawing shows the one-piece cast-iron chimney used on the first two 'Princess Royal' boilers. The drawing has, however, been amended with the external diameter reduced between cap and saddle and the rebate filled by welded steel plates omitted. The original arrangement can still be seen faintly on the drawing though where it was rubbed out. According to the Mark and Quantities note, these modified chimneys were intended for Nos. 6203-6212 but, as far as we are aware, the later type, with separate castings for outer and liner, the latter fitting inside onto a recess and having the blower ring and petticoat pipe attached to the bottom, were actually used.

CHIMNEY & PETTICOAT

Continued on pages 18/19.

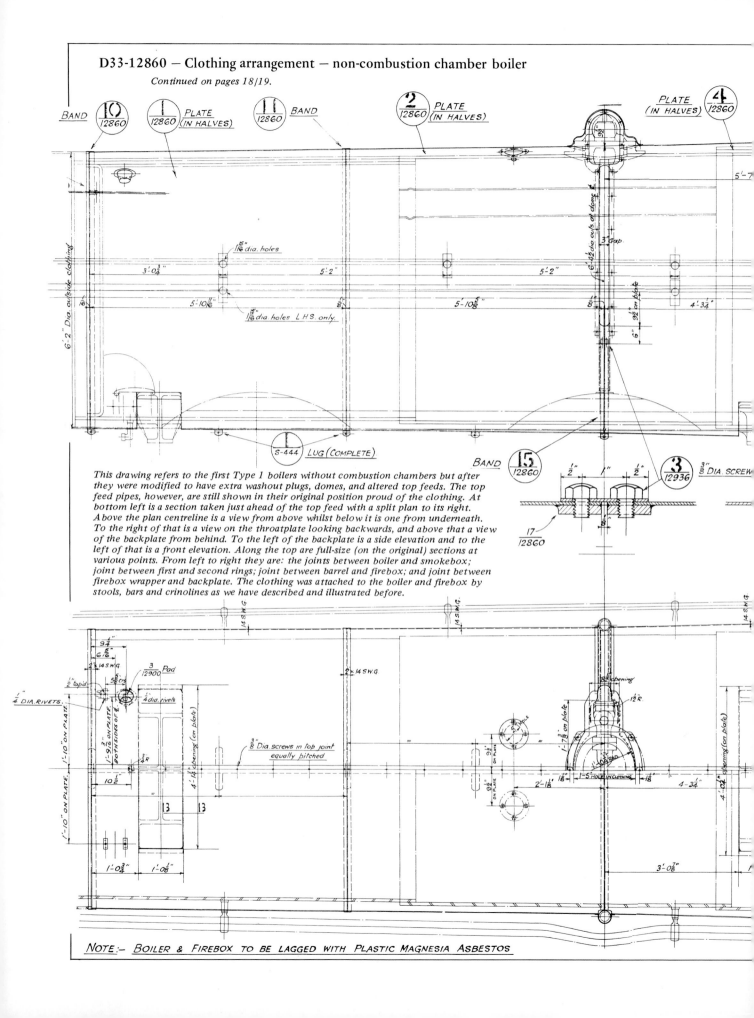

This drawing refers to the first Type 1 boilers without combustion chambers but after they were modified to have extra washout plugs, domes, and altered top feeds. The top feed pipes, however, are still shown in their original position proud of the clothing. At bottom left is a section taken just ahead of the top feed with a split plan to its right. Above the plan centreline is a view from above whilst below it is one from underneath. To the right of that is a view on the throatplate looking backwards, and above that a view of the backplate from behind. To the left of the backplate is a side elevation and to the left of that is a front elevation. Along the top are full-size (on the original) sections at various points. From left to right they are: the joints between boiler and smokebox; joint between first and second rings; joint between barrel and firebox; and joint between firebox wrapper and backplate. The clothing was attached to the boiler and firebox by stools, bars and crinolines as we have described and illustrated before.

NOTE:- BOILER & FIREBOX TO BE LAGGED WITH PLASTIC MAGNESIA ASBESTOS

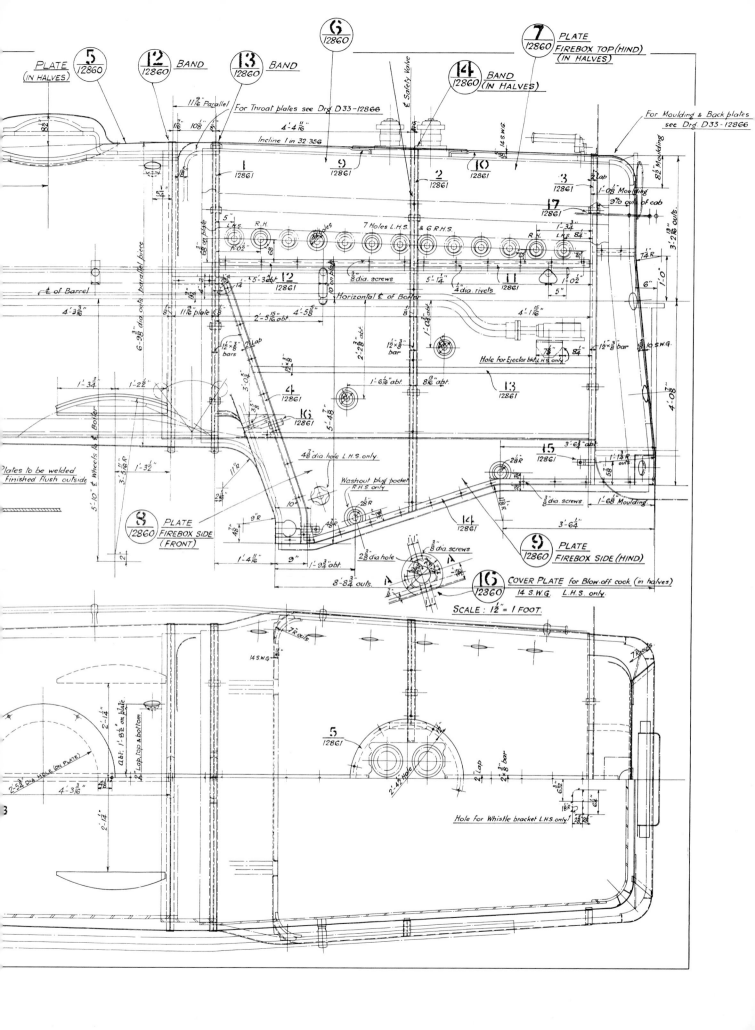

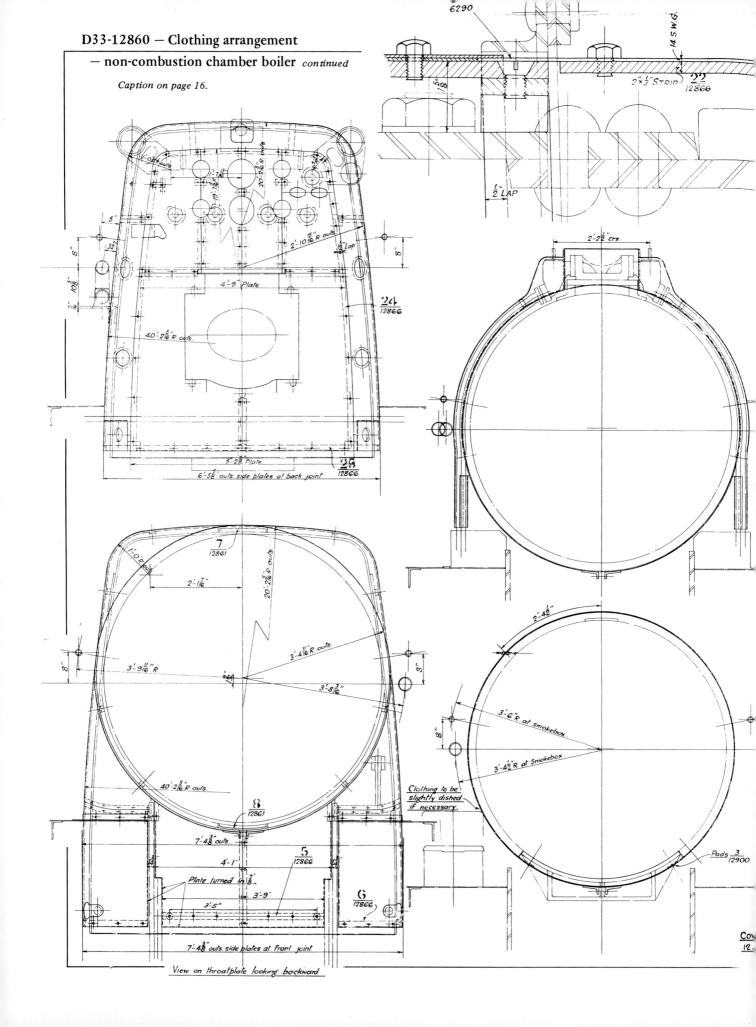

D33-12860 – Clothing arrangement
– non-combustion chamber boiler *continued*

Caption on page 16.

View on throatplate looking backward

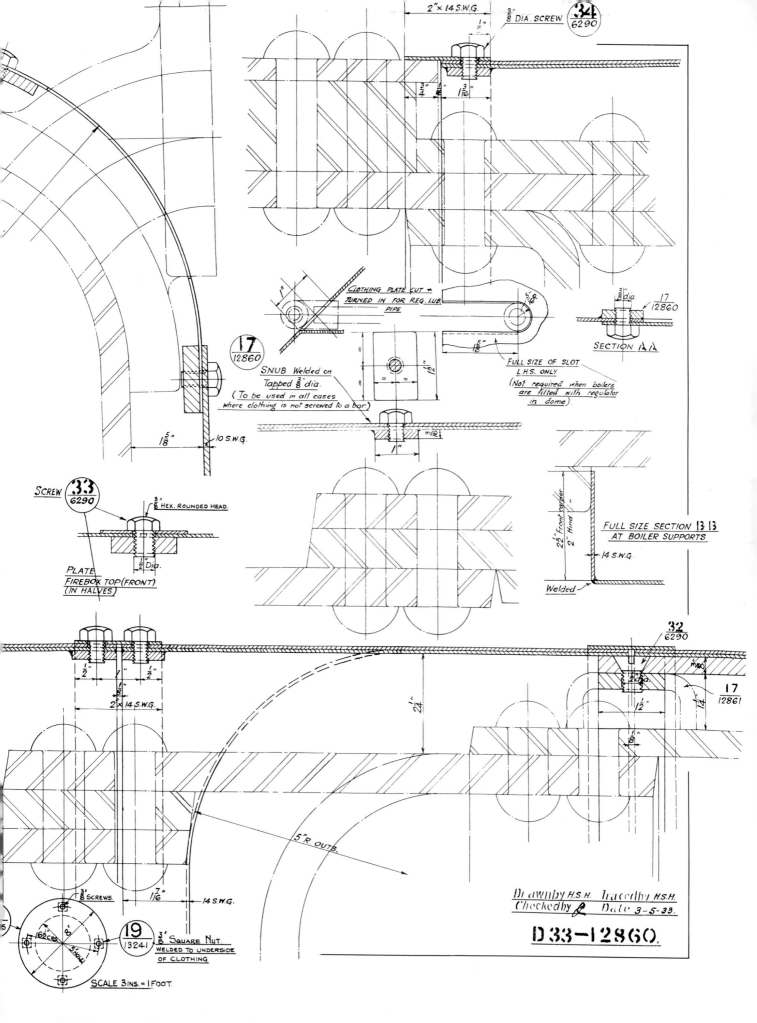

2"× 14 S.W.G.

³/₈" DIA. SCREW 34/6290

17/12860

SECTION AA

Clothing plate cut & Turned in for Reg. Lub. Pipe.

5/16"R

5/16"

Full size of slot L.H.S. only
(Not required when boilers are fitted with regulator in dome).

17/12860
³/₈"dia.

SNUB Welded on Tapped ³/₈"dia.
(To be used in all cases where clothing is not screwed to a bar.)

1"

³/₁₆"

1⅝"

10 S.W.G.

17/12860

SCREW 33/6290

³/₈" HEX. ROUNDED HEAD.

PLATE FIREBOX TOP (FRONT) (IN HALVES)

½" Dia.

2¼" Front rafter

2" Hind

14 S.W.G.

FULL SIZE SECTION 13 13
AT BOILER SUPPORTS

Welded

½"   ½"

1"

2"× 14 S.W.G.

2¼"

5"R OUTS.

32/6290

³/₈"

17/12861

2"dia.

1½"

¼"

⅜"

³/₈" SCREWS

7/16"

14 S.W.G.

16²CRS.

8"

19/13241

½" SQUARE NUT.
WELDED TO UNDERSIDE OF CLOTHING

SCALE 3 INS. = 1 FOOT.

Drawn by H.S.H.   Traced by H.S.H.
Checked by   Date 3-5-33.

D33-12860.

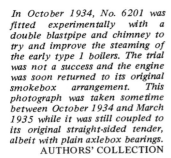

In October 1934, No. 6201 was fitted experimentally with a double blastpipe and chimney to try and improve the steaming of the early type 1 boilers. The trial was not a success and the engine was soon returned to its original smokebox arrangement. This photograph was taken sometime between October 1934 and March 1935 while it was still coupled to its original straight-sided tender, albeit with plain axlebox bearings.
AUTHORS' COLLECTION

As one of the measures taken to reduce the engine's weight, the barrel and firebox wrapper were made from 2% nickel steel. This enabled thinner plates to be used – ⅝ in for the front ring, ²¹⁄₃₂ for the middle and ¹¹⁄₁₆ for the rear – but the front tubeplate, top half of the throatplate, saddle plate and firebox backplate were still made from mild steel as it was more amenable to flanging. Because the same tubeplate was used, this boiler had an outside diameter of 5ft 8⅝ in at the front but the rear was kept at 6ft 3in. Firebox wrapper plates were ⅝ in thick. Altogether, this saved 1 ton 16cwt compared with the first two boilers.

Because the steam temperature required for operation of the turbine was considerably higher than that expected from the low superheat boiler designed by Jack Francis, a new internal layout was devised. Francis had by that time left Derby and returned to Crewe so the job was given to E. A. Langridge.[15] Since the original superheater had sixteen flues, each containing two elements, the header had 32 locations. Langridge therefore decided to use 32 flues arranged in four rows, each one containing a bifurcated element. Diameter of the elements was slightly reduced to 1¼ in. From each location on the saturated side of the header a downcoming pipe ending in a forged branch led to two elements, the return ends being similarly joined before entering the dry side of the header via a riser. Because of the extra sixteen flues, the number of small tubes was reduced to 110. Basic construction followed that of the first two boilers except that the firebox wrapper was a single plate. By the time this boiler was made, the ashpan cleaning apparatus was reckoned to be of doubtful value and so was omitted from it and from all future construction.

Whilst this modified boiler was being designed and built, attempts were being made to solve the steaming problems that Nos. 6200 and 6201 were having. Various different superheater elements were tried and in October 1934 No.6201 was fitted with two blast pipes and an elongated stovepipe chimney. The exhaust from the outside cylinders was directed to a blast pipe in the normal position but a further blast pipe was placed ahead of it and took the inside cylinder exhaust. Each chimney orifice was smaller than the original, so a crescent-shaped plate was welded into the rear of the existing hole in the smokebox wrapper before a new, elongated hole was cut and the double chimney fitted. The experiment was not a success and the engine was de-modified after a short time.

In the event, the third boiler wasn't used on the turbine engine but was fitted instead to 6200 in April 1935 and that engine's boiler was modified at Crewe to have the same, improved type of superheater. Concurrently, the smokebox regulator valves were removed and a conventional dome-mounted regulator fitted. This was because of problems associated with distortion of the original regulator valve faces caused by the different temperatures on the dry and saturated sides of the superheater header in which it was located. The long regulator rod also gave trouble due to excessive flexing and so the dome was positioned where the steam collector had originally been just in front of the firebox. The superheater header was not replaced, however, and retained the original valve faces. Once this boiler was ready, it was fitted to 6201 in November 1935 and the displaced unit was modified in the same way. Thus, of the first three boilers, two had domes by 1936, although 6200 did not run with a domed

boiler until June 1937. The top of the dome cover was 13ft 2in above the rails.

THE COMBUSTION CHAMBER BOILERS

Because of the problems being experienced with the original boilers, Stanier had already ordered a rethink on the design and Langridge was given the job of improving it. Derby Drawing Office had been aware of its two main weaknesses ever since the original inception, the first of which was that the tube ratios were unsatisfactory. Although the tube length had been kept down to 20ft 9in by using a sloping throatplate, the ratio of total surface area to cross section available for gas flow, or free gas area, was still too high whereas the ratio of free gas area to grate area was low.[16] Langridge therefore incorporated a combustion chamber in front of the firebox in order to reduce the tube length further, as had been done in the design for the Fowler Pacific. That scheme, however, had been for a 5ft long combustion chamber built up from multiple plates and Langridge wanted to avoid the maintenance pitfalls that would probably have resulted from such construction. Consequently, he decided on a single-piece, pressed throatplate, the size of which was limited by the capacity of the press in Crewe Works. Thus it was that the new boiler had 19ft 3in long tubes and an 18in long combustion chamber, the addition of which resulted in several other alterations to the rear ring of the barrel, firebox and grate. The bottom half of the Belpaire ring was eliminated and the outer throatplate riveted directly to the barrel. Then, in order to maintain adequate water space between inner and outer throatplates, the copper tubeplate was raised and shortened by ¹¹⁄₁₆ in and the bottom of the third ring of the barrel was angled down so that the rear was ⁹⁄₁₆ in lower than the front. Finally, the shape of the grate had to be altered with the front narrowed to 6ft 10¾ in and the back widened to 6ft 4in, which kept the grate area almost the same at 45.1 sq ft. In order to accommodate the new grate, the foundation ring and back-plate were also altered. It was these differences in the third ring and the firebox that required alterations to be made to the locomotive frames and cabs.

The second problem, which was common to several early Stanier boilers, was that Swindon-style low-degree super-heat, whilst successful on the Great Western, was not suited to LMS operating conditions.[17] The longer continuous runs and lower calorific value coal generally available meant that a much higher super-heat was essential. Langridge's intention was to use 114 small tubes and the same 32 double-return element superheater as that of the modified original type 1 boiler with 1⅛ in elements. Stanier, however, remained to be convinced about the need for so many elements and so the first four of the 1935 boilers had just 24 flues with 1¼ in elements and 141 small tubes. The modified boiler originally intended for No.6202, however, was still not achieving the steam temperature required by Metropolitan Vickers for the turbine and eventually approval was given for Langridge's 32 double return elements to be used on subsequent production. The number of small tubes was reduced to 112 with two extra washout holes being provided in the front tubeplate in place of two tubes (the 16- and 24-flue layouts had originally been designed with 170 and 143 tubes respectively and later altered for the same reason). The first of these 32-element boilers (which was actually numbered ahead of the 24-element units) went to No. 6202 and had the wall thickness of the elements reduced to 13swg. The remainder, however, reverted to 11swg. Tubes for both layouts were 2¼ in diameter.

A further two type 1 boilers, originally intended as spares, were made in 1935. In the event, the first of them was fitted to No.6212, the boiler meant for that engine having gone to the turbine locomotive, and was a 'standard' 32-flue, 112-tube dome-less boiler. The second, however, was different again and was designed to produce even higher temperature steam for No.6202. It had 40 flues in five rows, each flue containing three one-inch elements

emanating from a single downcomer and ending in a single riser to the dry side of the header. These were known as trifur-cated elements and were closely similar to the German Wagner elements.[18]

Stanier had introduced seal welding of boiler joints, which then became standard on the LMS, and we believe that these two boilers were the first type 1s so treated. According to anecdotal evidence, this technique was probably due to Fell, the boiler shop foreman. Circumferential joints between the barrel plates were welded on the outside for 2ft either side of the bottom centreline after riveting. Joints between firebox wrapper and barrel, throatplate and doorplate were also seal welded, as were those between the front tubeplate and barrel. The top-feed man-hole was seal-welded to the barrel whilst the safety valve mounting, washout door pads and various pads for backplate fittings were welded to the outer firebox and riveted.

All the 1935 boiler barrels and firebox shells were made from 2% nickel steel plates but, because of the combustion chamber and other constructional differences, they were heavier than the third of the early boilers. The cupronickel stays in the firebox were replaced by copper ones in the first six but subsequent ones used another copper/nickel alloy called monel metal.[19] The washout plugs on the barrel were moved higher up and there was an extra one on each side of the firebox, making eight in all on the left and seven on the right at crown level. Additionally, there were two washout doors under domed covers on each shoulder.

Rather than being proud of the clothing as on the first three boilers, the water feed pipes on the 1935 units were hidden beneath broad clothing bands between the horizontal centreline and the clacks. The atomiser steam cock was moved to below the ejector exhaust, where it was fitted without a cover, leaving a smaller cover over the regulator lubricator pipe. Clothing details and external dimensions were as for the first three boilers except that maximum width at the throatplate was only 7ft 0⅝ in. Whereas plastic magnesia had been used to lag the entire boiler and firebox on the early boilers, the combustion chamber units had it only on the firebox backplate. The rest was lagged with a material called Alfol. Whether this was because of the difficulty that was apparently encountered in getting the plastic magnesia to stick to the plates we don't know. In 1940 the specifi-

As described below (in the text), No. 6212 was built with a smokebox door in what can only be described as the old Derby style that was fastened by eleven dogs around the rim.
AUTHORS' COLLECTION

cation for lagging the boilers was altered to an asbestos mattress, still with plastic magnesia on the backplate. The latter material was also specified for the area around the firebox roof stay nuts, although this, too, eventually ended up as a mattress.

Although we can find no documentary evidence, we assume that problems must have been experienced with the smoke-box doors settling on 6200 and 6201, as 6203 onwards had a support bracket fitted to the right-hand side of the smokebox. Rather than the normal type of smokebox door, the last engine constructed, No.6212, was built with one reminiscent of the old Derby style fastened by eleven dogs around the rim. The alteration was reportedly ordered by R. A. Riddles but we can find no reason why it was done.[20]

The chimney construction differed from that of the first three. There were separate castings for outer and liner, the latter fitting inside onto a recess and having the blower ring and petticoat pipe attached to the bottom. Thus the outer profile was subtly different with larger radii top and bottom and hardly any parallel section. At 2in, the rim was also ⅞ in deeper. Although the two types of chimneys remained with their own boilers, the shapes were so similar that it is sometimes difficult to tell them apart in photographs.

Steaming qualities of the type 1 boilers were still not completely satisfactory, however, and in tests conducted in 1937 it was confirmed that the tube ratios were large-ly to blame.[21] As a result, an instruction was issued in July of that year to increase the small tube diameter from 2¼ in to 2⅜ in

D35-13925 — Smokebox arrangement — combustion chamber boiler

The smokebox arrangement for Nos. 6203-6212 after removal of the spark deflector plates and replacement of the jumper top blast pipe is shown in this drawing. The layout is closely similar to D32-12678 but the ejector exhaust and blower ring are not combined. The former is still basically the same as before but the blower steam pipe starts at the tubeplate, about halfway up the right-hand side of the plan view, and runs about two-thirds of the way round the inside of the liner before turning across to the top of the blast pipe. It ends in a perforated blower ring around the blast orifice. The chimney illustrated is one of the later ones formed from two separate castings, one inside the other, with no steel ring around the outside. The petticoat pipe and choke are dimensioned differently as well. Note that the drawing illustrates a boiler with three rows of superheater flues.

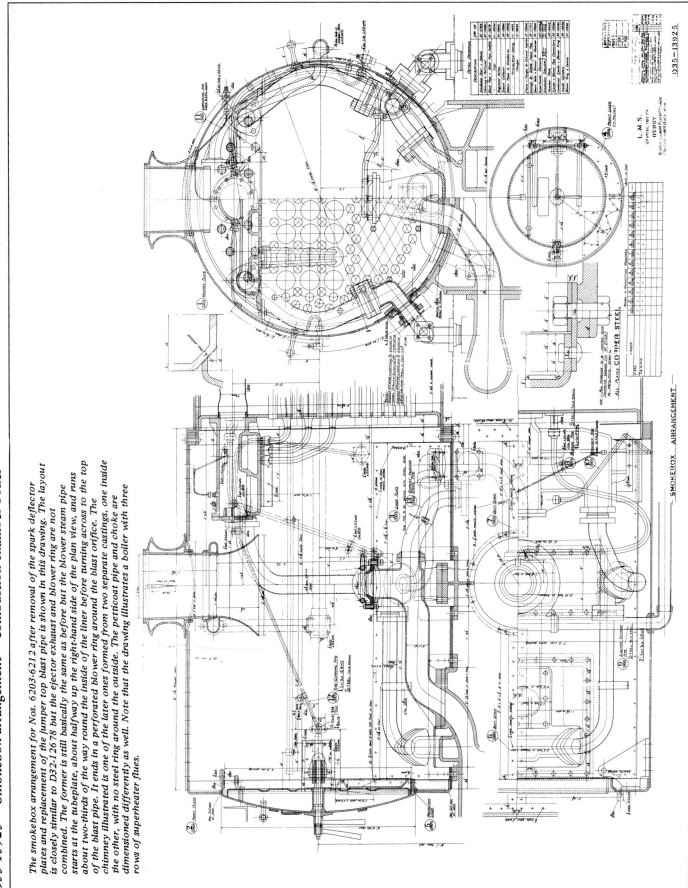

D34-13845 – Ashpan arrangement

This rather complex looking drawing shows the ashpan arrangement of Nos. 6203-6212. At top left is a side elevation with the assembly sectioned along its centreline and below that is a half plan. Below the half plan is a scrap view showing the left-hand edge and side door control mechanism. At the right-hand side are various cross-sections taken on planes as indicated by their nomenclature. Around these sections are full-size (on the original) scrap sections showing various fastenings and joints. As can be appreciated, the linkages to the ashpan doors were complicated and it is easy to understand why they sometimes jammed. The locking mechanism added to the side doors in 1942 is not shown on this drawing; a note was added referring to a new drawing D42-16447 for details.

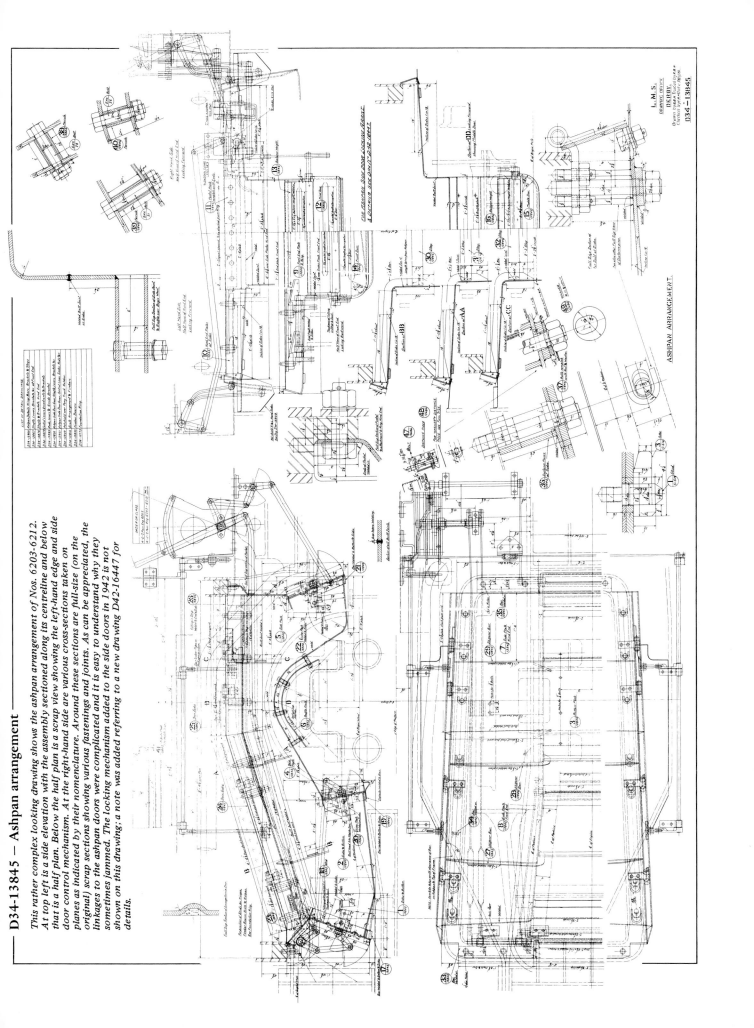

ASHPAN ARRANGEMENT.

L. M. S.
DRAWING OFFICE
DERBY.
D34–13845.

Drawing continues on pages 26/27 with caption.

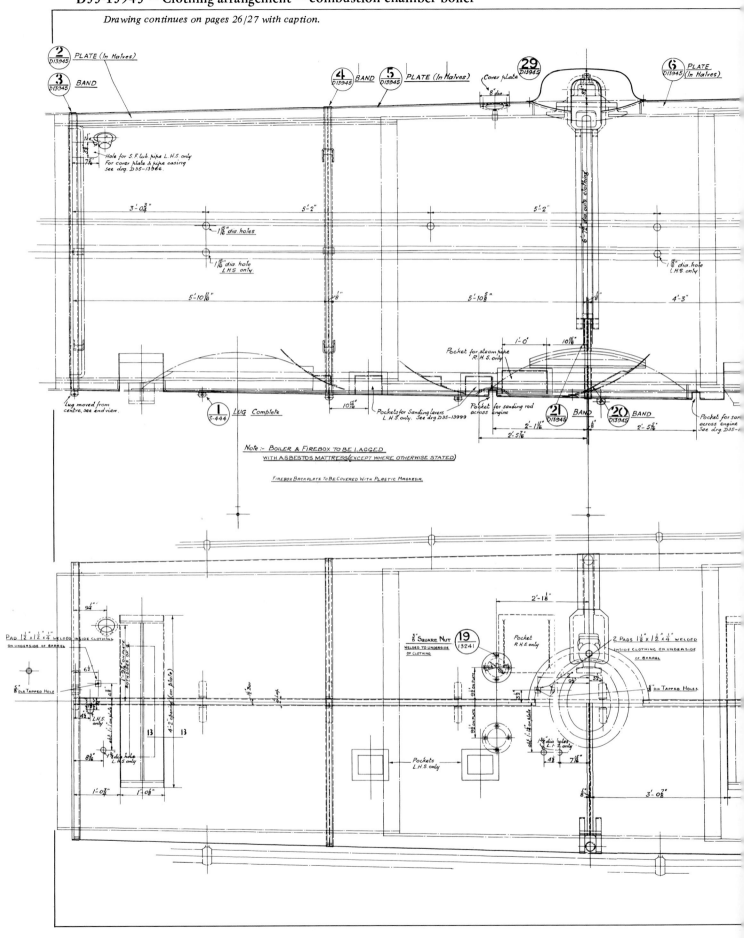

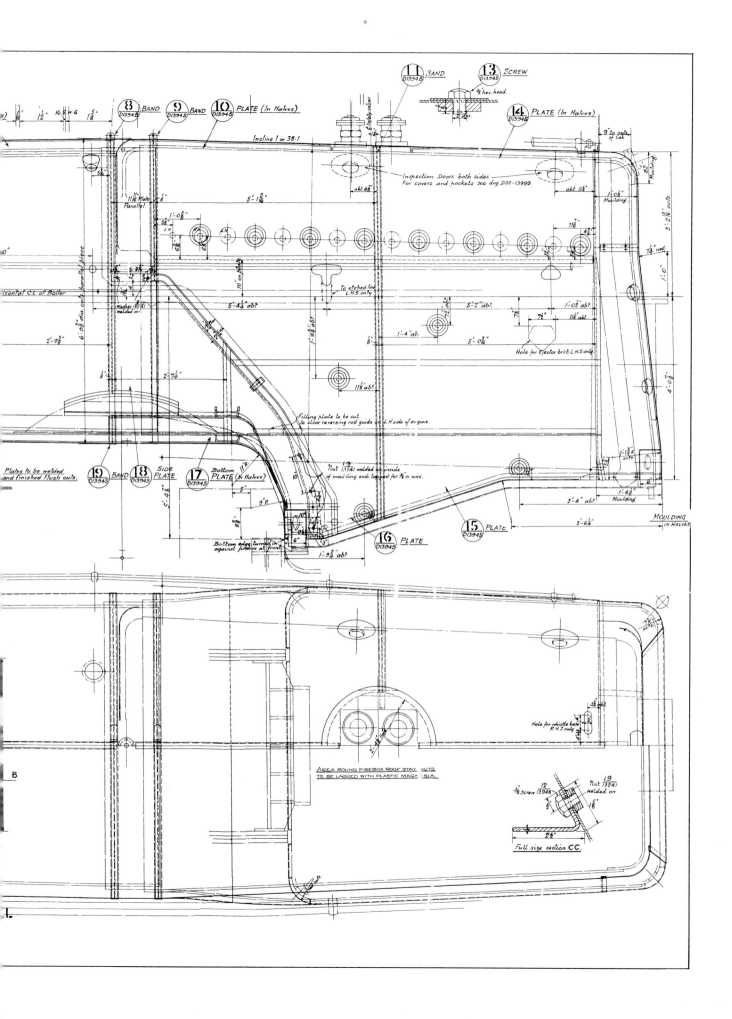

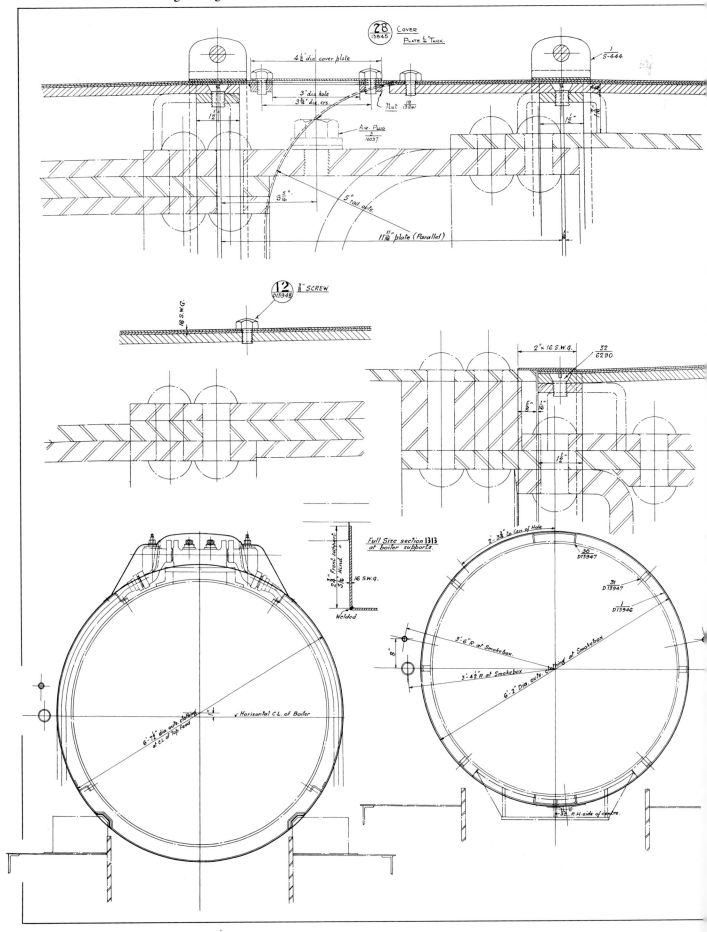

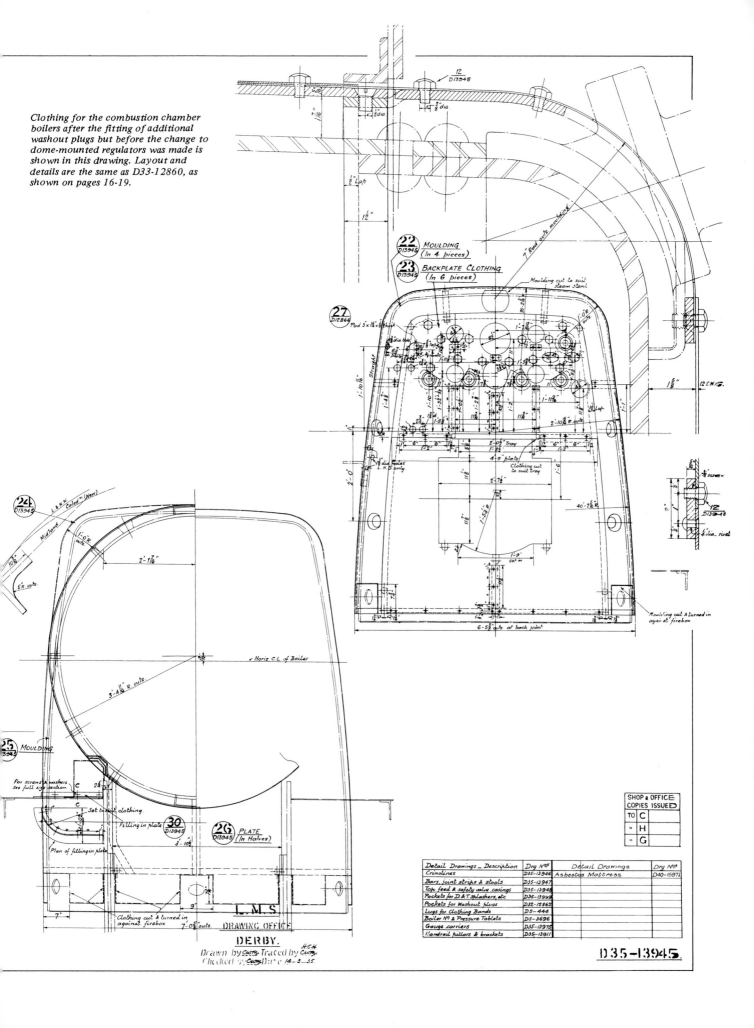

Clothing for the combustion chamber boilers after the fitting of additional washout plugs but before the change to dome-mounted regulators was made is shown in this drawing. Layout and details are the same as D33-12860, as shown on pages 16-19.

L.M.S
DRAWING OFFICE
DERBY.
Drawn by Curtis Traced by Curtis
Checked by Curtis Date 14-3-35.

D35-13945.

SHOP & OFFICE COPIES ISSUED		
TO	C	
"	H	
"	G	

Detail Drawings _ Description	Drg Nos	Detail Drawings	Drg Nos
Crinolines	D35-13946	Asbestos Mattress	D40-15971
Bars, joint strips & stools	D35-13947		
Top feed & safety valve casings	D35-13948		
Pockets for D & T splashers, etc	D35-13999		
Pockets for Washout plugs	D32-12862		
Lugs for Clothing Bands	DS-444		
Boiler Nº & Pressure Tablets	DS-3696		
Gauge carriers	D35-13975		
Handrail pillars & brackets	D35-13911		

once stocks of the former had been used. In order to preserve the thickness of the bridges in the copper tubeplate, the wider tubes were narrowed to 2¼ in diameter at the firebox end. The 24-flue boilers were modified to the 32-flue arrangement between 1943 and 1952 and all four of them, together with four of the other 32-flue boilers, had the number of small tubes increased to 123. The 110-tube boiler originally built for No.6202 had the number of small tubes increased to 112 and the second turbine boiler was fitted with 101 tubes. Thus, there were eventually the following type 1 boilers:

Three without combustion chambers, with 32-element superheaters and 110 tubes.
Eight with combustion chambers, 32-element superheaters and 123 tubes.
Two with combustion chambers, 32-element superheaters and 112 tubes.
One with combustion chamber, 40-element superheater and 101 tubes.

Although mainly used on 6202, when that engine was out of service the 40-element boiler was fitted to 6210 from 1943–1944 and 6204 from 1950–1952. After the rebuilt 6202 was damaged beyond repair at Harrow in 1952, its boiler entered the type 1 pool and was used on 6208 and

6212. More details will be found at Appendix B.

BOILER MODIFICATIONS
As well as the differences between the various boilers as built, other modifications were carried out on them. For the sake of simplicity, we will deal with the alterations in chronological order rather than by boiler type. For any that pertained only to one particular boiler or type we will define which ones were affected. If no particular ones are mentioned, the alteration can be taken as applying to all of them.

D49-2007 — Boiler arrangement with combustion chamber (part of)
A new arrangement drawing for the combustion chamber boilers modified to have dome-mounted regulators was prepared in 1949. Part of it, showing the dome mounted on the second ring just in front of the firebox, is reproduced here.

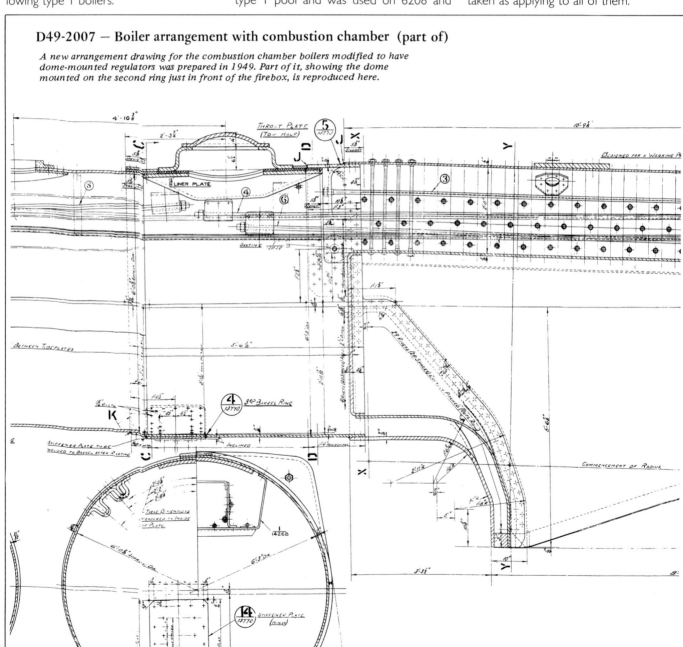

Within two years of being built, Nos. 6200 and 6201 had door support brackets fitted to the right-hand sides of their smokeboxes. From 1936 onwards, hinged crossbars for the dart fastening of the doors were fitted to all of them. At about the same time, their ashpan washout system was removed.

Job No.4982 of December 1935 directed that the main steam pipe joint clips were to be altered to four-bolt type as the engines passed through for general repair. This was in common with all other LMS taper-boiler engines.

Instructions were given in March 1936 to fit continuous blowdown, which was a constant slight drain of water from the boiler whenever the regulator was open, in order to reduce the concentration of harmful salts in the boiler water. Originally, the water was taken through a cooling pipe in the tender tank before being discharged under the right-hand side of the buffer beam. Following representations from the Civil Engineer that the right-hand rails, fixings and sleepers were being corroded and damaged, however, the blowdown was redirected into the ashpan around 1949 or 1950.[22]

A trial undertaken in 1937 entailed lagging the superheater header, steampipes and the front 4ft 6in of the flues on No. 6211 in order to raise the steam temperature. The measures resulted in an increase of 48 degrees but were expensive and reduced the free-flow gas area through the flues. Hence the trial was not pursued and no more engines were modified.

So that regulators could be set to the drifting position, Job No. 5059 was issued in March 1938 for stops to be fitted on the regulator stuffing boxes and catches to regulator handles. The modification was to be carried out as engines passed through the shops for repairs and were applicable to many Stanier classes.

When Robert Riddles had directed that 6212 be fitted with its dog-ring smokebox door, Roland Bond apparently tried to countermand the order but was too late to prevent it happening. It is unsurprising, therefore, that a normal type of door was fitted during a heavy repair finishing in August 1939.

Three other alterations were ordered in 1939. They were:

Job No. 4991 issued in January for the fitting of new bronze link couplings in both header and dome type regulators to prevent sticking – also applicable to the 'Coronations'.

Job No. 5113, also issued in January, for the provision of steel rather than copper blower and ejector exhaust pipes – also applicable to other Stanier taper-boiler engines.

Job No. 5141 of August for the fitting of non-ferrous firebox stays in triangular areas at top corners of the lowest firebox side plates.

Problems were encountered with freezing-up of the exhaust steam injectors during severe winter weather. Starting in 1940, therefore, cocks were fitted to the injector bodies so that they could be drained when the engines were standing.

During the Second World War, the production of special bifurcated elements ceased and standard Superheater Company 1⅜ in return elements were used (boiler 9236 was fitted with bifurcated instead of trifurcated elements at the same time). Bifurcated elements were reintroduced after the war but following nationalisation BR standard 1½ in double-loop elements replaced them.

The smokebox deflector plates were always a source of trouble and required constant attention. Since they could be removed for maintenance, many shed foremen left them off altogether rather than try to keep them serviceable. It probably came as a relief, therefore, when it was ordered in 1942 that they be removed and stored as a wartime measure. In the event, they were never restored and when the smokeboxes were altered after the war, their fittings were removed.

Several other alterations were ordered in 1942 to the following Job Numbers:

5059 – provision of catches and stops on regulator handles and stuffing boxes.
5274 issued in February – new standard brick arches using standard type firebricks.
5305 issued in August – provision of larger injector steam valves.
5309 issued in September – altered top feed clackbox connections with copper joint ring – fitted to all Stanier locomotives but later changed to Metaflex type joints to an unknown Job number.
5236 issued in December – all engines to have ashpan sidedoor locking arrangement plus eyebolts and hooks to hold doors open and operating linkage from cab removed - system previously fitted to 6210 as a trial.

On 3rd April 1946, Job No. 5391 to financial authority NWO 6453 was issued for the addition of two washout plugs at the front of the barrel on several classes of taper boilers including the type 1s. We don't know the actual dates of modification, but all were reported complete by 1952.

The idea of the feed trays being removable for cleaning proved in practice to be much more difficult than had been imagined. Consequently they were replaced by simple deflector plates after 1949. In 1951, the top feed pipes on the first three boilers, which were originally proud of the boiler clothing, were moved below the level of the clothing panels and broad cover strips fixed over them.

Because of the alterations to the firebox and grate, the combustion chamber boilers required design changes to the frames and cab on Nos. 6203 onwards. Although the necessary alterations to Nos. 6200 and 6201 were authorised in 1941, they were not carried out until 1952. Until then just the first three boilers, two having domes and one that was domeless, were used on them. After 1952, they could accept any of the type 1 boilers. Starting in 1950, Nos. 6204, 6208, 6210, 6211 and 6212 were modified so that they could take the three earlier boilers. Details of when the different types were fitted are at Appendix B. Between January 1952 and December 1957, the domeless boilers had their regulators altered and domes fitted. At the same time new top feed covers were fitted and the regulator oil pipes and covers were removed from the smokebox sides. When steam-operated cylinder cocks were fitted to the engines from 1956, the atomiser steam cocks were also removed from the left-hand sides of the smokeboxes.

It seems strange that the majority of the type 1 boilers weren't rebuilt with dome-mounted regulators until the 1950s and we are happy to include here some speculations on the topic made by David Jenkinson and Bob Meanley. David Jenkinson supposes that:

'Wartime problems would, of course, be part of the story, but I am inclined to think that it may have been mostly cost-based. The two original boilers had to be fully reconstructed to accept higher superheat, in which case the simultaneous fitting of dome regulator and separate top feed in 1935/6 (which was, by then, standard LMS practice – hence its presence on the new boiler for 6202) made sense. But this was not the case with the last short-firebox boiler or any of the original long-firebox examples for that matter, all of which were built in 1935 and had high degree superheat from the start. Boilers normally lasted for about 15 years before major repair and/or replacement, so it probably made much financial sense to defer the fitting of dome regulators on these otherwise fully satisfactory high superheat boilers until a more comprehensive midlife overhaul was needed – and the dates of conversion fit this theory.'

Bob Meanley is of the opinion that:

D32-12585 – Inside cylinders

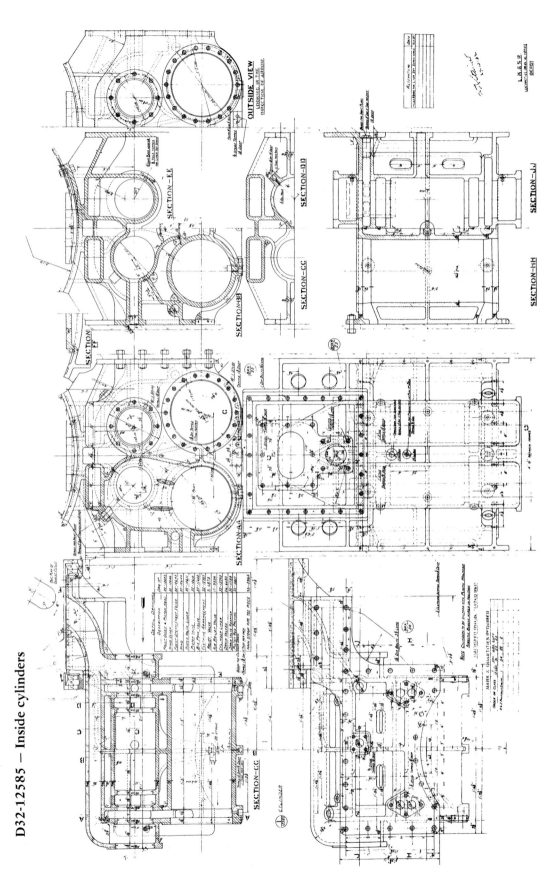

This drawing was issued for the manufacture of the inside cylinders on 6200 and 6201. A later version, dated 1934, was prepared for the main production batch of engines showing the different main steam pipes with which they were built. Also, as with the 1934 outside cylinder drawing, it omitted the bypass valve ports and facings as well as the sighting plugs and bosses. At the bottom left-hand corner of the drawing is an external side elevation whilst above that is a section taken on a plane through the centrelines of cylinder and valve chest. To the right of that is a split front elevation. To the right of the centreline is an external view whilst to the left is a transverse section taken on a vertical plane through the forward cylinder drain. To the right of that are sections taken at the rear part of the saddle, the centre of the cylinders, and the rear exhaust passage. Below them are lateral sections taken on two vertical planes through the top part of the valve chest – their positions are shown by the letters CC and DD on the side elevation at the top left-hand side. At the far right-hand side of the drawing is an outside view. At bottom middle is a plan view looking from above and at bottom right are two horizontal sections. To the left of the centreline is a section taken on a horizontal plane through the cylinders and above it one through the valve chests. The bypass valve ports and passages can be seen clearly on the side elevation at bottom left, where the diamond-shaped flanges indicate their position, as well as on the plan and lower right horizontal section. Sighting plus bosses are shown on the top middle view and section.

'It was probably as much to do as anything else with wear and tear on the regulator valve faces, which were likely to have been approaching scrapping thickness in an otherwise serviceable header (of which two survive to this day). It would have been cheaper to fit a dome regulator than renew the header.'

CYLINDERS AND MOTION

The four cylinders were 16¼in diameter and 28in stroke. Again, GWR practice was followed inasmuch as drive was divided between leading and intermediate coupled axles. The horizontal inside cylinders and valve chests were in a single iron casting positioned over the leading bogie wheels and drove the leading coupled axle. Their forward position was evidenced by the prominent fall plates with tail rod covers that protruded above the frames on the front platform. The outside cylinders and valve chests, also cast-iron, were inclined at 1 in 35 and positioned adjacent to the rear bogie wheels driving the intermediate coupled axle. This arrangement was seen as beneficial for two reasons. Firstly, the divided drive reduced the strains and wear that would have resulted from applying the effort of all four cylinders to one axle. This was held to have been a contributing factor to the problems experienced with the frames of the 'Claughtons'. Secondly, a better weight distribution was achieved on the bogie. Unlike contemporary GWR locomotives, however, each valve was driven by its own independent Walschaerts gear, rather than using just two sets of valve gear with rocking shafts. According to Eric Langridge, this was largely because it was realised at Derby that the latter arrangement resulted in uneven steam distribution. That Stanier approved the extra expense and weight of the adopted layout suggests that maybe he was not completely convinced of the benefits of Swindon's design. He would, of course, have been well aware of its drawbacks. Later events with No. 6205 and the 'Coronations', however, were to show a change of mind. One of the drawbacks of the cylinder layout was the difficulty of access to the inside motion, particularly above the bogie, which lengthened the preparation time involved when working a 'Lizzie'.

Steam was delivered to the valve chests by pipes running from the dry side of the superheater header and round the inside of the smokebox to branches leading to inside and outside cylinders. Those to the outside cylinders passed through the wrapper and then back to the tops of the steam

chests. Those to the inside cylinders contained very sharp bends, so from 6203 onwards their attachment to the steam chests was altered to ease them and give better internal streamlining. When Nos. 6200 and 6201 received new cylinders, they too had the later-pattern steam pipes fitted. In 1939, instructions were issued to fit glands to the outside steam pipes to prevent movement and steam leakage.

Eight inch diameter, inside-admission piston valves with ¼in lead and 1¾in lap were used. Although they were a fairly standard LMS pattern there was, unlike on Derby's previous designs or the later 'Coronation' Class, no exhaust clearance. Experience with the 'Royal Scots', Fowler 2–6–4 tanks and Horwich moguls had proved the benefit of multiple, thin valve rings and six of them, each ¼in thick, were used on the 'Princess Royals'. Maximum travel of the valves in fore gear was 7$\frac{9}{32}$in on Nos. 6200 and 6201 whereas the rest were arranged to have 7¼in travel on the outside valves and 7$\frac{5}{16}$in inside. Valve spindle crosshead guides were initially gunmetal but from January 1938, split cast-iron ones were substituted as the engines passed through the works.

When the 1935 engines first appeared, there were several reports from enginemen that they were not as powerful as 6200 and 6201. Stanier and Chambers thought that the problem might have been due to a slightly reduced port opening on the outside cylinders and suggested increasing the lead slightly. A set of valve heads was made for No.6206 with the lap decreased by $\frac{1}{16}$in and lead increased by the same amount, after which the engine underwent a series of trials. We haven't seen any published results of the trial runs, nor do we know whether the altered settings were adopted for the remainder of the main batch of locomotives. Our copy of the 1935 outside motion arrangement drawing, which was updated in 1938, shows the original figures with no mention of any alteration.

Near the front and rear of the valve chests were bosses with tapped holes in the castings that enabled sighting of the steam ports through the steam passages. These were closed off in normal circumstances by plugs that protruded through the cylinder clothing just below the platform angle. When viewed from the front they were sixty degrees from the vertical and were referred to as 'sighting plugs'. They were common to many Stanier engines and, as far as we are aware, their

purpose was to enable setting of the valves to be undertaken visually. Sometime after the original design had been finalised, however, the method of setting the valves changed and the sighting holes were no longer required. Hence, the 1934 drawing for the cylinders does not show them but they still appeared on the main production batch of engines, which suggests that the drawing originally included them but was amended. Replacement cylinders had the bosses, holes and plugs omitted and the clothing panels patched. The earliest dated photograph we have seen of an engine without the plugs is one of 6211 taken on 22nd February 1947, which was four days after it re-entered traffic following a heavy general repair. The next is one of 6210 taken in May 1948, the engine having undergone a heavy repair the previous August. Potentially, the earliest for which we have evidence, however, is 6205. It was photographed without the plugs whilst still in LMS crimson livery, suggesting a date before the middle of 1947. Assuming such a date, its most recent heavy repair had been in April 1946. Unfortunately, a lot of the above is conjecture and we have no hard facts except the dates of 6211's and 6210's photographs. Once again, if any readers can help we would be obliged.

All four valves were driven by independent sets of Walschaerts gear, all controlled by a single screw reverser. Because of the distance between reverser and weighshaft, as well as the offset needed to clear the wide firebox, the reach rod was in two portions, each connected to a transfer shaft alongside the left-hand rear splasher. Nos. 6200 and 6201 had this shaft at the rear of the splasher but on later engines built with combustion chamber boilers it was located in front of the splasher. The resulting increased length in the rear portion of the reach rod necessitated a support bracket and roller being mounted alongside the firebox, the lower edge of the rod being shaped to remain in contact with it at all stages of travel. The reach rod operated a transverse shaft to which the outside valve gear lifting links were attached and from which an auxiliary rod ran inside the left-hand frame to another weighshaft for the inside motion. The weighshaft lever protruded above the platform and on Nos. 6203 6212 was covered by a prominent slotted fairing in front of the intermediate splasher. Balancing of the reversing gear was by a spring attached to an arm on the reversing shaft and the maximum cut-off obtainable was 73%.

D32-12591 – Outside cylinder

Although a drawing was prepared in 1934 for the cylinders on the main production batch of engines, photographic evidence shows that all the locomotives were actually built with the type shown here, albeit with thicker bolting flanges. At top left is a sectioned side elevation taken on a plane joining the axes of cylinder and valve chest looking in towards the locomotive frames and below it is a horizontal section through the exhaust passage. At bottom left is an external top view. To the right of the sectioned side elevation is a front elevation and two cross-sections, one taken at the centre of the casting and the other at the centre of the rear drain. Below the front elevation is a full-size (on the original) detail of one of the studs and, to the right of that, a section at the bypass valve facing. The bypass valve ports and passages can be seen on the front elevation and cross-sections. Below the section A-A is a section through the valve chest showing a lubrication union at the top and sighting plug about 60 degrees to the right. At the bottom, to the right of the top view, is a horizontal section through the cylinder and at the bottom right is an external side elevation showing the inside face of the casting and flange for attachment to the frames. As with the inside cylinders, the 1934 drawing had the bypass valve ports and passages omitted and sighting plug bosses and plugs rubbed out.

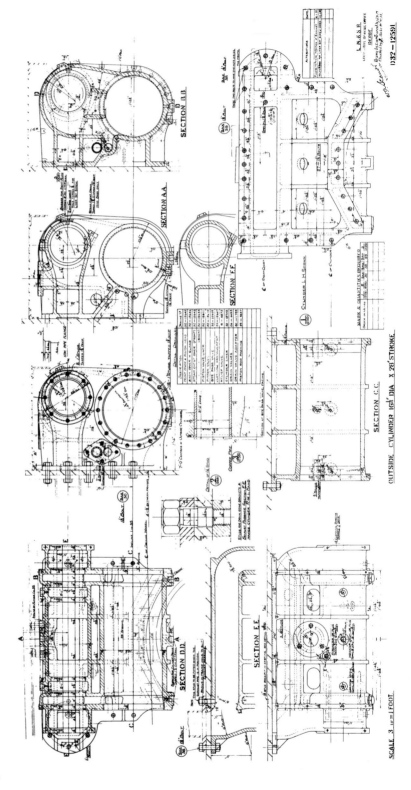

Design of the cylinders followed standard Derby practice with Fowler/Anderson bye-pass valves and large compression relief valves. Bye-pass valves allowed communication between the two ends of the cylinders when steam was shut off, thus avoiding the pistons acting as vacuum pumps and drawing in detritus from the smokebox when the regulator was closed. Stanier, however, thought that the risk of a bye-pass valve failure causing complete loss of power in a cylinder outweighed the benefit when coasting and so they were left out. The 1932 drawing from which the cylinders were made, however, incorporated the necessary steam passages and flanges, so they actually appeared on the engines and had blanking plates over the ports. Replacement cylinders made to the 1935 drawing had the passages and ports omitted. The engines were built with diamond-shaped holes in the frames just behind the buffer beam where the bye-pass valve flanges would have been bolted on. Stanier also changed the design to have smaller compression relief valves than originally intended.

Anti-vacuum, also called air relief or 'snifting', valves were provided for each cylinder, their function being twofold. Firstly, they had partially the same effect as bye-pass valves in preventing at least some ingestion of smokebox gases during admission when the engine was coasting. They also allowed cold air to mix with any hot gases that did get into the cylinders, thus preventing the temperature from rising sufficiently to burn the lubricating oil. If not prevented this could lead to carbon build-up, which was a particular problem with superheated engines. Previous Derby practice had been to fit both bye-pass and anti-vacuum valves and many enginemen disliked the absence of the former, averring that the engines did not coast as freely without them. The official technique when running without steam on non-equipped locomotives was to select 45% cut-off so that wear on the connecting rod big ends was avoided, the position being indicated by a button on the reverser scale marked with a D. This was known as the drift position.

Air relief valves were generally fitted to the saturated side of the superheater header but Derby favoured connecting them directly to the steam pipes or cylinders, outside ones on the 'Lizzies' being visible at the front of the external steam pipes. Initially they were the type that had been designed at Derby in 1917, consisting of a gunmetal piston in an iron casing with a series of holes around the base, the top being connected to the steam pipe. When there was steam pressure in the pipe, it acted on the top of the piston and held it down, closing off atmospheric air. When steam was shut off, however, the pressure above the piston fell and atmospheric pressure lifted it, allowing air to enter the cylinder via the holes in the casing. Although effective, the valves tended to chatter at low speed and wore rapidly so, starting in 1935, various modifications were tried. In 1940 a cast-steel valve design was introduced and found to be satisfactory, resulting in Job 5351 being issued under the authority of NWO 6319 to fit it to several locomotive classes including the 'Princess Royals'. Although we can't find records of when individual engines were modified, the job was reported complete in 1953.

The cylinder cocks were mechanically operated but the long and complicated linkages were troublesome. Eventually, in 1956, it was decided to fit steam-operated cocks and all except 46204 were altered between then and 1958. The cocks were not BR standard ones but were the LMS type originally used on the Caprotti-geared Class 5. Modified locomotives could be identified by the much less obvious discharge pipes that replaced the original ones extending forward from the cocks and clipped together near the cylinder fronts. At first, there was no access provided in the cylinder clothing for the steam chest drain or its neighbouring oil pipe adapter for the top barrel feed. This meant that the clothing had to be removed for any work to be done, which proved irksome, and so from 6203 onwards a small circular hole with a cover plate secured by four bolts was fitted. After a few years, the hole and its cover were elongated to an oblong and by the mid-1940s all the engines were so fitted. Under the clothing, the cylinders were lagged by plastic magnesia blocks wired in place.

Outside-cylinder exhaust channels passed through the frames and into a casting that also formed a saddle at the centre of the smokebox. The inside-cylinder exhausts passed over the top of the steam chest and merged together at the hind end, where they passed through the cylinder casting extension that formed the front smokebox saddle. Both sets of exhausts then joined into a single blast pipe casting with a nozzle to the rear and a Swindon-style jumper top. This was designed to lift when the exhaust pressure rose, thus increasing the diameter of the orifice and reducing the back-pressure to the cylinders to give a freer exhaust. Opinion was divided on the effectiveness of these devices and they frequently gave trouble, mainly due to accumulated carbon jamming them. As a result, starting in 1944, they were replaced by conventional blast pipes.

Problems were encountered with movement of the outside cylinders caused by twisting and racking moments on the intermediate section of the frames. As described later, various modifications were made to the frames, culminating in replacement of the front portions on most of the engines. This, however, didn't prevent loosening and movement of the outside cylinders. The cure was to weld 1in wide steel strips, known as 'shear strips', to the frames so that they fitted inside the flanges at front and rear of the outside-cylinder castings. The faces of the strips were then heat treated to relieve stresses and machined. The cylinder flange faces were also machined and interference fit keys driven between them and the shear strips before the latter were tack-welded in place. This achieved two things – firstly it reduced the possibility of the cylinders moving and secondly gave an indication if they did by the weld cracking. The alteration was carried out from 1953 onwards and was then used for outside-cylinder engines on other BR regions as well as the LMR.

Twisting of the frames also caused fractures of the exhaust passages from the inside cylinders and, as a result, between May 1953 and March 1956 all the locomotives were fitted with cast-steel inside cylinder blocks having cast-iron liners. In the cases of 46206 and 46207, this was coincident with the outside cylinder fixing improvement and front frame replacement described later.

Box pistons with three rings were screwed onto 3¼ in diameter piston rods on all the engines as built. Fatigue fractures in the piston rods began to appear at the roots of the threads and so, starting in 1943, new pistons and rods were fitted. The rods were lengthened and the pistons, instead of being screwed directly to them, were held against collars on the rod by left- and right-handed nuts with locking tab washers. The new pistons had two rings and bronze piston carriers and modified front cylinder covers were fitted in order to clear the locking nuts.

Lubrication of valves and cylinders was by mechanical lubricators on the platform.

D33-12817 — Inside motion arrangement — 6200 & 6201

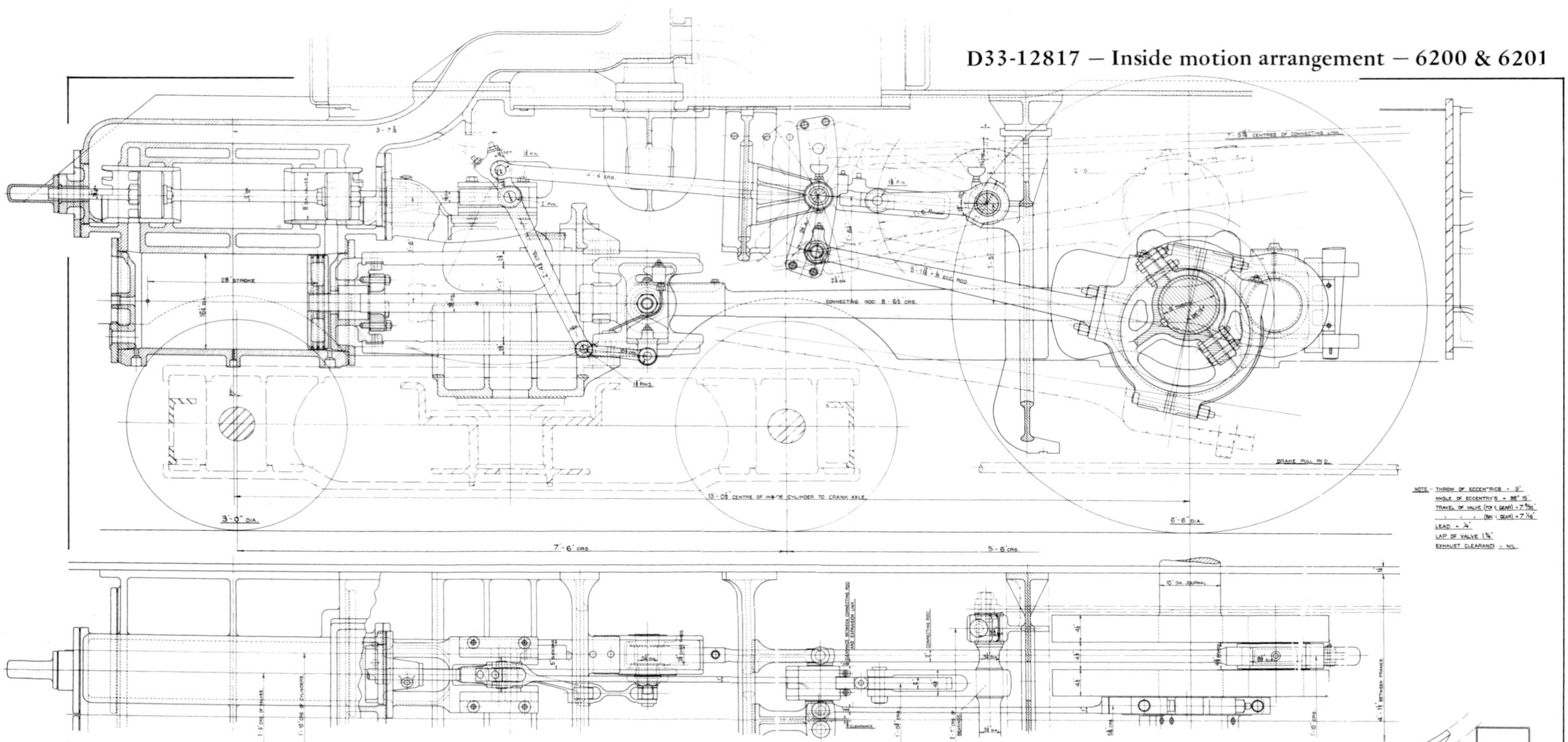

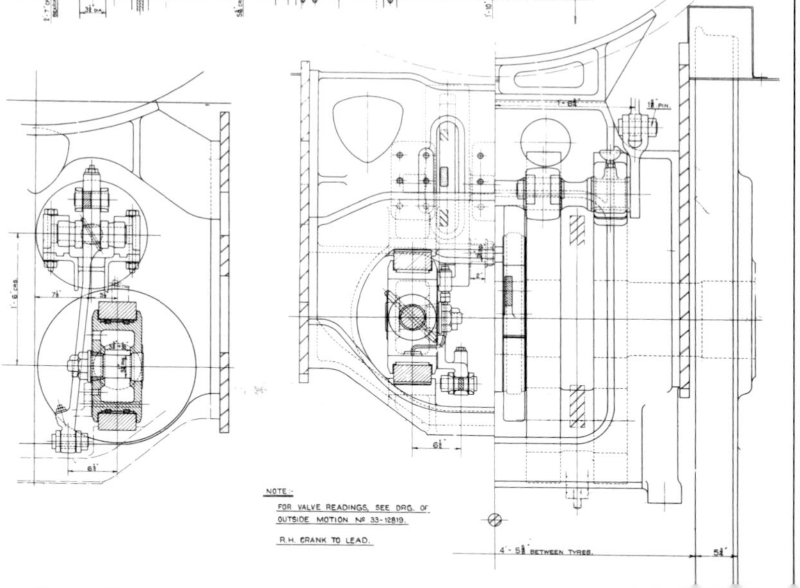

The inside Walschaerts motion is shown in this drawing prepared in 1933 for the first two engines. The general layout is applicable to all the class except that the maximum travel in full forward gear was increased by 1/32in on Nos. 6203-6212, needle rollers were used on some of the bushes, and fabricated motion plate, expansion link carrier and combined boiler support, stretcher and brake hanger bracket were used rather than the cast ones shown here. We have described the function of Walschaerts gear before, the only difference here being the way in which the eccentric rod was driven. Rather than being connected to a return crank from one of the driving wheel crankpins, as was usual practice for outside motion, the eccentric rod derived its movement from an axle-mounted eccentric. To the right of the side elevation are three half-sections taken at various stages. The top, split section to the left of the centreline looks back from in front of the motion plate to the expansion link carrier whilst that to the right looks back to the boiler support, lifting link carrier and leading brake hanger bracket. This was originally a single casting but in the 1940s was split into two. Below is a half-section looking forwards towards the cylinders and valve chest.

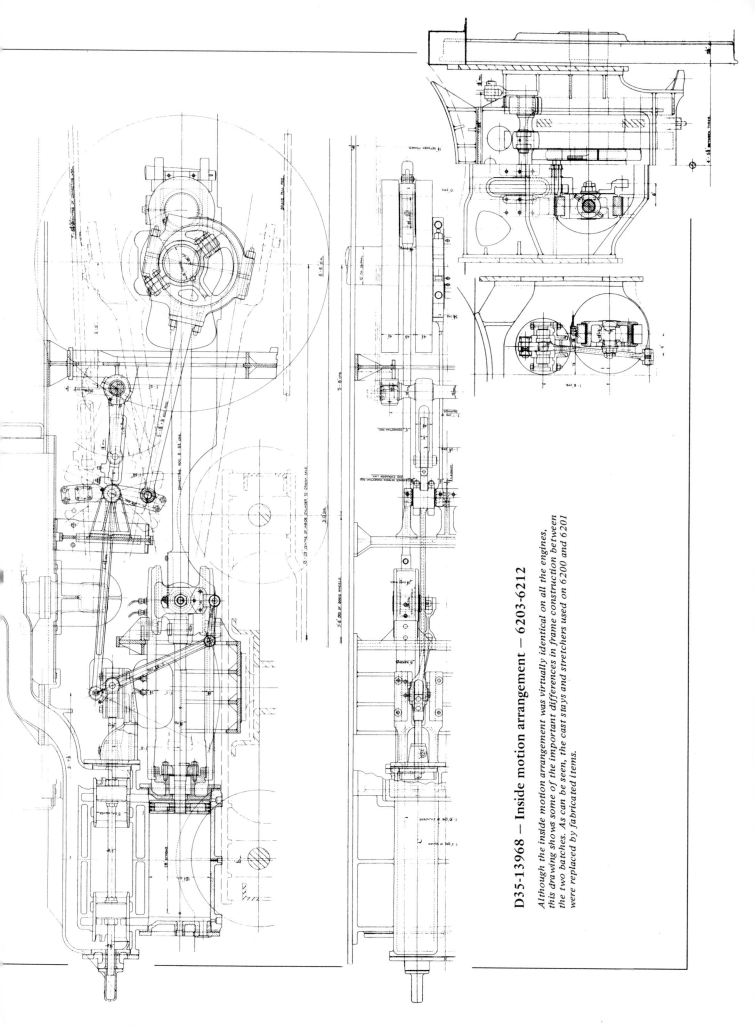

D35-13968 — Inside motion arrangement — 6203-6212

Although the inside motion arrangement was virtually identical on all the engines, this drawing shows some of the important differences in frame construction between the two batches. As can be seen, the cast stays and stretchers used on 6200 and 6201 were replaced by fabricated items.

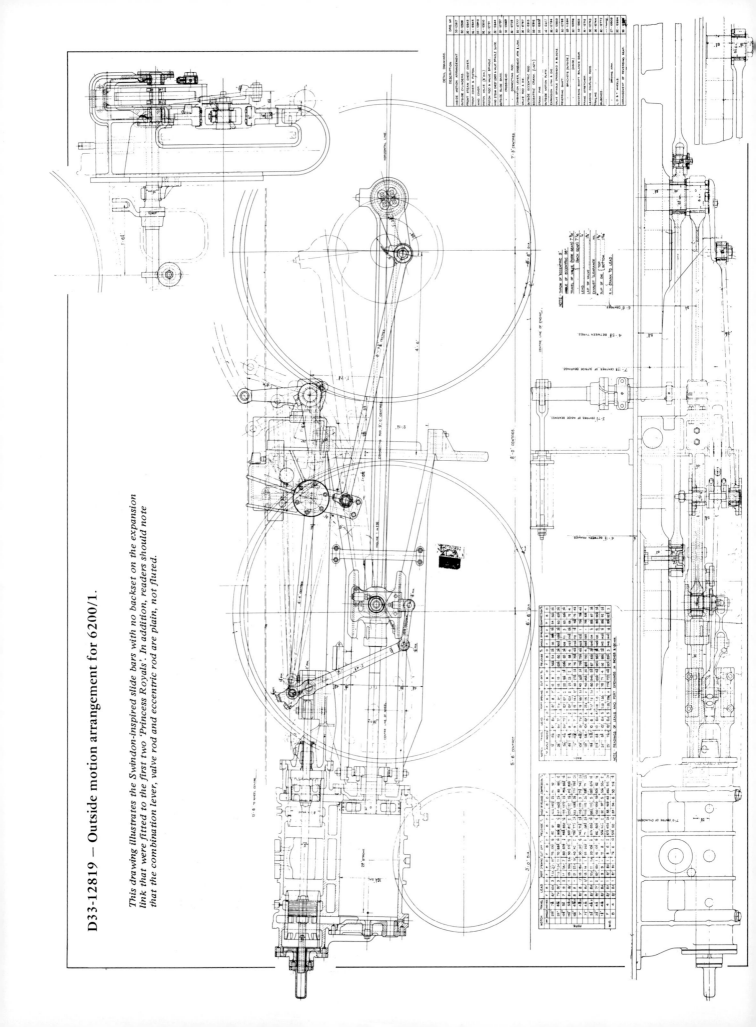

D33-12819 – Outside motion arrangement for 6200/1.

This drawing illustrates the Swindon-inspired slide bars with no backset on the expansion link that were fitted to the first two 'Princess Royals'. In addition, readers should note that the combination lever, valve rod and eccentric rod are plain, not fluted.

Atomised oil was supplied to the front and rear of each steam chest, whilst that to the cylinder barrels, piston rod glands and valve spindle glands was fed through back-pressure valves directly from the lubricator. Oil was atomised by steam from the saturated side of the superheater header. Originally, a valve operated by a feed from the mechanical lubricator directed steam to the atomiser when the engine was in motion. There were reportedly some problems with this arrangement, however, and Job No. 5175, issued in August 1939 to the financial authority of NWOX 6826, directed that Nos. 6200 and 6201 were to have the pump-controlled atomisers replaced by cylinder-cock-controlled ones. Since the Job refers only to the first two engines, we must assume that 6203–6212 were fitted with the latter system from new. When the cylinder drain cocks were open, no steam was available to the atomiser. A shut-off valve was provided on the smokebox side but since it was essential for it to be open whilst the engine was running, a telltale jet of steam came from the valve if it was closed.

Connecting rods were close-grained manganese molybdenum steel, inside ones being plain, rectangular section whilst out-side ones were fluted. Big ends on the inside rods were a departure from previous LMS practice as they had cottered, forked ends rather than straps and bolts. In the early 1950s, tell-tale devices that emitted a strong smell when a certain temperature was reached were fitted into holes bored in the inside big-end brasses so that the driver would be alerted to overheating. These devices, popularly known as 'stink bombs', were the subject of Job No. 5555 issued in May 1950 and although we don't have records of all the 'Lizzies' being modified, the job was reported as complete in March 1954.

Coupling rods, also close-grained manganese molybdenum steel, were plain, rectangular cross-section and 'fishbelly' profile. Stanier did away with fluting because the steel used was more elastic and better able to resist permanent deformation when placed under great strain such as that following a slip. He therefore believed that fluting would have been not only superfluous but also counter-productive. The outside connecting rods were made with a thinner section for weight considerations and were consequently fluted. The coupling rods had plain bushes pressed into the ends with whitemetal liners flanked by bronze side bearings or oiling rings. The latter had numerous oil retention holes to provide effective lubrication and so reduced side wear on long non-stop runs. All motion bushes on Nos. 6200 and 6201 were bronze with oil lubrication whereas the 1935 engines had grease-filled needle rollers on the motion and ball races for the outside return crank and eccentric rod pins. During World War 2, however, a shortage of such bearings forced a return to bronze bushes, albeit grease lubricated on the later locomotives.

Outside slidebars and motion brackets were different on Nos. 6200 and 6201 from those on the other engines. The former were clearly modelled on Swindon ones, having a deep T section and chamfered ends that earned them the nickname of 'rabbit ears'. They were supported at the rear by the cast-steel motion brackets located between them and the frames, inside the connecting rods, and projecting above the platform and outside the platform angles. The upper parts of the ribbed castings enclosed the tops of the expansion links and extended below the edges of the platform to hold their trunnion bearings. Clips connected the rear ends of the

This detail view of **Princess Elizabeth** *shows the 'rabbit ear' slidebars and type of outside motion bracket peculiar to 6200 and 6201. As can be seen, the motion bracket casting projected through the platform and interrupted the angle, which was attached to it. The number of oil boxes for lubricating the slidebars, valve spindle, lifting links, etc, can be seen, as can the position of 6200's and 6201's makers' plates. The picture was taken in BR days when there was only one oil box on the upper slidebar, a large plate was fitted in the cylinder clothing for access to the steam chest drain, and there were no sighting plugs on the steam chest itself. When the engine was built there were two oil boxes, two plugs and no access. The second oil box was restored sometime after this picture was taken. It had also been fitted with steam sanding; a comparison with the photograph on page 6 of the engine as built will show the difference. The absence of diamond-shaped holes in the front frames indicates that they had been replaced as described in the text. Note the stay from footstep support to frame, the clip between the slidebars outside the connecting rod, and the fact that the upper rear fixing bolt on the clip was missing.*   AUTHORS' COLLECTION

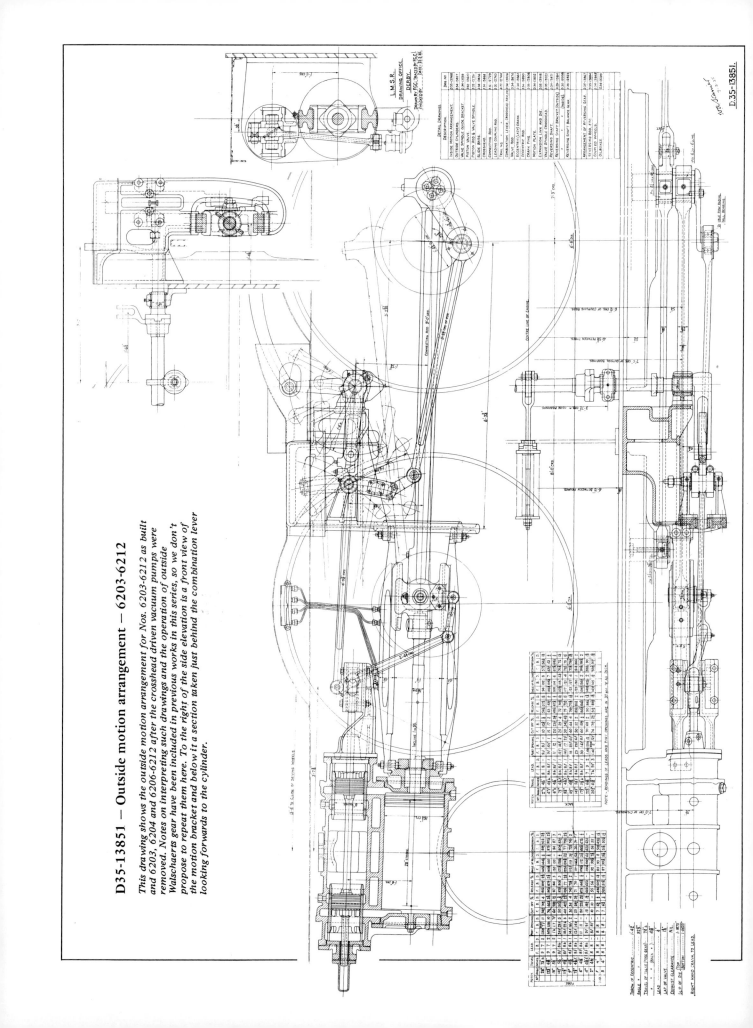

D35-13851 — Outside motion arrangement — 6203-6212

This drawing shows the outside motion arrangement for Nos. 6203-6212 as built and 6203, 6204 and 6206-6212 after the crosshead driven vacuum pumps were removed. Notes on interpreting such drawings and the operation of outside Walschaerts gear have been included in previous works in this series, so we don't propose to repeat them here. To the right of the side elevation is a front view of the motion bracket and below it a section taken just behind the combination lever looking forwards to the cylinder.

outside bars and lubrication was from two oil boxes on the upper slidebar and one bolted to the crosshead. In the 1950s the forward oil boxes were removed from the slidebars on some engines but seem to have been restored soon afterwards.

Nos. 6203 onwards had rectangular-section fluted outside slidebars, shorter than the first two engines, supported by prominent motion brackets that projected outside the connecting rod and extended above the footplate to the top of the main frames in a rectangular covered box to allow clearance above the expansion links. It also formed part of the platform angle. The expansion link trunnion bearings were in triangular, ribbed brackets bolted to the backs of the motion brackets. The front ends of both types of slidebars were bolted to brackets cast into the cylinder back covers.

Inside slidebars were rectangular-section Derby type on all the engines, supported at the rear by a motion plate that was an upward extension of the bogie stretcher. Inside eccentric rods were attached to the bottoms of the expansion links and the link trunnions had their bearings in rearward triangular brackets bolted to a stay between the frames called the expansion link carrier.

The cast-steel crossheads originally had gunmetal slides with whitemetal bearing surfaces, large rectangular holes being cut in the mainframes above the bogie for access to the inside ones. The frame flexing referred to earlier also led to problems with overheating of crossheads until alterations (described in the section on frames) were made, starting in 1936. Attachment of the outside eccentric rods to the expansion links differed between the first two engines and the rest. Nos. 6200 and 6201 had the pins set in the lower extremities of the links themselves whereas the others had them set into offset extensions, or tails, protruding from the bottoms of the links.

Between 3rd February and 11th May 1938, No. 6205 underwent a heavy general repair during which its valve gear was radically altered. Instead of four sets of motion, the reverse of GWR practice was used with the outside gear driving the inside valves via rocking levers. A similar arrangement, albeit with the outside cylinders further forward and the rocking levers attached to the outside valve spindles behind them, had been used on the 'Coronation' Class engines, the first of which had appeared in June and July 1937.

On 11th May 1938, No. 6205 re-entered traffic after repair with only two sets of valve gear that drove the outside valves directly and the inside ones via rocking shafts from forward extensions of the spindles. The most obvious alteration was to the motion brackets, which were strengthened to take the extra strain of operating two valves each. The structure looked somewhat crude and immediately identified the locomotive for the rest of its life. This photograph was taken shortly after modification when the engine was being indicated – the rear of the left-hand shelter and pipe from the cylinder leading into it can be seen. Note the extra section of balance weight on the leading coupled wheel necessitated by the alteration and that the crosshead-driven vacuum pump had been removed. The altered profile of the sand pipes when steam sanding was fitted is also apparent, as is the sandbox filler with a knob on top, just behind the reversing rod fairing. Later on, the latter were replaced by lids with recessed tops and handles cast in.

AUTHORS' COLLECTION

On 6205 the rocking arms were driven from the front of the valve spindles, which, as far as Derby Drawing office was concerned, was a less satisfactory arrangement. Because the strain on the outside valve gear was increased by having to drive four valves, the motion brackets were altered to large tripod structures that immediately identified the engine. The drawing schedule called for new leading splashers, outside valve rods, combination levers, connecting links and eccentric rods as well as alterations to the connecting rods and crossheads so that needle roller bearings could be fitted. That 6205's modification was intended as a trial is undoubted – several contemporary commentators have stated as much and the financial authority had an experimental number – but events after the war suggest that the intention was to alter the rest of the class. In May 1941, however, it was minuted that the modification was satisfactory but that 'in the conditions then prevailing (i.e., there was a war on) it was not desirable to convert the remainder'.

That 6205's gear was 'satisfactory' was not universally held to be true and it had been an expensive exercise costing £1,164. Comments made to one of us by some inspectors in the 1950s suggest that 6205 was considered a rough-running engine compared with the rest of the class. This was held to be partially due to the different inclinations of inside and outside cylinders requiring universal joints on the rocking levers, possibly exacerbated by slightly different valve events. In the early 1950s it was proposed that the whole class, with the exception of 6205, be fitted with derived valve gear, but the alterations were to have been much more extensive. So that the rocking levers could be simplified, modified 'Coronation' Class cast-steel inside cylinders were to be used, lined to 16¼ in and mounted at an inclination of 1 in 35 to match the outside cylinders. The valve chests were to have been thick-walled with 8in bores to suit the 'Princess Royal' valves. In the event, the proposal came to nothing and 6205 remained the only one of its kind, retaining the 1938 derived gear until withdrawal.

We have never seen any official reason for the wish to alter the 'Princess Royal' valve gear. The obvious thought is that it was intended to simplify the gear, making it easier and less expensive to maintain as well as reducing preparation time. Given the problems that were encountered with

D37-15117 — Arrangement of rocking gear for inside motion

This drawing shows how the inside valve travel on No. 6205 was derived after the modification carried out to its motion in 1938. The drawing was ordered on 1st November 1937 and completed four weeks later. On both side elevation and plan, the cylinder and valve chest are sectioned to show details of the front gland through which the extended spindle passed. The front elevation at top right is sectioned through the rocking lever.

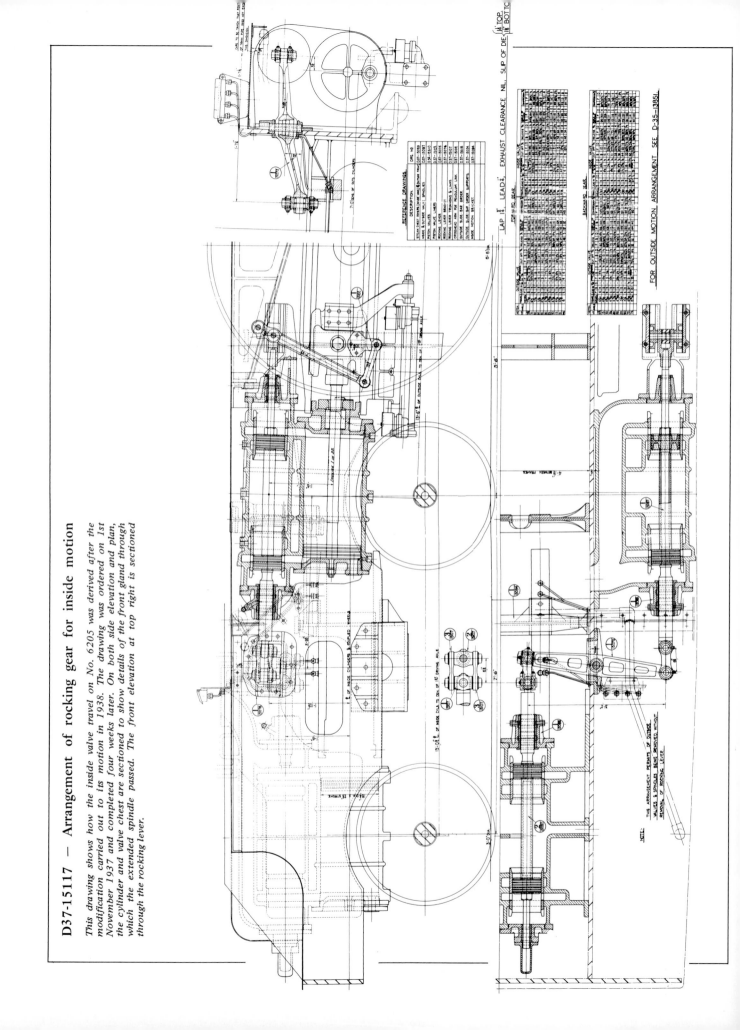

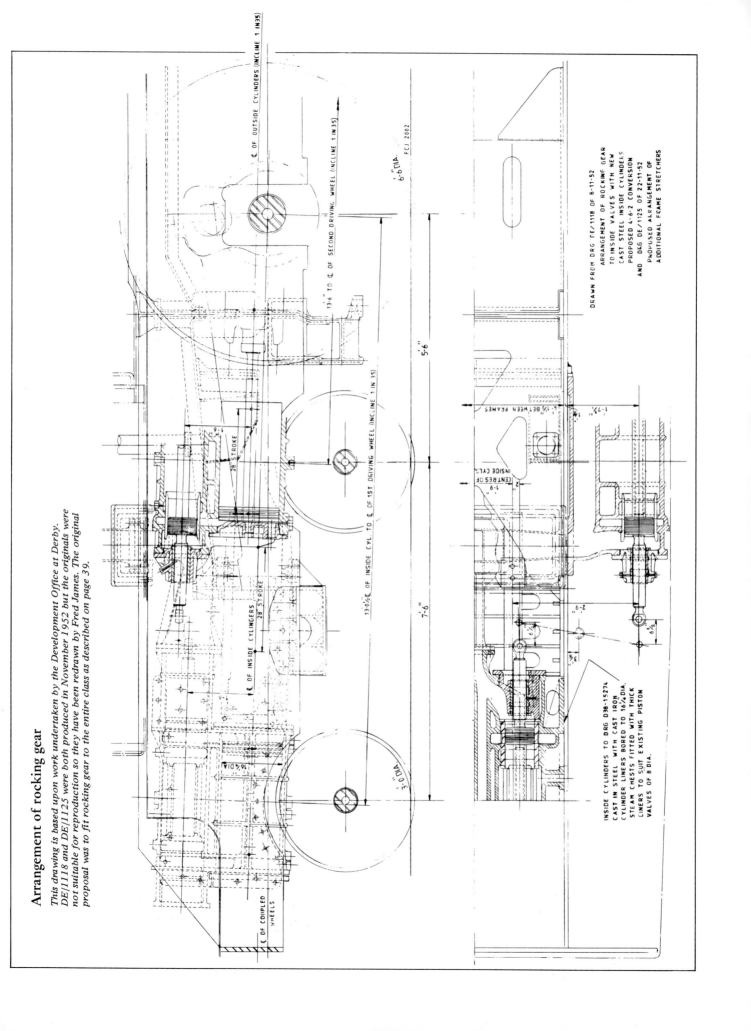

Arrangement of rocking gear

This drawing is based upon work undertaken by the Development Office at Derby. DE/1118 and DE/1125 were both produced in November 1952 but the originals were not suitable for reproduction so they have been redrawn by Fred James. The original proposal was to fit rocking gear to the entire class as described on page 39.

℄ OF OUTSIDE CYLINDERS (INCLINE 1 IN 35)

FCJ 2002

6'-6" DIA.

13'-6" TO ℄ OF SECOND DRIVING WHEEL (INCLINE 1 IN 35)

5'-6"

28" STROKE

28" STROKE

℄ OF INSIDE CYLINDERS

13'-0½" OF INSIDE CYL TO ℄ OF 1ST DRIVING WHEEL (INCLINE 1 IN 35)

7'-6"

16¾" DIA.

3'-0" DIA.

℄ OF COUPLED WHEELS

DRAWN FROM DRG DE/1118 OF 8-11-52
ARRANGEMENT OF ROCKING GEAR
TO INSIDE VALVES WITH NEW
CAST STEEL INSIDE CYLINDERS
PROPOSED 4-6-2 CONVERSION
AND DRG DE/1125 OF 22-11-52
PROPOSED ARRANGEMENT OF
ADDITIONAL FRAME STRETCHERS

4'-1½" BETWEEN FRAMES

1'-9" CENTRES OF INSIDE CYL.

1'-7½"

2'-9"

6½"

6½"

3⅝"

INSIDE CYLINDERS TO DRG D38-15274
CAST IN STEEL WITH CAST IRON
CYLINDER LINERS BORED TO 16¼" DIA.
STEAM CHESTS FITTED WITH THICK
LINERS TO SUIT EXISTING PISTON
VALVES OF 8" DIA.

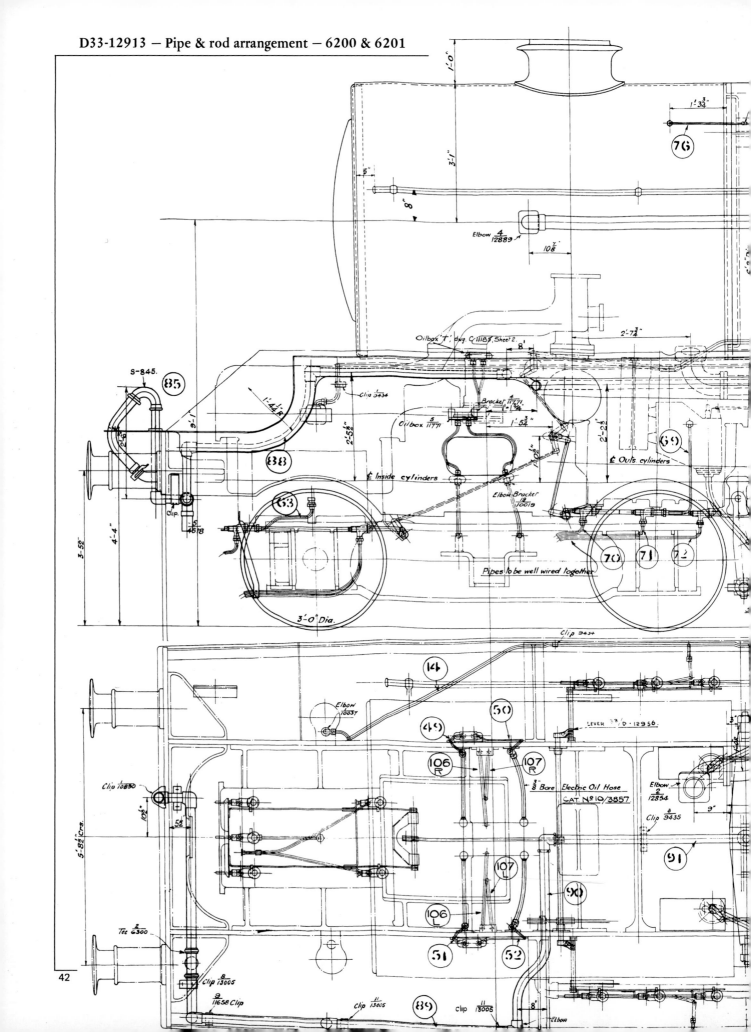

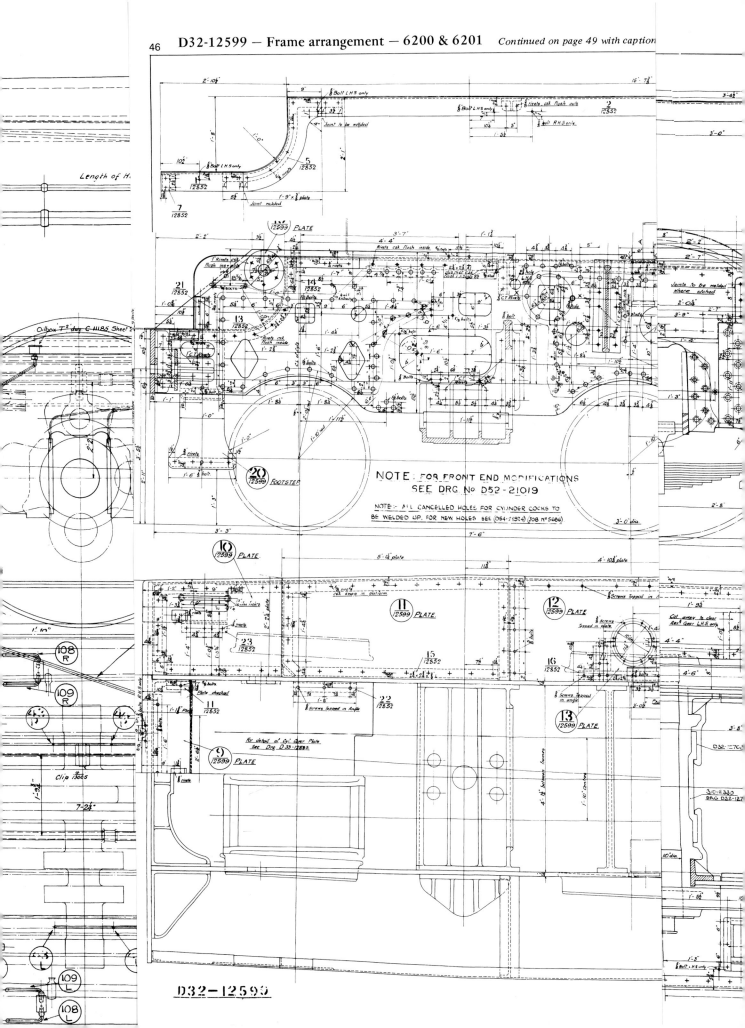

NOTE: FOR FRONT END MODIFICATIONS
SEE DRG N° D52-21019

NOTE:- ALL CANCELLED HOLES FOR CYLINDER COCKS TO
BE WELDED UP. FOR NEW HOLES SEE (D54-21574) (JOB N° 5686)

D32-12599

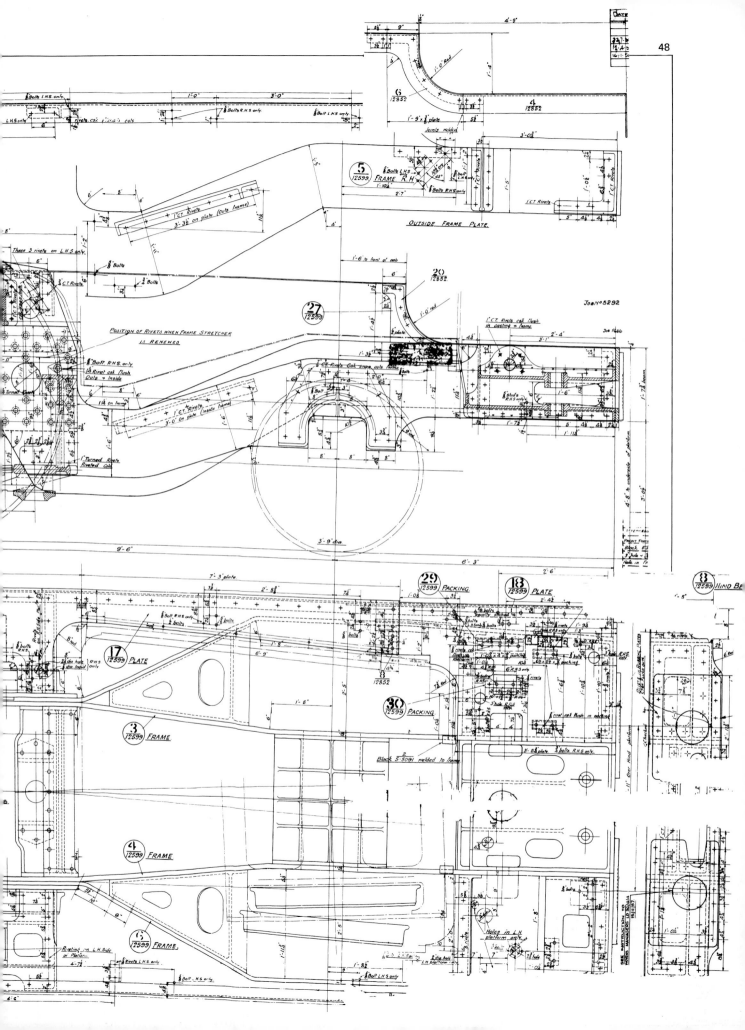

D32-12599 — Frame arrangement — 6200 & 6201 *continued*

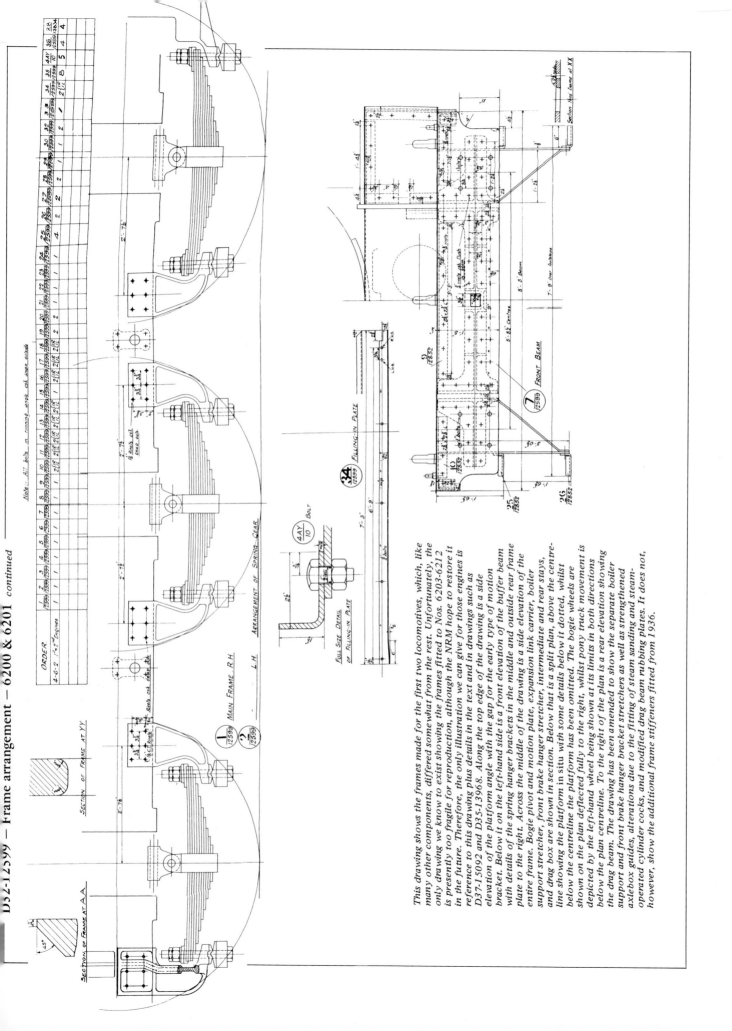

This drawing shows the frames made for the first two locomotives, which, like many other components, differed somewhat from the rest. Unfortunately, the only drawing we know to exist showing the frames fitted to Nos. 6203-6212 is presently too fragile for reproduction, although the NRM hope to restore it in the future. Therefore, the only illustration we can give for those engines is reference to this drawing plus details in the text and in drawings such as D37-15092 and D35-13968. Along the top edge of the drawing is a side elevation of the platform angle with the gap for the early type of motion bracket. Below it on the left-hand side is a front elevation of the buffer beam with details of the spring hanger brackets in the middle and outside rear frame plate to the right. Across the middle of the drawing is a side elevation of the entire frame. Bogie pivot and motion plate, expansion link carrier, boiler support stretcher, front brake hanger stretcher, intermediate and rear stays, and drag box are shown in section. Below that is a split plan, above the centre- line showing the platform in situ with some details below it dotted, whilst below the centreline the platform has been omitted. The bogie wheels are shown on the plan deflected fully to the right, whilst pony truck movement is depicted by the left-hand wheel being shown at its limits in both directions below the plan centreline. To the right of the plan is a rear elevation showing the drag beam. The drawing has been amended to show the separate boiler support and front brake hanger bracket stretchers as well as strengthened axlebox guides, alterations due to the fitting of steam sanding and steam- operated cylinder cocks, and modified drag beam rubbing plates. It does not, however, show the additional frame stiffeners fitted from 1936.

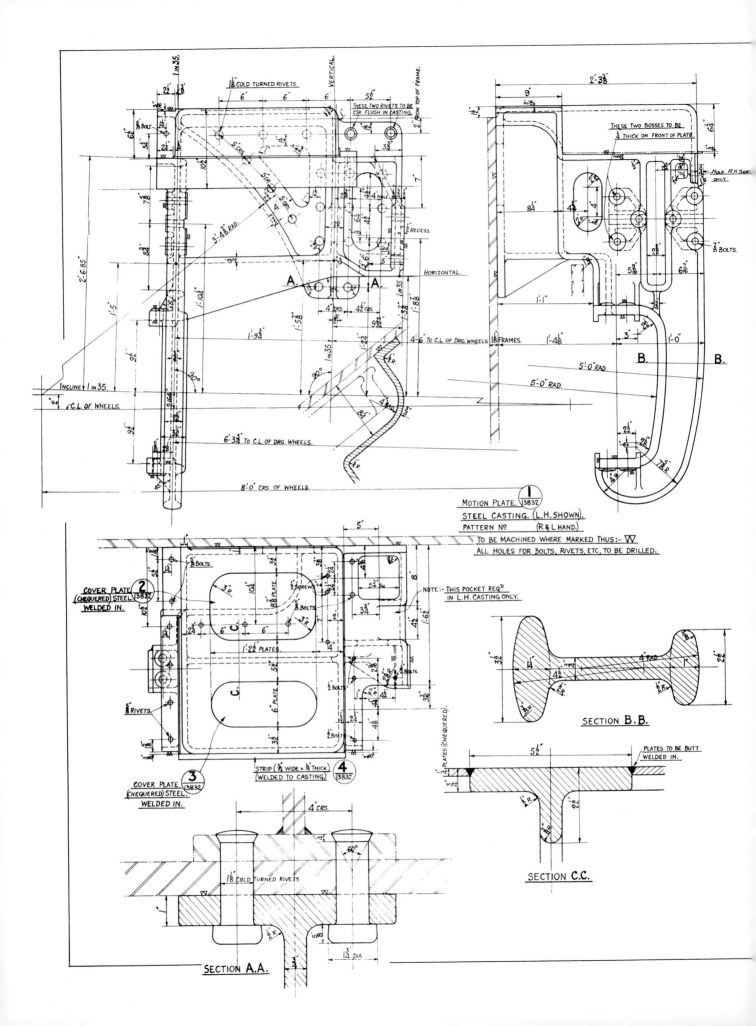

MOTION PLATE. ①/3832
STEEL CASTING. (L.H. SHOWN).
PATTERN Nº (R & L HAND.)
TO BE MACHINED WHERE MARKED THUS:- ⱲⱲ
ALL HOLES FOR BOLTS, RIVETS, ETC, TO BE DRILLED.

COVER PLATE ②/3832
(CHEQUERED) STEEL
WELDED IN.

COVER PLATE ③/3832
(CHEQUERED) STEEL.
WELDED IN.

STRIP (¾" WIDE × ⅛" THICK)
(WELDED TO CASTING) ④/3832

SECTION B.B.

SECTION C.C.

SECTION A.A.

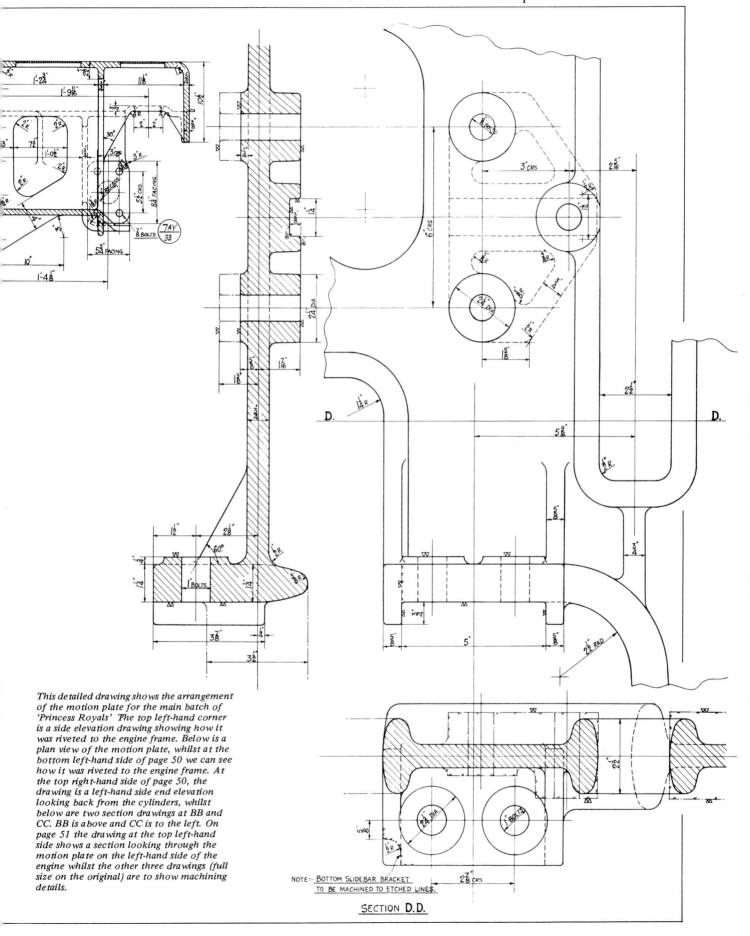

This detailed drawing shows the arrangement of the motion plate for the main batch of 'Princess Royals' The top left-hand corner is a side elevation drawing showing how it was riveted to the engine frame. Below is a plan view of the motion plate, whilst at the bottom left-hand side of page 50 we can see how it was riveted to the engine frame. At the top right-hand side of page 50, the drawing is a left-hand side end elevation looking back from the cylinders, whilst below are two section drawings at BB and CC. BB is above and CC is to the left. On page 51 the drawing at the top left-hand side shows a section looking through the motion plate on the left-hand side of the engine whilst the other three drawings (full size on the original) are to show machining details.

NOTE:- BOTTOM SLIDEBAR BRACKET
TO BE MACHINED TO ETCHED LINES.

SECTION **D.D.**

D37-15092 – Frame alterations at front end – 6205
Drawing on facing page

When 6205 was altered to have derived valve gear in 1938, it also had extra frame stays fitted between the outside cylinders. As we commented in the text, this may have been at least one reason for eliminating the inside motion, which idea was also revived in 1953. The drawing shows the extra horizontal plate between the combined boiler support, stretcher and brake hanger bracket and the motion plate, which replaced the gussets on the other engines. The plates were cut away at the sides to clear the sand boxes. There was also an additional full-width horizontal stay forward of the motion plate. This drawing was prepared by Fred James from a copy of the original that had been reduced to A4 size. As there were a large number of dimensions that were not easy to read, only those that are legible are quoted. However, it has been related to other known frame drawing dimensions, such as those on D32-12599 and D35-14252.

D35-14252 – Arrangement of additional frame stiffeners

One of the measures taken to reduce the amount of flexing in the frames, which led to problems such as overheating of the crossheads, was to add substantial steel gussets. They were fitted between the bogie frame stretcher/motion plate and expansion link carrier stays as well as to the intermediate stretchers. Large stiffening plates were also fitted between the frames over the leading coupled axle. These alterations are shown in this drawing by the heavy, solid lines on both plan and side elevation.

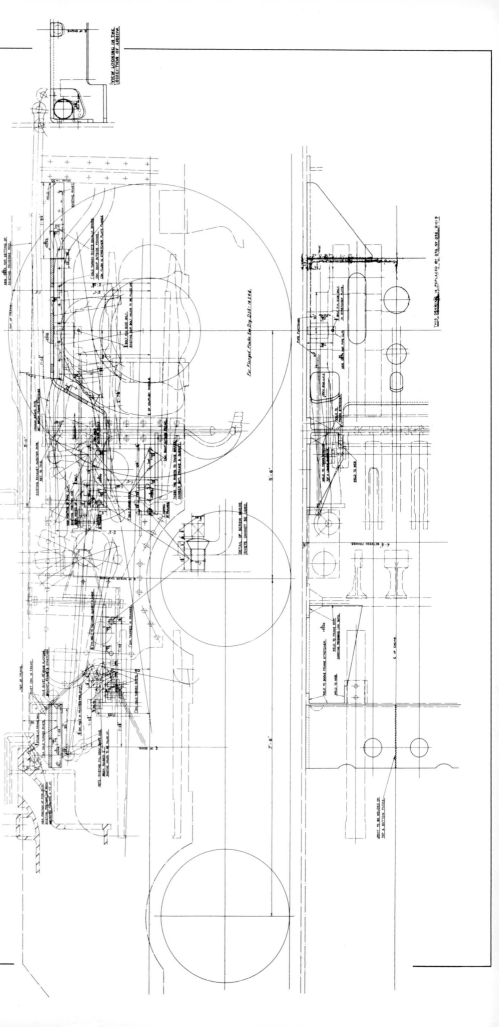

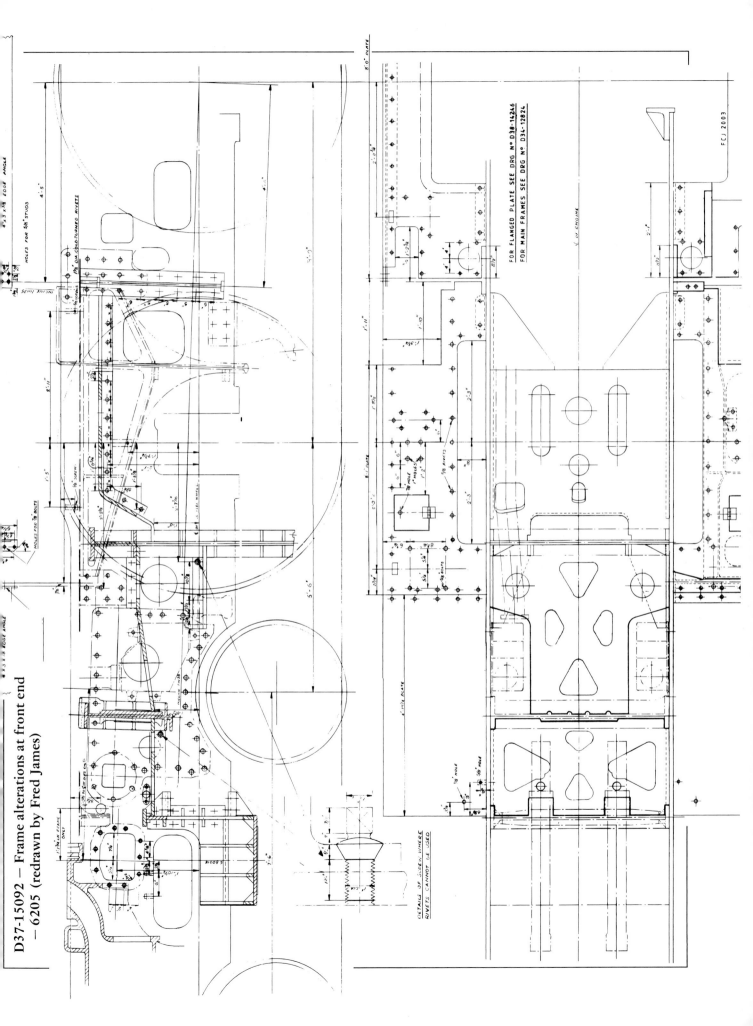

D37-15092 – Frame alterations at front end – 6205 (redrawn by Fred James)

D52-21019 – Modifications to front end of frame

This 1952 drawing shows the new frame front ends fitted to all the locomotives except, possibly, 46212 from 1952 to 1956. It also shows the two separate castings that replaced the combined stretcher, boiler support and leading brake hanger brackets on 46200 and 46201. At the top right-hand side of the drawing are details of the shear strips and keys fitted to prevent cylinder movement with a full-size (on the original) section through them. Whether or not 46212 was ever fitted with new front frames, it was included in the list of locomotives to which this drawing applied. Note that there was no separate drawing issued for modifying 6203-6212 and that the slotting details for all of them were incorporated into the same drawing, D52-21020, referred to at bottom right. There were, however, separate drilling drawings issued because of the different pipe work arrangements of the two locomotive types.

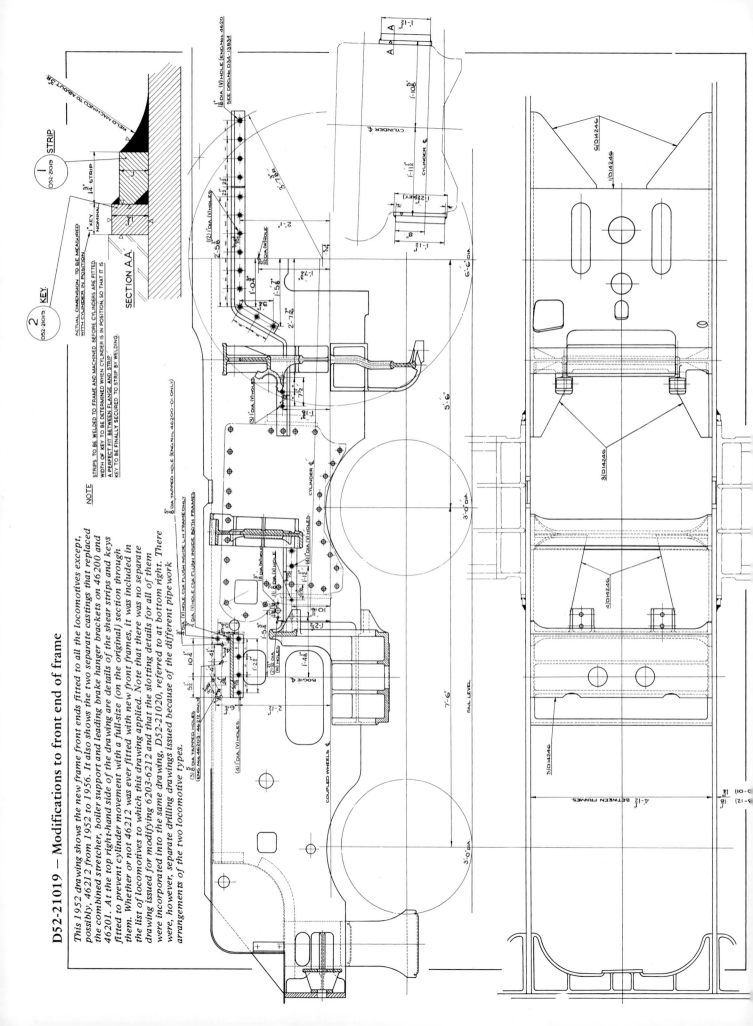

the frames, however, it is also possible that it was meant to free up space so that further stays could be incorporated, as was done with 6205.

FRAMES

The steel mainframes on 6200 and 6201 were 1¼ in thick and spaced 4ft 1½ in apart. The design concept was to use relatively little staying for such long frames but to make them from fairly thick material, thus building in a measure of flexibility. There was, however, a concern that the force trying to spread the tops of the frames, induced by the weight of such a large boiler as that on the 'Princess Royals', would be transmitted into frame closure at the lower edges. Apparently, this had been seen on other large-boilered engines. Cross stays were therefore used as a preventative measure. Design of the rear frames was closely similar to that of the aborted Fowler Pacific and quite unlike anything used previously. The main frames finished at the rear of the trailing coupled wheels, in front of the firebox throatplate, with the trailing truck under, and cab mounted on, shallower, upswept splice frames lapped and riveted inside them. There were two frame plates each side, the inner ones being 1¼ in thick and the outers 1in. Inner frame plates were set inwards slightly from the front, then for two-thirds of their length were parallel at 2ft 10½ in spacing, with the centre casting for the trailing truck and the drag box fixed between them. The outer plates were splayed outwards quite markedly from the front, ran parallel to just past half way and then had a slight inward set at the rear. Maximum width was 7ft 11in. Between the two on each side were gusset stays at the front and vertical and horizontal stays at the rear. The drag beam was joined to all four plates and the drag box. Because the lapped joints were potentially weak spots, they were welded along their outer seams as well as being riveted.

As one of the measures to reduce the weight of the engines, the frames on Nos. 6203 et seq were made from higher-tensile strength steel plate. This allowed reduced thickness to be used – 1⅛ in for the main frames, 1in for the inner rear extensions and ⅞ in for the outer ones. The spacing was the same as on the first two engines so the overall width was ¼ in less. Further weight savings were made by fabricating some frame components, such as stays, brackets, gussets, motion plate and stretchers, rather than using castings. These alter-

ations also reduced the cost. The frames were ½ in shallower above the bogie and ¼ in shallower from bogie to leading coupled wheels than 6200's and 6201's. The combustion chamber on the later boilers meant that the shape of the top rear corners of the frames was altered slightly to have a larger radius, whereas the lower corners were sharper. The frames of 6200 and 6201 were altered to match when they were made compatible with the later boilers in 1952.

Instead of hornblocks, separate axlebox guides were fixed to the sides of the horn gaps with stays bolted to the bottoms of the guides rather than being fixed directly to the frames. The underhung coupled axle springs were different from those that had been used before, the *Railway Gazette* describing them as having been the subject of special attention. The plates were made from silico-manganese steel and the buckles were connected to the undersides of the axleboxes by links and pins passing through them. The spring ends of the outer links had cup-shaped bearings to allow more freedom of movement and each link was independently adjustable with threaded ends and nuts. When the necessary adjustment had been made, the nuts were locked by pins. Unfortunately, the threads corroded and fretted in service and subsequent adjustment was often difficult at best. Between the links and the spring brackets were dampers made from alternating thin steel plates and rubber pads. Had a third reciprocating engine been built instead of 'Turbomotive', it would have had equalising beams between the intermediate and rear coupled axleboxes on each side. This can still be faintly seen on some drawings but we don't know why they were only incorporated into the design for the third engine, nor why 6202 didn't have them when actually built. Spring hanger J beams differed slightly between the first two and the rest, later ones being 'Coronation' pattern.

Probably the most immediate improvement Stanier made to LMS locomotive design was the GWR style of axlebox that he brought from Swindon. Even after Derby had started to use generous bearing surfaces, axlebox design had not been its strong point. Stanier's version consisted of a steel casting with pressed-in brasses and whitemetal liners and had excellent lubrication. Oil was fed under pressure to the top of each bearing, whence it was directed through small channels around the outside of the brass to oil grooves on the inside

surface. Additionally, each underkeep formed an oil reservoir containing a substantial horsehair and wool oil pad that was held against the axle by springs. Journals were 10in wide. Almost overnight, the incidence of hot boxes that plagued LMS locomotives was reduced by as much as 90% due to this change in design.[23]

Because of problems with cylinder movement and overheating of crossheads attributed to flexing of the frames and/or motion plates, various alterations were carried out from 1936 onwards. Some of the frame stay flanges were stiffened and substantial steel gussets added between the bogie frame stretcher/motion plate and expansion link carrier stays as well as to the intermediate stretchers. Extra plate stays were also fitted between the frames over the leading coupled axle. When 6205 had its valve gear altered in 1938, it also had extra stays fitted between the outside cylinders.

On 6200 and 6201, the front boiler support, weighshaft bearing and spring attachment bracket for the leading coupled wheels was a single casting that also formed a frame stretcher. It was prone to fracturing and from March 1942 its lower portion was replaced by a more substantial casting to Job No. 5292. The boiler support section was retained as a separate item. The main production batch of engines had a fabrication that doesn't seem to have been as liable to fractures and we don't know whether all of them were modified.

As previously stated, the outside cylinders on the 'Princess Royals' tended to work loose, which led to leakage where the exhaust channels passed through the frames. Despite the frame alterations described earlier, the problem persisted. In fact, it got worse on some engines because the fixing holes became elongated and fixing the cylinders properly was virtually impossible. Even the addition of the shear strips outlined earlier would not help unless the fixings were restored. In November 1951, No. 46203 was found to have loose cylinders only six months or so after receiving a heavy general repair at Crewe and was taken to Derby Works for rectification. This was the only occasion on which a Stanier Pacific underwent a heavy repair other than at Crewe and was probably so that it could be close at hand for the Regional CM&EE and his staff to observe and supervise the process.

In addition to the elongated fixing holes, fractures were developing in the front

Most of the visual differences between the first two engines and the main production batch are well illustrated by this study of 6203 Princess Margaret Rose *taken in the summer of 1936. The chimney had a subtly different profile and the atomiser steam cock was moved to below the ejector exhaust pipe, the small regulator lubrication valve still being in its original position. The combustion chamber boilers, which were not seen on 6200 or 6201 until 1952, had their Belpaire corners above the centres of the trailing splashers rather than over the hind edges, the washout plugs at the rear of the second ring were higher up, there was an extra washout plug on each side of the firebox, and there were washout doors on the firebox shoulders. Top feed pipes were hidden underneath the boiler clothing. The motion brackets were quite different, being outside the connecting rods, and the tops of the expansion links were covered by large boxlike fairings on the platform. The reach rod transfer shaft was further forward, near the leading edge of the trailing splasher, and there was a support roller alongside the throatplate with the lower edge of the rod shaped to remain in contact with it at all stages of travel. The weighshaft lever was covered above the platform by a prominent slotted fairing and there were circular access holes with cover plates in the cylinder clothing. The return crankpins had ball races rather than plain bearings, shown by the domed brass cover. The axles were bored out and the pony truck axlebox covers were different; No. 6203 had plain bearings, so its covers were relatively flat. When built, the engines were coupled to curved-sided 9-ton tenders, as seen in this photograph. Their first paint scheme was the same as the earlier engines with gold, shaded black transfers. By the time the picture was taken, 6203 had been fitted with steam sanding.*

AUTHORS' COLLECTION

frame sections at the leading horn gaps, 46203's left-hand one being affected. It was estimated that to weld up the defective areas and then re-drill the cylinder fixing holes would be costly and probably unsatisfactory. The answer arrived at instead was to cut off and replace the whole front end from the centre of the leading horn gaps forward – a total of 16ft 3in. The locomotive was stripped down and the front frames cut off. New, pre-shaped and drilled plates were then butt-welded to the frames, the joints dressed and the welds x-rayed to check for soundness. Shear strips, as described earlier, were welded to the frames before re-assembly to restrict cylinder movement. The repair took a long time and it wasn't until March 1952 that the engine was returned to traffic.

At the same time as 46203 was at Derby, Nos. 46200 and 46201 were at Crewe being repaired and as soon as the frame modification was deemed successful they were similarly treated. Their new front frames were to the same profile as those on 6203 *et seq* rather than that originally used. We have been able to confirm that all but one of the remaining engines were rebuilt in the same way, the last of them probably being done by February 1956. Since the diamond-shaped holes

This close-up view of 6201 Princess Elizabeth *was taken at Tewkesbury in the mid-1960s. Note the holes drilled in the front bogie stretcher for the fitting of the AWS receiver, the lack of diamond hole in the front frame above the bogie wheel, lack of cylinder drain pipes, and bored-out axles. All these details would have been different when the engine was built.*

AUTHORS' COLLECTION

above the leading bogie wheels originally intended for the bye-pass valve flanges were not required, they were omitted from the new plates. This fact can be used to detect which engines were altered. The only one about which we are unsure is 46212, as we have not seen any photographs taken during the relevant period showing its front frames in sufficient detail.[24] The length of time it took to deal

with locomotives was considerable, seemingly around 100 days, which in the early to mid-1950s was over twice the time normally taken for a heavy general repair. Thus, although the process wasn't recorded in the history cards, we have been able to identify likely periods when it happened for each engine, backed up in the majority of cases by photographic evidence. These dates are given at Appendix C.

Between December 1956 and November 1958, strengthened leading and intermediate axle box guides were fitted to all the engines as part of Job No. 5755, which applied to the 'Coronations' as well. The modification was occasioned by some rivets securing the guides to the frames working loose because of the longitudinal forces on driven axles. Replacement guides had broader flanges and were secured by twelve, rather than eight, rivets.

WHEELS, BRAKES AND SANDING

In the 1920s, LMS thinking had been that 6ft 9in was the preferred driving wheel diameter for an express passenger locomotive. The 'Lizzies', however, had 6ft 6in coupled wheels because, as an official LMS leaflet stated, the smaller diameter was desirable in order to obtain maximum power combined with free-running. The fact that the GWR 'King' had 6ft 6in wheels may, of course, also have had something to do with it. A reduction of a mere three inches would seem to be a trivial thing but R. A. Riddles later said that it made a significant difference and he regretted persuading Stanier to increase the coupled wheel diameter of the 'Coronations' to 6ft 9in (based, he said later, on a remark by J. E. Anderson that locomotives lost efficiency beyond a certain piston speed; whatever the truth of that remark, slipping certainly resulted).

The 20-spoke wheel centres were cast-steel with Stanier's hallmark triangular section rims, designed to make them stiffer than plain section rims and to give the tyres a better foundation. On 6201 and 6202 they were slightly wider than the LMS norm at 5¾ in and had 3in thick tyres attached to them by Gibson rings. The remainder reverted to 5½ in. Axles were 10in diameter, solid steel on Nos. 6200 and 6201, whereas those on subsequent engines were bored out 3¼ in, chiefly to save weight. Nos. 6200 and 6201 were subsequently altered to match.

The engines were dynamically balanced for all the rotating and 50% of the reciprocating masses. The balance weights were another departure from previous LMS practice with steel plates riveted onto inside and outside faces of the wheels and the space between them filled with the appropriate amount of molten lead and antimony. In shape they were all truncated crescents, those on the intermediate coupled wheels covering seven spokes whilst smaller ones on the others only covered

five. Extensions of the crank sweeps balanced the big ends of the inside connecting rods. No. 6205 had extra weights fitted to its intermediate coupled wheels when its valve gear was altered in 1938.

Along with most other six-and eight-coupled LMS locomotives, the 'Princess Royals' were the subjects of instructions issued in July 1940 aimed at increasing the sideplay on leading and trailing coupled wheels, bogies and pony trucks. The measures were intended to enable the engines more readily to traverse sharp curves in yards and depots but did not reduce the minimum radius over which they were allowed. Job No. 5155 applied to the 'Lizzies' and involved machining ⅛ in off the inside faces of leading and trailing coupled wheels. There were also some alterations to the bogies and trucks, as described later.

Locomotive brakes were actuated by a steam cylinder mounted inside the frames between intermediate and trailing coupled wheels. Those on the tender, although initiated by the same brake valve, were separate and are discussed later. Only the coupled wheels were braked, the hangers and blocks being ahead of each one with beams between their lower extremities, operated by a central pull rod from the cylinder. At first, the brake blocks were peculiar to the Pacifics but in the interests of economy it was decided in September 1939 that standard blocks would be used and the brake hangers modified accordingly. Brake hangers originally were retained on the top pins by split pins but they were prone to breaking and in December 1943 a start was made on replacing them with clips.

Vacuum for the train brakes was generated by an ejector plus a crosshead-driven pump mounted below the left-hand outside slidebars on Nos. 6200 and 6201 when they were built and by LMS combined ejector plus pump on 6203 et seq. The ejector was mounted on the left-hand side of the firebox just in front of the cab, the exhaust pipe running along the side of the boiler just below the handrail and entering the smokebox to join the ejector exhaust ring at the base of the chimney.

The crosshead pump was intended to maintain the vacuum in the train pipe when running, the ejector only being used to create the vacuum following a brake application. The pumps, however, were unreliable, costly to maintain and were thought to be a contributory factor in cases of left-hand piston rod fractures in the crossheads. In 1938, Stanier reported to

the Mechanical and Electrical Engineering Committee that it was common practice for small ejectors on standard engines to be used regularly for maintaining the vacuum against leakage, even though the crosshead pumps were operating. He recommended that as it was unnecessary for both appliances to be used, the pumps should be removed from all 885 engines fitted with them. Accordingly, Job No. 5088 with the financial authority of NWO 5149 was issued for their removal and, as a consequence, 6200 and 6201 were fitted with combined ejectors.

All were built with gravity sanding, or trickle sanding in LMS parlance, although the operating rods were steam powered on 6203–6212. The Great Western used gravity sanding on all its locomotives and Stanier decided that the complication of steam sanding was unnecessary. It seems strange that he did this since not only had it been found necessary on many parts of the LMS system previously, but also *Launceston Castle* had suffered when climbing Shap during its loan service in late 1926 because its gravity sanding proved ineffective in the weather conditions. Sand was applied in front of the driven, i.e., leading and intermediate coupled, wheels for forward running and behind the latter for travelling tender first. Fabricated steel sandboxes were positioned between the frames with filling pipes extending up above the platform. The front pipes were taller than the others in order to clear the outside steam pipes and all were originally fitted with slightly domed lids having knobs on top. In the mid- to late 1940s, they were replaced by lids having concave tops and integrally cast handles.

The engines were also built with hot water de-sanding apparatus – manually operated in the case of Nos. 6200 and 6201 but steam operated on the rest. This directed a jet of hot water onto the rails to the rear of the trailing coupled wheels when sanding was applied whilst running chimney first. It had been determined some years before on the Metropolitan Railway that sand left on the rails could disrupt electrical continuity between them and the wheels of locomotives and rolling stock, which would interfere with signalling track circuits. This was primarily due to over-zealous use of hand sanding because of its relatively poor effectiveness in some situations. Experiments had started in 1922 with desanding equipment designed to clean the sand off once it had done its intended job and the hot water system was

This drawing shows the original gravity sanding and hot water de-sanding gear fitted to Nos. 6203-6212. Unlike the equipment on 6200 and 6201 as built, the cocks for both sanding and de-sanding gear were steam operated on the main production batch of engines, although there were only three cylinders for the six sand valves. The other three valves were operated by bellcranks and links. The drawing has been amended to show the altered set of the leading sand pipes used from 1936 to enable easier oiling of the inside expansion links. The later steam sanding without de-sanding arrangement was not only more effective but was also less complicated mechanically.

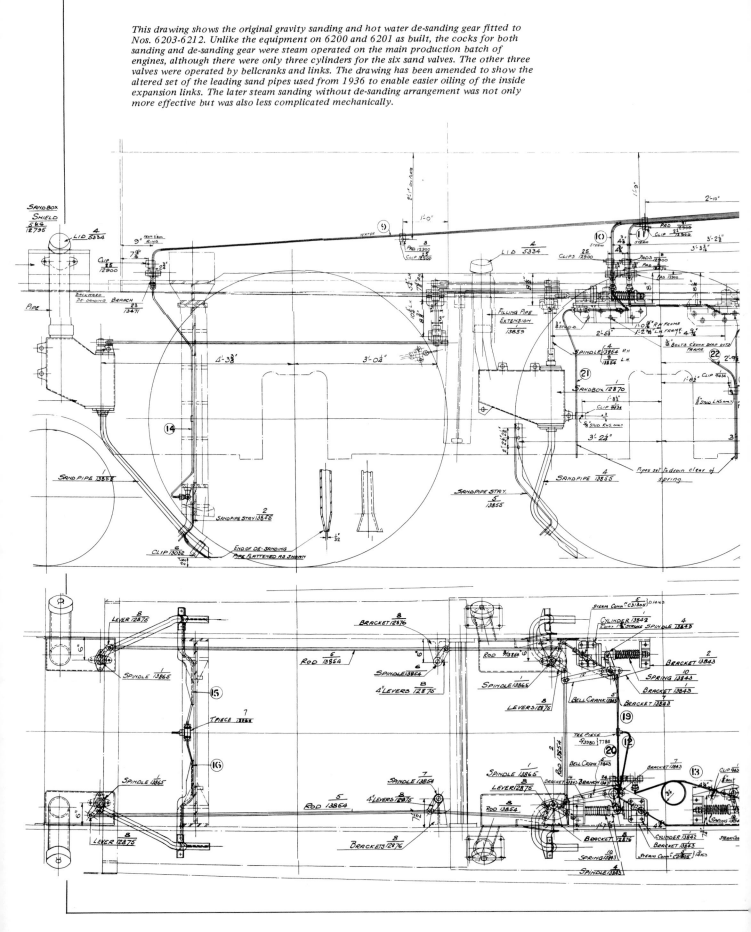

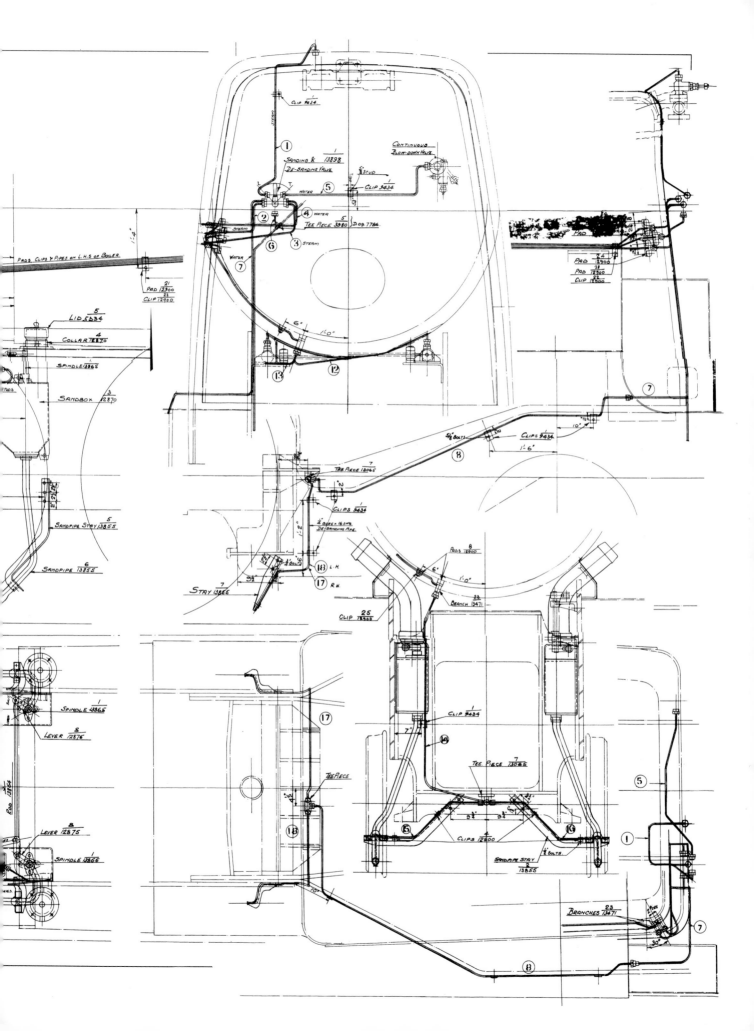

D32-12629 – Bogie arrangement

All the bogie modifications referred to in the text have been incorporated in this drawing. The side elevation is split, the portion to the left of centre being a section through the middle, whilst to the right is an external view. The plan below it, however, is wholly an external top view with internal components shown by broken lines. To the right are various cross-sections and end views. Top left is a half-section on a transverse vertical plane taken through the centre of the bogie whilst adjoining it to the right is one taken at the centre of a side control spring. Bottom right is a half-section taken at the centre of one of the axles and adjoining that to the left is an external end elevation. As noted in the text, the bogie was absolutely symmetrical except for the life guards, holes for which were only drilled at one end.

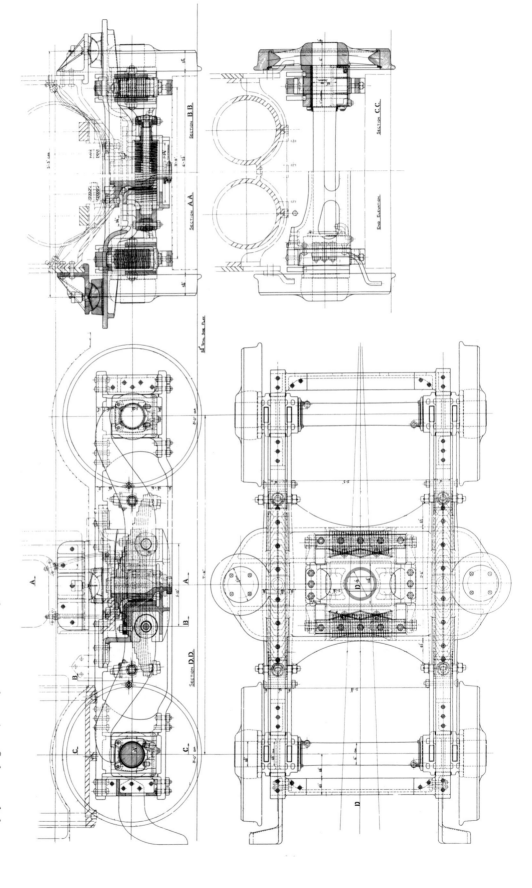

adopted on the LMS from late 1923. At about the time the 'Lizzies' were being built, however, the Civil Engineer had decided that damage was being caused to the track by the de-sanding equipment. As a result, the apparatus was soon removed and subsequent engines built without it.

By 1936, it was also apparent that gravity sanding on Stanier locomotives was not satisfactory. Not only was sand getting blown away from the wheels' path before it could do any good, but any slight dampness in the boxes was leading to blockages in the delivery pipes and preventing it from reaching the rails at all. NWO 4714 detailed the installation of steam sanding to Job No. 5019 in September of that year. Nos. 6200, 6203 and 6211, however, had already received 'unauthorised' equipment (i.e., prior to the new work order being issued) in April and May and the rest of the class was fitted by October 1937. Steam sanding, being generally more effective at getting sand to where it was needed, usually resulted in less being used. This in itself reduced the amount left on the rails and probably achieved as much as water de-sanding had. Thus, the de-sanding equipment was removed.

BOGIE AND PONY TRUCK

The type of bogie Stanier used was another great improvement on what had gone before on the LMS. The principle of side control had been introduced to the GWR in 1903 on the De Glehn compound Atlantics and developed by that company for all its subsequent bogie engines. The type was consequently known on the LMS as a 'French' bogie, that on the 'Princess Royals' having bar frames to save weight. Side control was effected through lateral coil springs in a central casting that engaged on a pin fixed to a casting between the locomotive frames immediately behind the inside cylinders. Lateral movement allowed was 2⅞ in each way. Wheelbase was 7ft 6in and the nine-spoke cast-steel wheels were 3ft diameter with triangular-section rims and Gibson ring tyre fixing, as on the coupled wheels. Axlebox guides were fixed between top and bottom frame bars with gunmetal axleboxes having oil reservoirs in the underkeeps and lubricating pads similar to those used on the coupled wheels. Equalising beams containing single, inverted, leaf springs, similar in construction to those on the coupled axles, bore on the tops of the axleboxes.

A notional 21 tons was transferred from locomotive frames to the bogie via side bolsters set at 5ft 5in centres. Steel bolster castings riveted to the main frames had spherical seatings underneath engaging in bearing cups that were free to slide on brass pads fixed to the tops of lateral extensions to the bogie centre casting. Lubrication of the slides was effected from a small oil cup on top of the bolster at each side. The bogie was completely symmetrical except that the hind ends weren't drilled for the life guards. In drawing D32-12640 for the bogie axlebox guide and stretcher, the holes and bolts for attaching the life guards were amended 'front end only'. This suggests the commonly-held belief that bogies were reversed from time to time was probably not true. The tyres were provided with special, 5 5⁄16 in thick T profile flanges, back-to-back spacing being reduced by ⅛ in to 4ft 5½ in to provide an additional wear allowance. It was normal practice to change wheelsets from front to back and vice-versa at intervals to equalise flange wear.

One of the drawbacks to the side bolster bogie was that if uneven wear occurred on coupled and bogie wheels, or tyre thickness differed due to differential turning, weight distribution would be affected. If the coupled wheel tyre diameter reduced more rapidly, weight would be transferred to the bogie and vice versa. On 2nd April 1940, Job No. 5207 was issued to resolve the problem. Bogie wheel types were permitted to be a maximum of ¼ in

thicker or ¾ in thinner than coupled wheels and, within those limits, different sizes of bolster pads were to be used when the difference was ¼ in or greater. When, starting in 1940, the coupled wheels had their boss faces skimmed for negotiating sharp curves, sideplay of the bogie was also increased. Other modifications to the bogies included the fitting of improved lubricating pads for the journals and stronger side control springs, both to Job No. 5413 starting in May 1945. Nos. 6203 and 6204 had the main bearing springs strengthened and new bottom frame bars fitted in December 1947. It would appear that these alterations were in the nature of a trial as they predated the issue of Job No. 5491 to the financial authority of NWO X9953 in January 1948. In March 1948, No. 6206 was similarly modified but authority was then cancelled and there is no record of any other locomotive being altered.

The pony truck was outside-framed and also used bolsters for weight transfer but they were between the wheels at 2ft 8½ in centres. The bolsters were mounted on castings riveted to the inner rear frame extensions whilst the bearing cups and pads slid on the centre truck casting. This centre casting was larger and more complicated on 6200 and 6201 than it was on subsequent engines as built. There was a cast-steel open frame from the front of the truck to a pivot point 6ft 10in ahead of the axle centre, the pin being carried in a

This close-up view of No. 6201's lower cabside and pony truck was taken on the same date as the view shown on page 56. The device below the cabside was the live steam injector.

AUTHORS' COLLECTION

D32-12747 – Pony truck arrangement – first two

The pony trucks differed in detail between the first two engines and the rest, as well as the type of axlebox varying as described in the text. This drawing illustrates the type originally fitted to 6200 and 6201. At top left is a split drawing showing a rear view to the left of the centreline and a section taken on a transverse vertical plane through the centre of the axlebox to the right. As with most arrangement drawings, components behind those in the foreground are shown dotted. At top right is a side elevation looking out from the longitudinal centreline, and below it is a split plan. Below the centreline is a view from above the truck with the positions of the locomotive frames and firebox shown chain dotted, whilst above is a section taken through two horizontal planes – one through the axle centre and one at the centres of the side control springs. As bottom left are side elevations and plan of an outside frame with hornguides and spring attachment bracket.

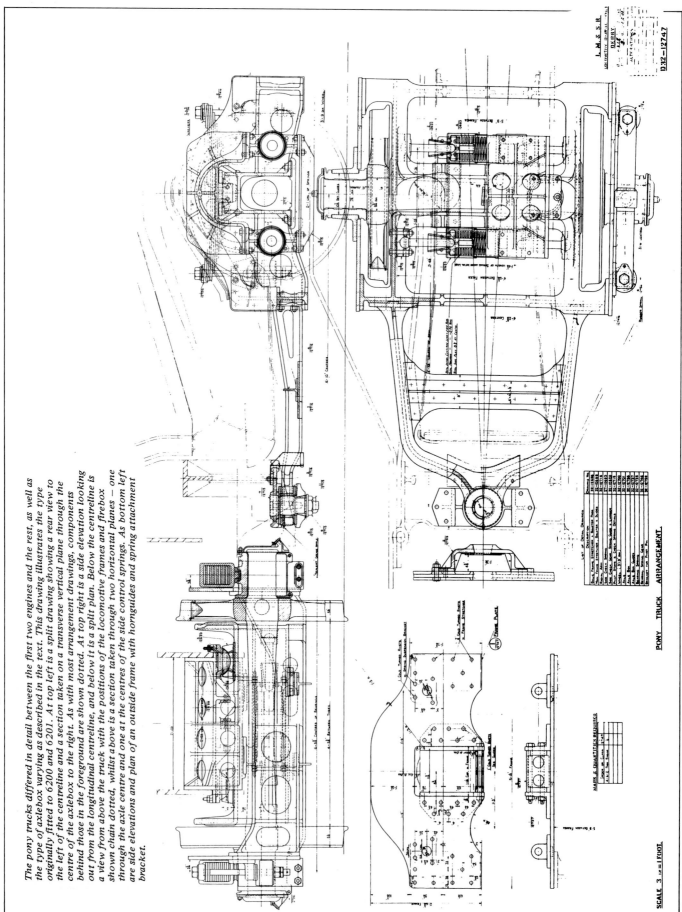

PONY TRUCK ARRANGEMENT

SCALE 3 IN = 1 FOOT

L.M.&S.R.
DERBY

D32-12747

D34-13877 – Pony truck arrangement

This drawing shows the type of pony truck as originally fitted to 6203-6212 with details of the frame alterations made when roller bearing boxes were fitted. As drawn, it illustrates one with a plain bearing axlebox but has notes concerning the alterations necessary for Hoffmann roller bearings. The latter needed an inch wider and ¼in deeper horn gap as well as some other detail differences. The layout of the drawing is the same as D32-12747 opposite.

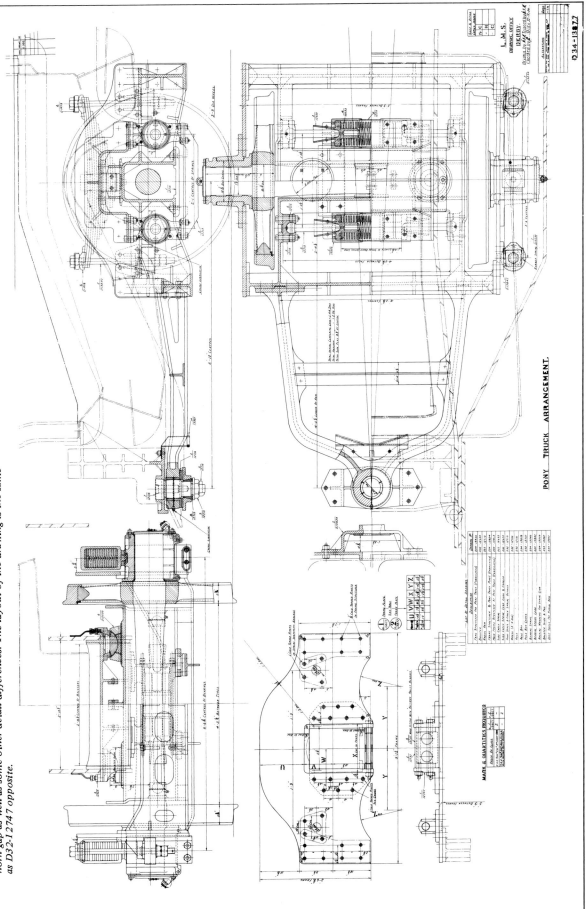

PONY TRUCK ARRANGEMENT.

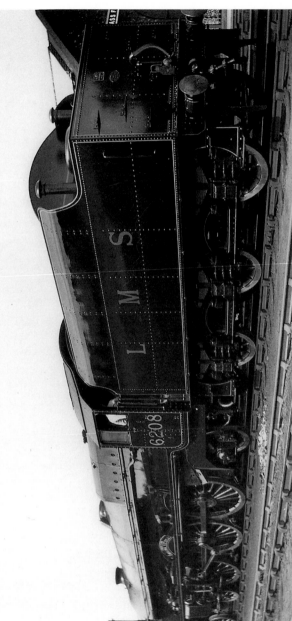

The first engine to be built with roller bearings to its truck axles was 6208, seen in this photograph outside the brass foundry at Crewe Works on 18th August 1935, two days after it officially entered traffic. The roller bearing axleboxes were quite distinctive, having relatively small diameter but pronouncedly domed end covers. In addition to the characteristics already noted for the main production batch, the support bracket on the right-hand side of the smokebox door can be seen.
W. L. GOOD

Another view of 6208, also taken two days after it was completed at Crewe Works, showing to advantage the characteristics of its 9-ton curved-sided tender No. 9129. Compared with the later 10-ton examples, the rear fender was further forward and the sides were not as deep. Unlike a great many Stanier tenders, all those allocated to 'Princess Royals' were built using snap-head rivets. Although the cab and tender insignia appear not to have had any shading, this is a trick of orthochromatic film and they were actually shaded black.
W. L. GOOD

stretcher between the locomotive main frames immediately forward of the firebox. Side control was again through lateral springs ahead of and behind the axle with a maximum travel of 4¼ in each way. The outside steel plate frames were 1in thick and set 5ft 9in apart. Gunmetal axleboxes were supported by overhung leaf springs having adjusting screws and steel strip and rubber dampers on the links. The frame attachment points were slightly different between the batches of locomotives. It has been suggested that 6200 was originally built with roller bearings to the truck axles but later altered to have plain ones. We have seen no evidence to support this and suspect that it may have been because the outside covers were different from later plain bearings examples, having some similarity to roller bearing covers. They were more prominent than the later plain bearing ones and had hinged lids to the reservoirs rather than corks, but were not quite as prominent as roller bearing ones and had a larger diameter. No. 6201 was built with plain bearings having the same type of covers as those just described. Nos. 6203–6207 were also built with plain bearings but the covers were flatter and had corks rather than hinged lids for the oil. The remainder were built with roller bearings having smaller-diameter, more prominent covers. In later years, engines could be seen with different bearings from those with which they were originally built, the alterations being easily detected by the outer covers. Since the horn-slots for plain and roller bearing axleboxes were different widths, we assume that the whole truck was exchanged. Wheels were 3ft 9in diameter, construction being as described previously.

As described in *LMS Locomotive Profiles* Nos. 2 and 3, there were several derailments in the early 1930s of swing-link trucks when engines traversed 1 in 8 crossings on curves at slow speeds. It was found that the centring force at the point where there was no inside check rail could move the truck sideways when it reached the gap in the crossing, causing the wheels to take the wrong road. At high speeds there was insufficient time for the truck to move enough and there was no problem on straight crossings. The solution was to fit ferrobestos pads (similar to car brake pads) that bore on the truck frames under spring pressure. The friction produced by these pads slowed down the sideways movement enough to prevent the outer wheel from entering the gap as it was traversing

it. By this time, side-bolster trucks and bogies were also being made with ferrobestos pads on one face of the sliding surface to avoid such problems and in October 1935 Job No. 5012 was issued for their addition to Stanier engines that had been built without them. At first, the modification was to be applied to both bogies and pony trucks but just over a month later the instruction was altered to apply only to the latter. The spring end shoes were modified in the 1940s under Job No. 5189, which introduced plate clips with 2⅜ in studs and split pins to the retaining clips. The provisions of Job No. 5207 in 1940, to compensate for the differences in wear between coupled and carrying wheels, were applied to pony trucks at the same time as they were to the bogies.

PLATFORM AND SPLASHERS
Width over the ¼ in thick steel plate platform was 9ft 0in, reduced at the cab to 8ft 11in and narrowing from above the bogie centre to 8ft 6in at the front. It was reinforced along the lower edge by angle-iron ⅜ in thick, 3in wide and 5in deep on the first two engines and 4in deep on the remainder. The 8ft 5in wide, 1¼ in thick steel buffer beam narrowed below the level of the angle to 7ft 8in and was flush-riveted on all engines as built. When 46203 left Derby Works in March 1952, however, her buffer beam had been replaced using snap-head rivets. As all Crewe repairs at that time used flush rivets, for a while this made her unique until flush rivets were used during her next repair in September 1955. Narrowing of the platform and buffer beam were for clearance purposes because of the long forward overhang on curves. Buffer casings were standard LMS Turton & Platt 'No-weld' type with raised footsteps on top. Nos. 6200 and 6201 were originally built with round-head buffers but it was found that buffer locking could occur on minimum radius curves in depots and sidings due to the long front overhang. Consequently, they soon had dished, oval plates riveted on to the heads in the manner of the parallel boiler 2–6–4 tank engines and the main production batch were built with them. Screw couplings were fitted to the front draw hooks of all the engines from the day they were built.

Steam heating was never fitted to the front of any 'Princess Royal'. The vacuum standpipe on No. 6200 was initially mounted so that it was completely above the front platform. Within a few weeks, how-

ever, it was shortened to what became the standard height with the dummy, or stowage point, adjacent to the bottom edge of the buffer beam and only about a third of the standpipe above the platform.

Footsteps were mounted on support plates riveted to the front platform and stayed to the main frames. The ends of the steps were turned up to give a more secure foothold than the older flat kind. Small steps were also riveted to the vertical portions of the front platform outside the frames of Nos. 6203–6212. The first two engines did not have these steps, nor were they ever modified to have them. Due to throwover of the hind end on curves there were no cab footsteps on the locomotive, those on the tender providing the only means of access.

As already remarked, the motion brackets extended above the platform and outside the platform angles, enclosing the tops of the expansion links. Both platform and angles finished either side of the bracket castings and were riveted to them.

Nos. 6200 and 6201 each had a Silvertown mechanical lubricator on either side of the platform just ahead of the leading splashers. That on the left had sixteen feeds and supplied the piston rod glands, steam chests, and cylinders. The right-hand one had twelve feeds, two of which were not used, and supplied the valve spindle glands as well as the coupled axleboxes. On Nos. 6203–6212, however, there were three lubricators, a twelve-feed one ahead of each leading splasher supplying the adjacent piston and valve spindle glands, steam chests and cylinders, and an eight-feed one just ahead of the right-hand intermediate splasher supplying the coupled axleboxes. Two feeds from the latter were not used.

As on contemporary Great Western locomotives, the intermediate splashers were set nearly 7in further out towards the edges of the platform than the leading or trailing ones in order to enclose the pipes to the top feed. Relevant measurements were 1ft 7¾ in from the edge of the platform to the inside faces of the splasher plates for intermediate ones and 2ft 2¹¹⁄₁₆ in for the rest.

Those locomotives of the main production batch altered in the 1950s so that they could be fitted with the first three boilers, i.e., 6204, 6208, 6210, 6211 and 6212, had minor alterations to their platforms. The different firebox shape meant that some cutting away and infilling was required and a new reversing rod guide was mounted slightly further out on the platform.

Following initial trials, Princess Elizabeth's tender received plain axlebox bearings, as seen in this photograph taken at Euston on 4th April 1934. It can just be discerned that oval plates had been riveted onto the locomotive buffers. The glass side screen, initially only provided on the driver's side, was folded back when the picture was taken and the rubber skirting on the gangway door can be seen. Note the stiffening angle and wing plate at the rear of the cab side and the slight bend apparent in the ejector exhaust pipe where it passed outside the top feed pipe.   L. HANSON

CAB

The cab had a ¼in steel-plate platform, ³⁄₁₆in sides and front, and ⅛in thick roof. It was generously proportioned, width overall being 8ft 10in and maximum height of the roof above the footboards 7ft 4¾in. The footboards were 5ft 9¼in above the rails. The rear of the cab was stiffened by 3in angle down the sides and round the inside of the roof with 10in wide wing, or backing, plates set at 90 degrees to the sides and stretching from the platform to the tops of the commode-style handrails. Twenty holes of ½in diameter at 2¼in pitch were drilled in the front plate just below the roof to admit cooling air and further ventilation could be provided by the sliding ventilator in the roof itself. The top of the ventilator was the highest point on the locomotive, being 13ft 3in above the rails. The radius of the roof at the overhang was sharper than it was between the cab sides in order to give loading gauge clearance because of the throwover on curves.

The cab shape was reminiscent of Horwich engines with two wooden-framed windows on each side. Both windows were able to slide, the rear inside the front one, in a cast channel. The front ones were later secured, possibly when blackout screens were fitted during the war. Front windows were hinged on their inside edges and held closed by spring-loaded catches. As built, Nos. 6200 and 6201 had a hinged

glass side screen outside the cab between front and rear side windows on the driver's side only. In 1934, similar screens were fitted to the fireman's side and 6203 *et seq* were built with two screens.

On the driver's side, a toolbox just over a foot wide and nearly two feet long was built in to the front corner of the cab. On the other side, the fireman had what was described as a cupboard, which was the same width but only half as deep. On 6200 and 6201, both had doors. The remainder, strangely enough, had lids on the 'cupboards' but doors on the 'toolboxes'. Tip-up seats were provided on both sides.

The wooden-plank cab floor was 13in above the platform. It has been related several times that the single-bore tunnel on the down main line at Linslade was such a close fit around the 'Lizzies' that the air pressure generated under an engine as it entered was sometimes sufficient to dislodge the floorboards. Whether the further embellishment that they were swept away and crews were left standing on the drag box is true or not, however, we can't say. Maybe a reader can add to the story. Folding gangway doors were fitted, held closed against the insides of the tender side plates by springs and having rubber sheet extensions to eliminate some of the draught that otherwise would have come underneath them. They also helped to prevent lumps of coal falling off the engine and causing damage or injury. These extensions

do not seem to have lasted very long and needed frequent replacement at various repairs.

Alterations to the cabs included the following:

Job No. 5013 of November 1936 – additional stops and guides fitted to gangway doors.

Job No. 4959 of August 1937 – thickness of window glass increased from ³⁄₁₆in to ¼in.

Job 5031 of February 1938 – spring-loaded front window catches, which proved troublesome, replaced by rotating handles and catches.

Job No. 5146 of September 1939 – stiffening brackets added to the insides of the wing plates to prevent fractures.

Job No. 5240 of February 1941 – fitting modified springs and guides on gangway doors as the originals were prone to coming off.

Job No. 5256 of August 1941 – modified front window fastenings so that the windows could be opened about 2in and locked in position – meant to improve ventilation when blackout screens were fitted at night.

Job No. 5354 of August 1943 – extension of fall plate sections to prevent them falling between engine and tender when traversing sharp curves.

Another unfamiliar feature, to LMS crews, of the 'Princesses' when built was the steam manifold in the cab above the firebox backplate. Consideration had been given to utilising a manifold in front of the cab when the Horwich mogul was being schemed but had come to nothing. Its addition was beneficial both to enginemen and fitters as it had its own steam supply shut-off valve as well as control valves for steam brakes, injectors, ejectors, regulator lubricator, whistle and carriage warming. Nos. 6200 and 6201 also had control valves for the ashpan flushing system. Layout of the other controls was determined by making a wooden mock-up and trying out various positions before finally deciding on their placement. Thus, the blower handle was placed in the centre of the boiler backplate where it could be reached by either driver or fireman. Unfortunately, neither could get to it if the firebox suffered a blow-back (although this was not exactly a common occurrence and the shovel or coal pick could be used).

There were whistle handles on both sides of the cab roof, but we have been told by people with first-hand experience that they were awkward to reach for some enginemen. Firedoors were the double, roller type with a single operating handle. The first three boilers had large, GWR-style firehole flaps with oblong slots in them. The rest had smaller flaps that still allowed firing when they were in position. The screw reverser was mounted on the driver's side toolbox with a prominent intermediate gear between the handle and the reversing screw because the reach rod was set well out to clear the wide firebox.

The regulator handles on the first three boilers were conventional, single-ended ones. The boilers made for 6203 onwards, however, had double handles, the two branches being set at about 120 degrees, so that the regulator could be operated from either side of the cab. This should not be confused with the two-handled regulator found on some Midland and LMS standard locomotives that was frequently referred to as a 'compound handle'.

Nos. 6200 and 6201 had what was declared to be the 'new standard' driver's brake valve for LMS engines. Rather than the standard LMS variety, they each had a

1. Regulator handle
2. Main steam valve for steam manifold
3. Live steam valve to exhaust injector
4. Live steam pipe to injector
5. Exhaust steam injector
8. Water feed pipe to injector
10. Injector overflow pipe
11. Water control gear for injector
12. Steam valve for live steam injector
13. Live steam pipe to injector
14. Live steam injector
15. Water feed pipe to injector
17. Injector overflow pipe
18. Water control gear for injector
19. Stop valve for ejector steam valves
20. Small ejector steam valve
21. Large ejector steam valve
23. Vacuum gauge
24. Driver's brake valve
25. Train pipe
26. Steam brake pipe
27. Steam brake cylinder lubricator
28. Drip valve for train pipe
29. Train pipe connection to tender
30. Vacuum relief valve
31. Steam brake pipe connection to tender
32. Stop valve to carriage warming reducing valve
33. Carriage warming reducing valve
34. Carriage warming pressure gauge
35. Carriage warming hose-pipe connection to tender
36. Water gauge cocks
37. Stop valve for steam sanding
38. Steam sanding valve
39. Side damper door handle
40. Front and rear damper door handles
41. Steam valve for boiler pressure gauge
42. Boiler pressure gauge
43. Whistle valve
44. Whistle valve handles
45. Blower valve
46. Sight feed lubricator for regulator valve
47. Steam valve for sight feed lubricator
48. Condenser coil for sight feed lubricator
49. Gauge glass test cock
50. Combined continuous blowdown, ash pan flushing and de-sanding valve
51. Gauge glass lamp
52. Washout plugs
53. Reversing screw handle
54. Cylinder drain cock handle
55. Driver's seat
56. Firehole door
57. Coal watering cock
58. Fireman's seat

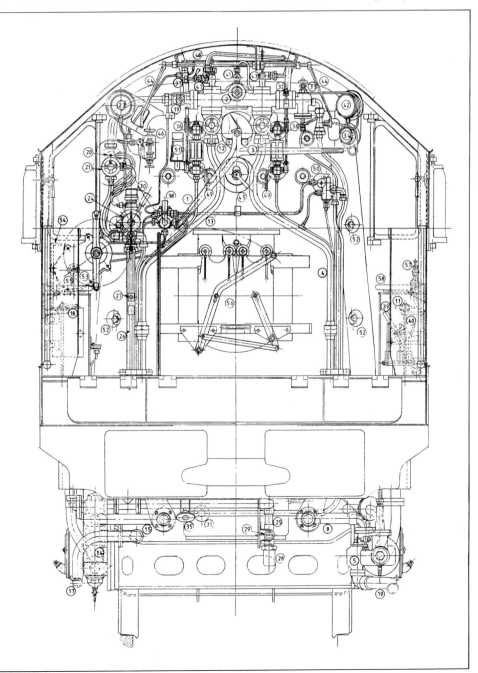

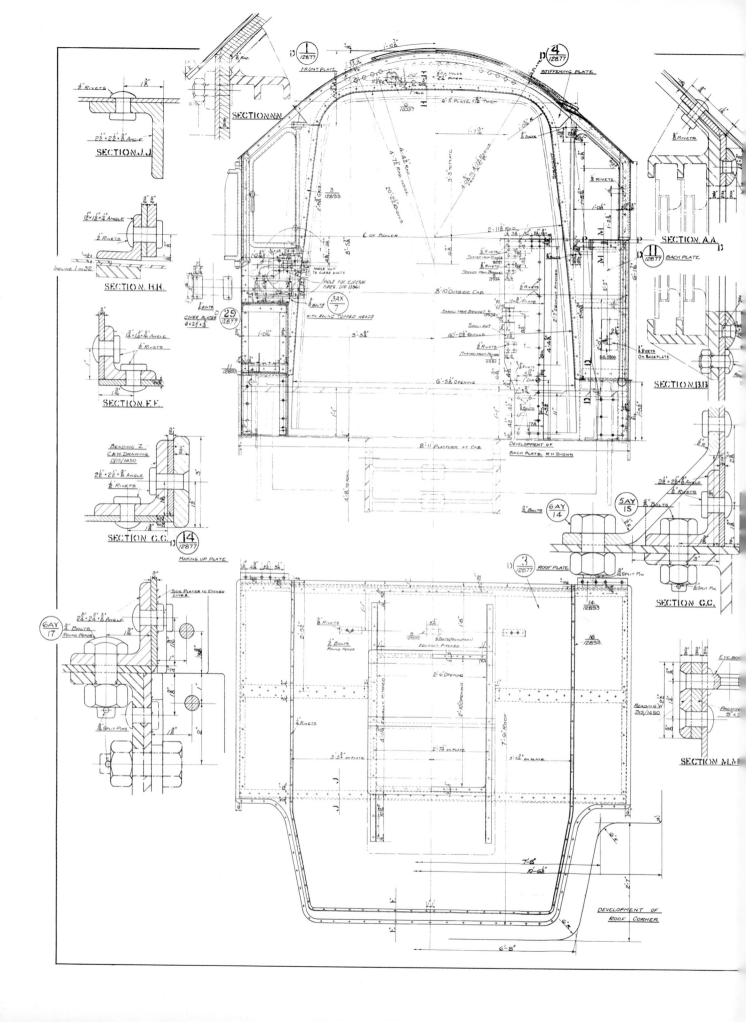

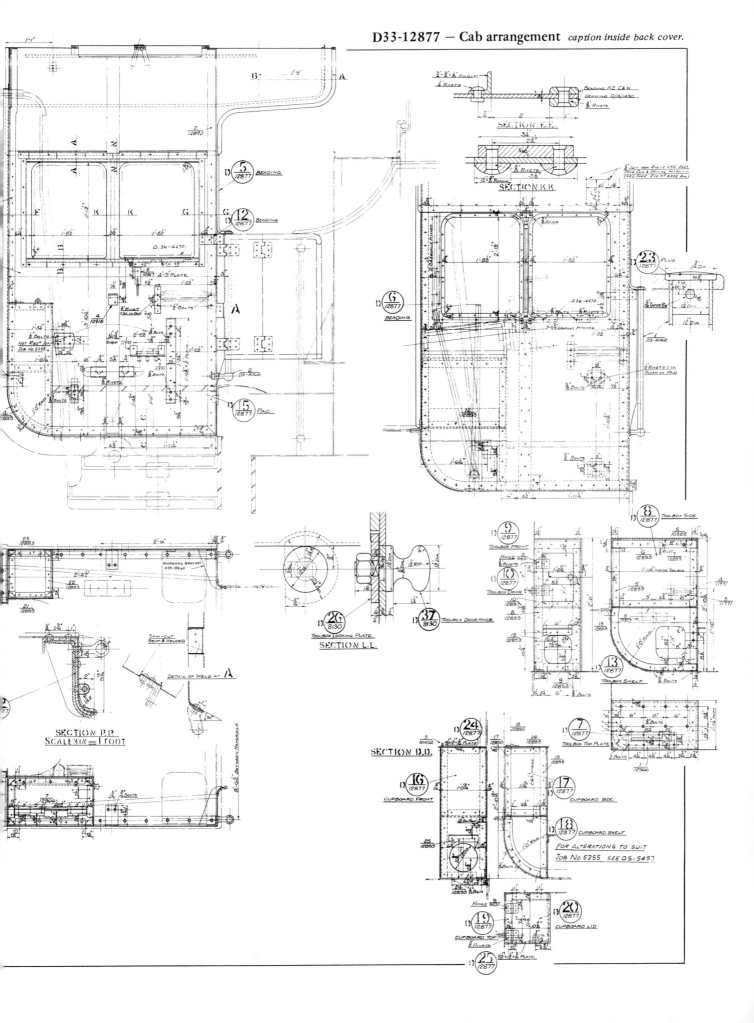

This study was taken at Crewe Works yard on 25th September 1938 and shows 6212 two days after it entered the Works for a heavy repair. Note that the left-hand crosshead and connecting rod had been removed. The non-standard smokebox fitted to the engine wasn't altered until its next heavy repair in July and August 1939. No. 6212 was one of the engines built with roller bearings to its pony truck axleboxes, the distinctive domed covers being apparent here. It had been fitted with a Hasler speed recorder the previous year, the gearbox for which can be seen mounted on a bracket from the platform and driven by a return crank on the trailing coupled wheel. The drive shaft ran horizontally from the gearbox before turning up to the front of the cab.

W. L. GOOD

Gresham and Craven valve with three positions of the handle – brake on, running, and ejector on – to suit the single-cone ejector and crosshead pump arrangement. Nos. 6203–6212, however, reverted to the standard LMS brake valve with separate ejector steam control and the first two engines were eventually altered to match. No. 6200 was modified in March 1947 but we don't have a date for 6201.

In 1941, Job No. 5255 was issued for the fitting of sand guns. The fireman could direct a stream of sand from the gun into the boiler tubes to scour them while the engine was running. There were problems with the connecting pipes from the sand hoppers to the guns being damaged, so, in April 1944, instructions were issued to replace the fixed pipes with flexible ones that could be removed when not in use. In service, the sand guns were unreliable as the nozzles got burnt and most firemen resorted to the simple alternative of flinging shovelfuls of sand through the fire hole and over the brick arch towards the tubeplate whilst the engine was working hard. The sand guns were removed in 1952–3 to Job No. 5663.

The water gauge frames originally fitted to the backplate had integral drain cocks. These were old-pattern standard with indi-vidual cocks and Job No. 5317 was issued in September 1942 to replace them with new standard frames having coupled shut-off cocks.

SPEED RECORDERS

When the 'Princess Royals' were built, the question of fitting speedometers, or speed recorders as they were then known, was unresolved. In view of the service accelerations being undertaken and further ones contemplated, however, the need for reliable speed recorders in the cabs of express passenger engines was becoming more pressing. In April 1936 the Traffic Committee recommended that various different types of recorders should be tried, the 'Princess Royals' to be fitted with Stone Deuta electrical instruments and eight 'Royal Scots' with Hasler mechanical recorders. The following November, however, it was reported that there would be difficulty in fitting the Stone Deuta equipment to the 'Princess Royals' so they would instead receive the Hasler type. The recorder was driven from a modified left-hand rear crankpin, the drive box being mounted on a 'ladder' bracket suspended from the underside of the platform. The flexible drive shaft ran horizontally back from the drive box, being clipped to the

outside rear frame extension, then turned up from a point above the pony truck axlebox to the front underside of the cab.

The Hasler recorders proved to be unreliable and in December 1937 it was decided that the standard equipment for the LMS would in future be that made by BTH, the type having already been ordered for 71 'Jubilees' the previous October. In January 1938, Job No. 5043 detailed its fitting to 998 locomotives and was extended in July 1940 to cover the 'Lizzies'. Problems with reliability, however, had delayed the programme and the outbreak of war exacerbated the situation such that in the end only Nos. 6210, 6200 and 6208 were modified in December 1940, June 1942 and October 1942 respectively. In June 1944 the CME directed that, owing to the difficulty in maintaining the BTH indicators in a satisfactory condition, which was aggravated by the difficulty in obtaining replacement parts, the instruments, together with all ancillary equipment, should be removed.

The following November, the directive was extended to cover the removal of all types of speed recorder then in use, including the Hasler models still fitted to some of the 'Princess Royals'. All equipment was to be stored for possible future use. Further trials with modified BTH and Smith-Stone speed indicators were ordered in 1949 but it wasn't until 1957 that anything was done to the 'Lizzies'. On 20th August 1957, Job No. 5794 was issued for the installation of Smith-Stone equipment in all the ex-LMS 4–6–2s 'in view of the increased number of high-speed trains now operating in this (London Midland) Region'. The work was carried out at Crewe and engines were called in specially to be fitted, all being completed by the end of December. Like the Hasler recorders, the Smith-Stone ones were driven by a return crank on the rear left-hand crankpin. However, instead of being attached to a long mounting bracket, the generator was simply mounted on the end of the crank and steadied by the armoured cable that curved up to the wheel size adjustment rheostat box clipped to the platform.

AWS

The idea of repeating signal aspects in locomotive cabs was one with which Stanier had been involved for many years before joining the LMS. In December 1914 he presented a paper on what was to become the Great Western Railway system at a symposium held by the Institution of Mechanical Engineers. The drawback to this system was that it depended on mechanical and electrical contact between a shoe on the locomotive and a ramp between the rails, so ice or other foreign matter, as well as poor adjustment, could negate the proper action. By the time he joined the LMS, a better system was in development that did not require physical contact. It was known as the Hudd system and its operation, similar to the later BR AWS, was described in *LMS Locomotive Profile No. 3* on the parallel-boiler 2–6–4 tank engines. Various trials were carried out and it would seem that it was intended for widespread use on the LMS until World War 2 interrupted. The bogie axlebox guide and stretcher drawing for the 'Princess Royals' was modified in February 1938 to show six holes in the front stretcher with a note that they were for fitting an ATC receiver bracket.[25] In the event, none was so fitted and it wasn't until twenty years later that the subject was raised again in the context of the 'Lizzies'.

In 1958, the fitting of the BR Automatic Warning System was authorised for the 'Princess Royals' at a cost of £302/9/0d per engine. The BR version of AWS was activated by magnets sited centrally between the rails about 200 yards on the approach

The Princess Royal *herself made a fine sight with her clean, crimson paintwork when photographed under the coaling stage at Camden. The protection plate for the AWS receiver and overhead warning flashes indicate that she was nearing withdrawal, but otherwise she looks like a locomotive in the prime of its life.* AUTHORS' COLLECTION

side of distant signals. The first one in the direction of travel was a permanent magnet but the second, positioned about 2ft 6in further on, was an electro-magnet that was energised only if the signal was clear. On the locomotive, a reservoir was evacuated by the ejectors. Once evacuated it did three things – balanced the train pipe vacuum in the AWS brake valve, closed a switch and energised the locomotive system from its battery, and evacuated a small timing reservoir. An electrically-operated valve in the driver's control unit then maintained the vacuum in the system and held the brakes off.

If the receiver passed over a magnet, a current was induced and a contact opened. If another magnet was passed within one second, the contact closed again and a bell rang in the cab to indicate that a distant signal was being passed at 'clear.' If, however, another magnet was not passed within

one second, a solenoid in the control unit was de-energised and a valve opened. This valve sounded a vacuum-operated horn and after approximately two seconds allowed air to bleed into the timing reservoir via a restrictor. Once the timing reservoir vacuum was destroyed, the AWS brake valve was actuated such that full brake application would result in about fifteen seconds. Movement of a reset handle on the control unit would re-energise the solenoid, whereupon the main reservoir would restore the vacuum, release the brakes and cancel the warning horn. In addition to the audible signals, a 'dart board' or 'sunflower' indicator on the control unit would show black when clear but, on receiving a caution signal that was cancelled by the button, would change to black and yellow segments. This indication would then remain until the next time a magnet was passed, when it would once more be activated according to signal aspect.

The system had 'fail-safe' features in that failure of the power supply to the electro-magnet between the rails would result in a 'caution' indication irrespective of the signal aspect. Also, an electrical power failure in the locomotive, once the vacuum had been established initially, would de-energise the solenoid and apply the brakes. Thus there were features of an automatic train control system as well as just warnings and some contemporary publications refer to 'Automatic Train Control' or 'ATC' as well as AWS.

The AWS signal receiver on a 'Lizzie' was mounted on the front bogie stretcher and was protected from damage due to the front coupling swinging against it by a guard attached to the buffer beam. The battery box was mounted on the right-hand platform in front of the cab with the vacuum reservoir in front of it adjacent to the rear splasher. The smaller timing reservoir was in front of the cab on the left-hand platform. The relay junction box was mounted inside the cab on the left-hand side, its lower mounting holes being 1ft 7⅜ in above the bottom edge of the cab side and hind ones 1ft 2½ in forward of the

rear edge. The bell and horn were on the inside of the roof, the horn just to the left of the ventilator and the bell level with the ventilator rear edge about halfway between it and the left-hand eaves.

No. 6201 was not fitted with AWS and there is no record of 6210 being fitted, nor have we seen any photographs of it so equipped. The remainder, however, were modified between March and November 1959.

TENDERS

We have included this broadside view of No. 6200 The Princess Royal *when it was still in works grey prior to entering traffic, in order to show the original style of straight-sided 4000-gallon tender coupled to the first two locomotives. A drawing of the tank arrangement will be found on pages 76/77.*

AUTHORS' COLLECTION

The tenders attached to LMS engines were never particularly large, the biggest associated with the 'Princess Royals' having a capacity for 4,000 gallons of water and 10 tons of coal. It wasn't short-sightedness on the part of Stanier, or anyone else for that matter, but a deliberate policy not to use anything bigger. On 27th April 1932, the Mechanical and Electrical Engineering Committee recommended that the pre-ferred size of tender for general purposes on the LMS was 3,500 gallons. If longer non-stop running or heavy haulage was required, it added, larger tenders may be necessary but rather than build anything above 4,000 gallons, it would probably be more economical to install extra water troughs. This was not only because of the extra cost incurred in building bigger tenders, but the potential expense of installing larger turntables to take longer engine/tender combinations. As it was, the

total wheelbase of a Stanier Pacific and 4,000 gallon tender required one of 70ft. It will be remembered that one of J. E. Anderson's objections to the Fowler Pacific project was the need for larger turntables. In the event, the vast majority of Stanier tenders had 4,000 gallon tanks.

The first two engines had tenders that were virtually the type designed for the Fowler 2–8–2, which would probably have also been used on the Pacific had it been built, with coal capacity increased to 9 tons. Three of them were built, numbered 9000–9002, the third of which was intended for 6202 but was actually paired with *Royal Scot* for its tour of America. Their appearance showed evidence of their lineage from the Midland's 3,500 gallon Deeley tenders, the main differences immediately apparent being the length and width of the tank, height of the coal plates, and design of axleboxes on two out of the

three. Wheelbase was 7ft 6in + 7ft 6in, the cast-steel wheels being 4ft 3in diameter and having triangular-section rims and fastenings as described for the locomotives.

The tender frame drawing indicates that 9000 and 9002 were built with roller-bearing axleboxes whereas 9001, which was coupled to 6201, had plain bearings. Although this is borne out by photographs of 9000, showing both number plate and axleboxes, and of 9002 when it accompanied *Royal Scot* to America, the majority of photographs of 6201's tender show boxes with plain bearings. However, we have three taken during 6201's first five months in service that show it coupled to a roller-bearing tender. Apart from tender 9001 being built with roller bearings and then altered, the only alternative would appear to be that 6201 ran for a while shortly after being built with 6200's tender. This seems unlikely as there is no record on either history card of an exchange and we have yet to see a photograph of 6200 with a plain-bearing, straight-sided tender. Neither could it have been tender 9002, as that would have been incompatible with a 'Lizzie'. We did consider that 6200 may have been photographed in the guise of 6201 for publicity purposes, as was later done when 6203 was pictured masquerading as all ten of the main production batch. This isn't valid though, as the pictures were taken when the locomotive was in crimson, rather than photographic grey, and in one it was fitted with indicator shelters. The photographs were taken in the first few months after building as they all show the engine with standard buffer heads and, in one case, without name plates. It would have been quite easy to convert the tender, even though plain-bearing axleboxes were two inches narrower, as the horn gaps were the same size for both types and only the width of the axlebox guides differed. Thus, we have come to the conclusion that 6201's tender, No. 9001, ran for a while with roller-bearing axleboxes despite the note on the frame drawing.

Outside frames were one inch thick and were slotted very much in the manner of Midland tenders. The outside springs had dampers of the type previously described where the hangers were attached to the frames. Between rear and intermediate buffer beams there were two longitudinal members, or inside frames, ⅝ in thick. The intermediate drawgear was controlled by a laminated spring housed in the tender drag box, the draw bar being connected directly to the spring buckle. There were also two side drawbars and two self-contained buffers spaced 3ft 8in apart that rode on case-hardened inclined plates riveted to the engine drag beam. Standard LMS pattern buffers were fitted to the tender rear buffer beam. Footsteps with turned-up ends were flush riveted to separate support plates, again of typically Midland profile, fixed to the underside of the platform at both leading and hind ends.

All wheels were braked by blocks behind them, which were operated by beams and pull rods connected to cranks on a shaft beneath the front platform. Further cranks on the shaft were operated by a steam cylinder and the hand brake. The steam cylinder was pressurised simultaneously with that on the locomotive when a brake application was made. The arrangement long used on Derby-designed tenders was for the hand brake handle to be mounted on top of a Midland-style cast-iron column on the front platform. For the 'Princesses' it had to be altered as the large throwover of the cab would have made the relative movement of the columns a hazard on curves. As a result, all their tenders had the brakes operated by a handle with a horizontal spindle mounted on the right-hand side of the front plate and connected to its linkage through bevel gears.[26]

The 4,000 gallon tank was 4ft high, 21ft long and 8ft 6in wide. The coal plates were straight and plainly Derby designed with concave front and rear top corners. Altogether, the sides were 6ft 5in high and 21ft 10¼ in long and the platform was 23ft 3¾ in x 8ft 11in. Construction of the tank used snap-head rivets, the top being horizontal for over half its length before sloping down at the front to a portion with a slight up-slope ending in a shovelling plate. The footplate was raised above the front platform to match the height of the cab floor and there was a folding door in a housing projecting forward from the front-plate for access to the coal space. Between the bottom of the door and the shovelling plate was a gap from which coal was taken. Toolboxes and lockers were provided either side of the coal space door and fire iron holders were on top of both the front plate and an intermediate curved support between the side plates.

A water scoop was fitted between intermediate and trailing axles. The operating linkage was controlled by a handle and bevel gears on the left-hand side of the front plate that were closely similar to the hand brake on the opposite side behind the driver. The water gauge was also behind the driver. Problems had been encountered with earlier tenders through coal dust and other detritus getting into the tanks via vent pipes in the coal space, so they were mounted behind the rear bulkhead. At first they were quite short, reaching only just above the level of the tank rear, but very soon after entering service were extended to the top of the side plates.

Nine tons of coal proved to be too much for the standard Derby tender design because it would not trim very easily, or shake down to the front, and the fireman had to spend a lot of time in the coal space trying to bring it forward. Not only could this be this dangerous if coal was still piled up at the sides and rear, but the weight distribution was less than ideal. The design was therefore altered and the

The rear of tender 9000, still in photographic grey, is seen to advantage in this photograph taken in June or July 1933. Note that the tank vents were still short and are only just discernible above the tank rear. Shortly after this picture was taken, they were extended to the top of the side plates. The three plates on the tank rear were, from top to bottom, tender number, makers and capacity. Their characters read 'LMS 9000 1933' on the numberplate, 'MAKERS LMS 1933 CREWE WORKS' on the makers' plate, and 'WATER CAPACITY 4000 GALLONS' on the capacity plate.   W. L. GOOD

Unlike the locomotive drawings, which were all prepared at Derby, those for the tenders were done at Crewe. This one was originally entitled '4,000 gallons tender frames with roller bearings for 4–6–2 engines' and was prepared for the first three Pacifics ordered, i.e. 6200-6202. According to a note on the drawing, tender Nos. 9000 and 9002 were made with roller bearings whereas 9001 had plain bearings. For reasons stated in the text, however, we have concluded that 9001 was actually built with roller bearings and later altered. Along the top of the drawing is a side elevation of one of the inside frames flanked by details of the footsteps and support plates. Below that is a side elevation of an outside frame, platform and angle with details of drilling and slotting. To its right is a section through the front drag box and the bracket for steam cylinder, water pipes and brake shaft. Further down is a longitudinal section between inner and outer frames showing the stays and drag boxes and, to its right, a lateral section showing frame stretcher, stays and tank support. At the bottom is a split plan with a view from on top of the platform above the centreline and one from underneath below it. At either side are end views of buffer and drag beams with internal details shown dotted. At far right of the drawing is a full-size (on the original) section through inner and outer frames, stays and tank support rotated through 90 degrees.

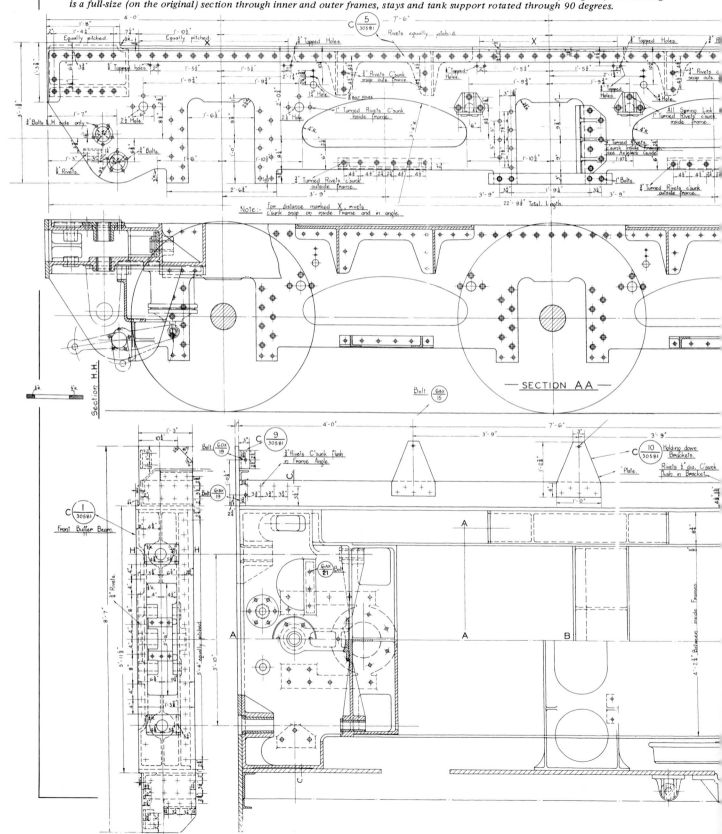

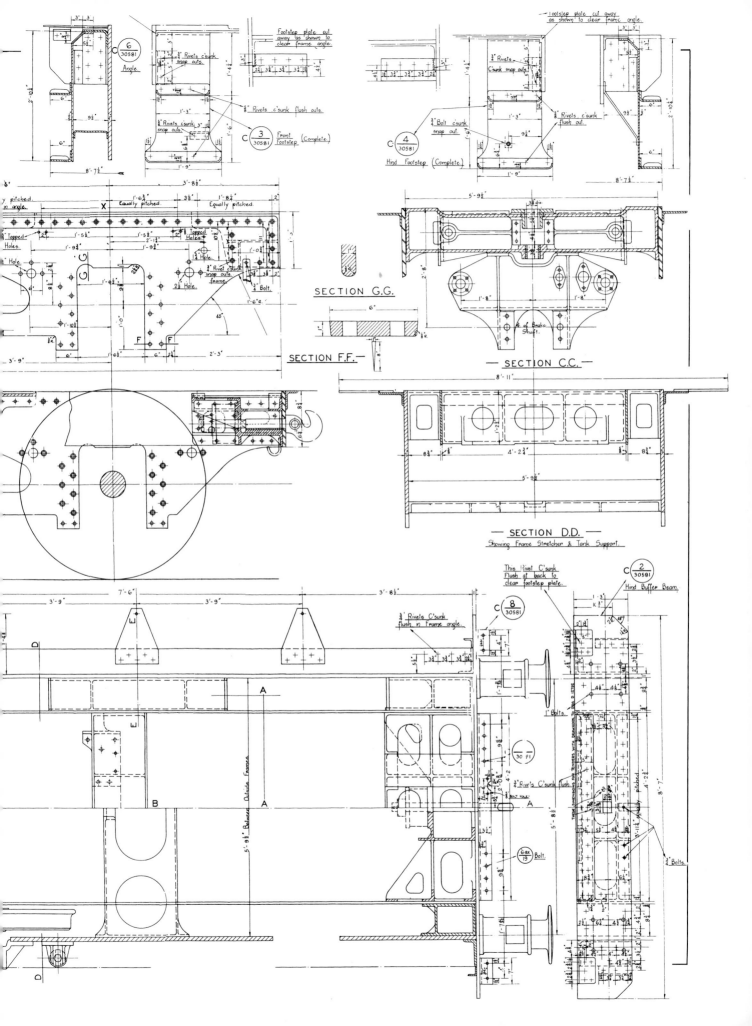

C30468 — 4,000 gallon tender tank arrangement — straight sided

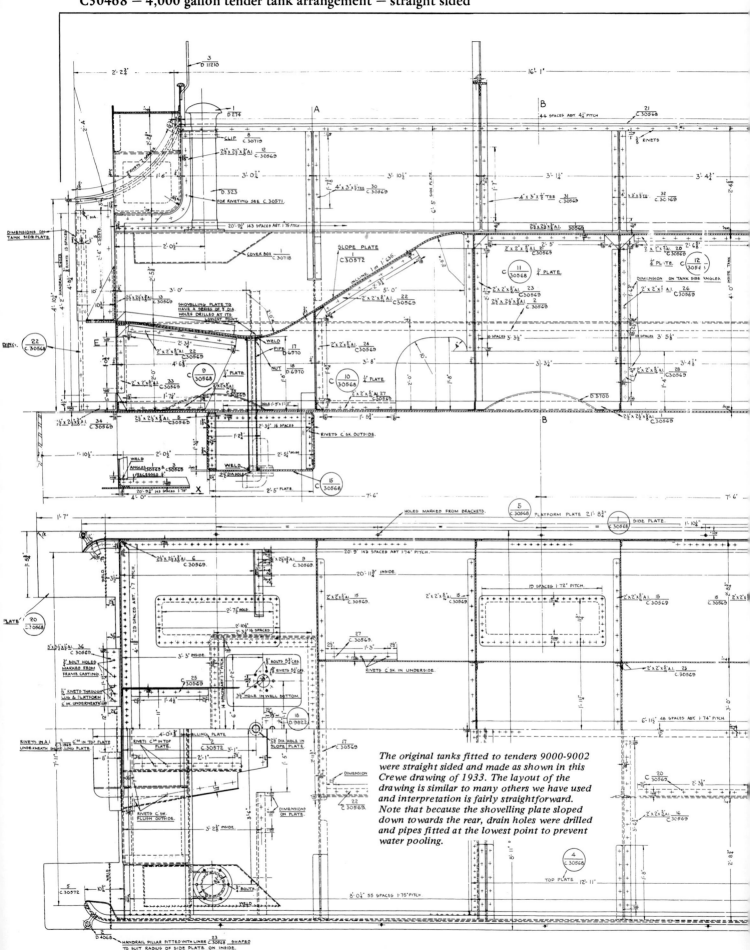

The original tanks fitted to tenders 9000-9002 were straight sided and made as shown in this Crewe drawing of 1933. The layout of the drawing is similar to many others we have used and interpretation is fairly straightforward. Note that because the shovelling plate sloped down towards the rear, drain holes were drilled and pipes fitted at the lowest point to prevent water pooling.

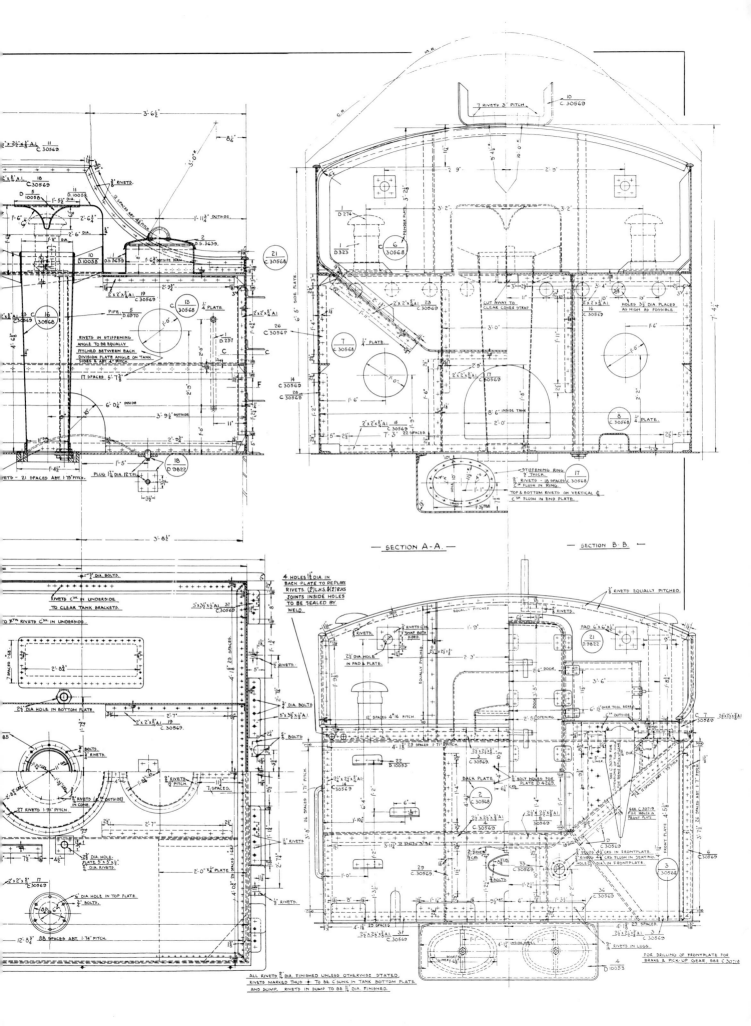

— SECTION A-A. —   — SECTION B-B. —

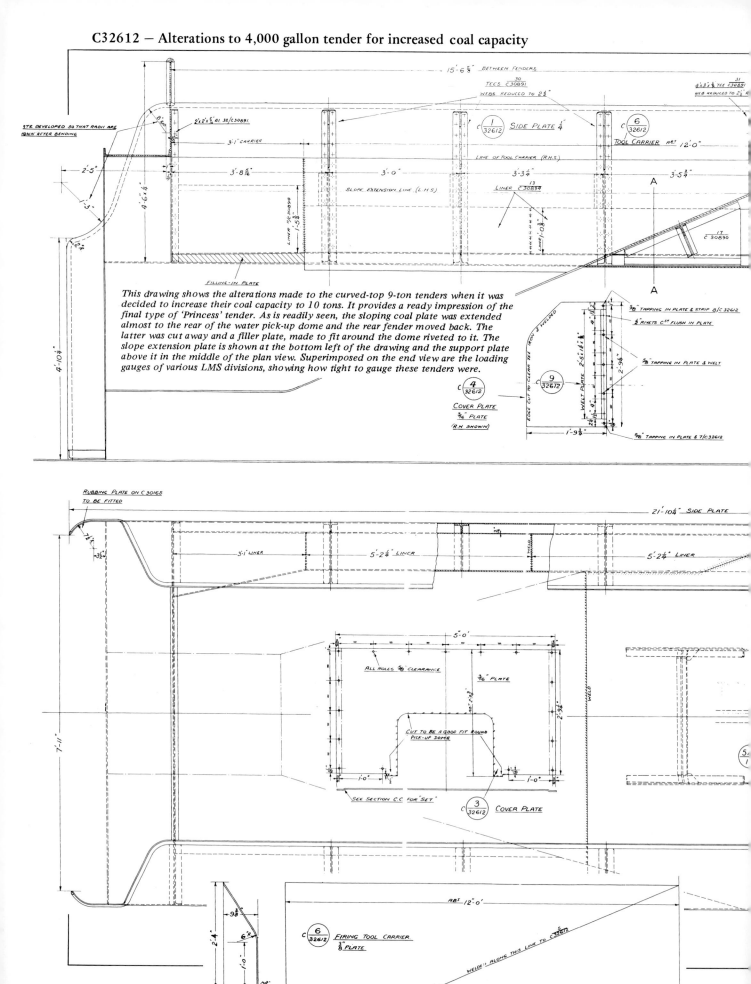

This drawing shows the alterations made to the curved-top 9-ton tenders when it was decided to increase their coal capacity to 10 tons. It provides a ready impression of the final type of 'Princess' tender. As is readily seen, the sloping coal plate was extended almost to the rear of the water pick-up dome and the rear fender moved back. The latter was cut away and a filler plate, made to fit around the dome riveted to it. The slope extension plate is shown at the bottom left of the drawing and the support plate above it in the middle of the plan view. Superimposed on the end view are the loading gauges of various LMS divisions, showing how tight to gauge these tenders were.

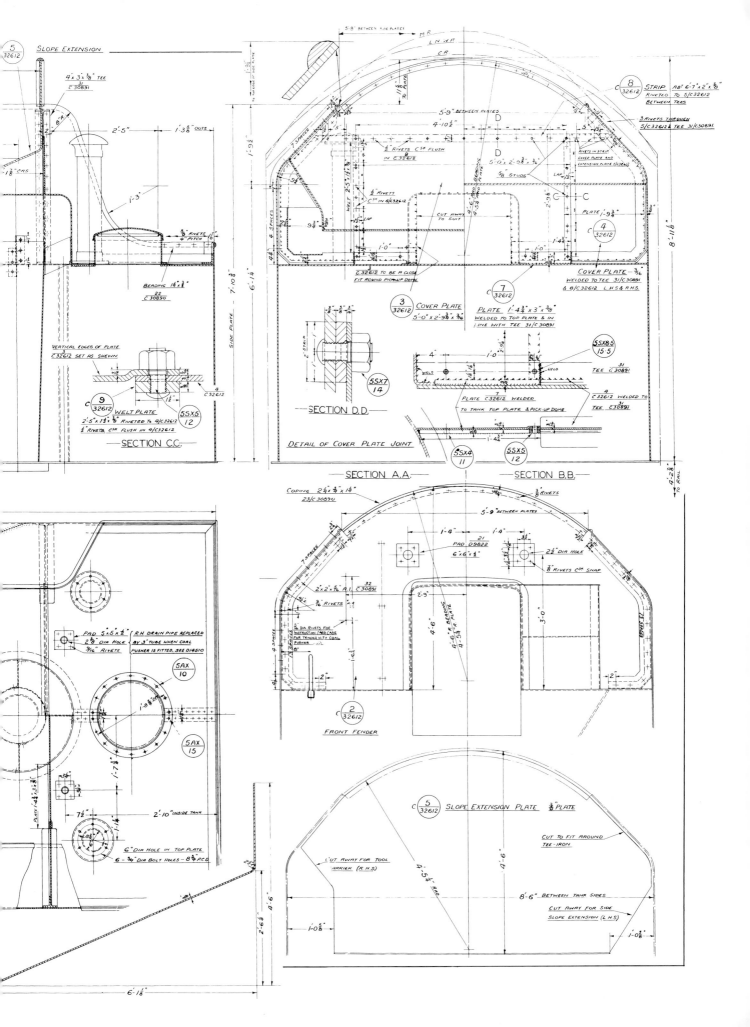

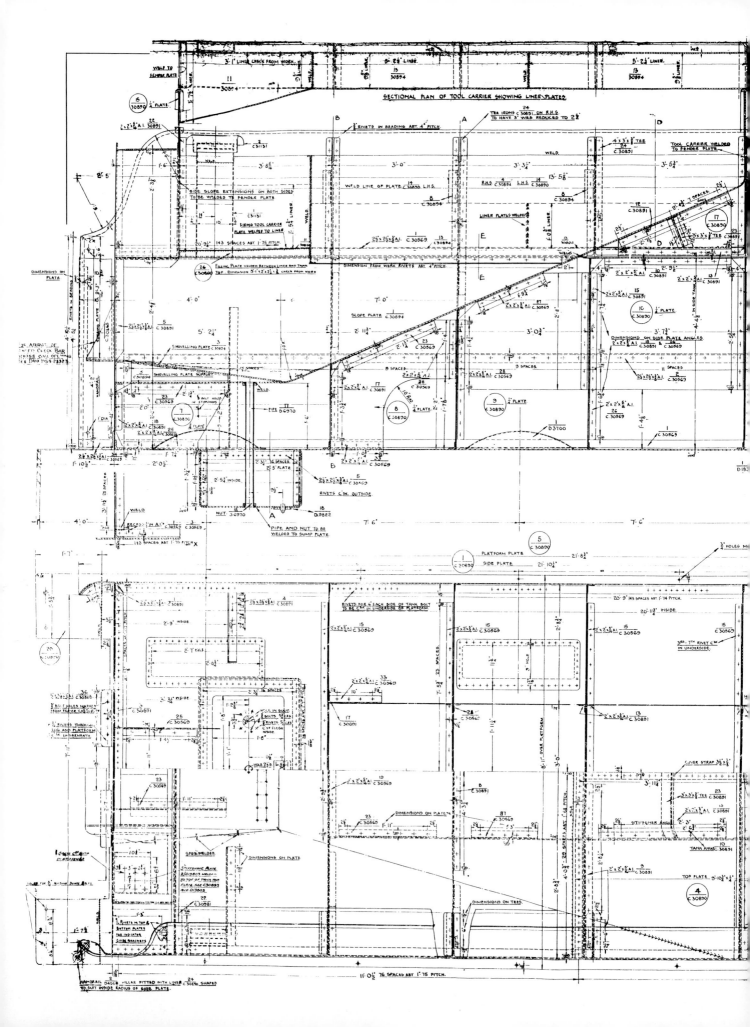

SECTIONAL PLAN OF TOOL CARRIER SHOWING LINERS PLATED

C30890 — 4000-gallon tender — tank arrangement

This drawing shows the tank arrangement for the 9-ton curved-side tenders introduced in 1935 and described on page 82.

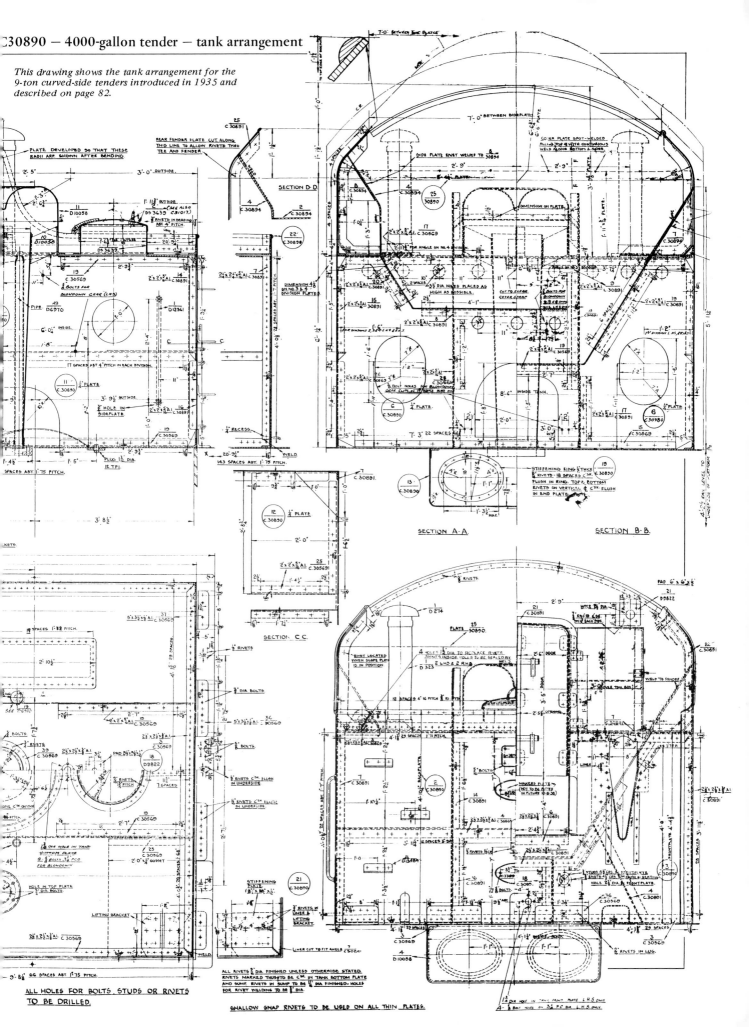

This photograph of the front of a 9-ton tender shows, to the left of the coal space doors (i.e. the right-hand side of the tender), the tunnel for housing the fire irons and, on the other side, the enginemen's locker. Next to that we can see the water level gauge and below it an indicator for the water scoop position, the plate reading from top to bottom 'OUT SCOOP IN'. The scoop operating handle with the legend 'WATER PICK UP' immediately below is seen next to the indicator with a chain attached to it from just below the water gauge so that the scoop could not lower inadvertently. The water valve handles are seen either side of the shovelling plate with their operating linkages coming up through the footplate and position indicator plates behind them reading, from top to bottom, 'SHUT WATER OPEN'. Outside the right-hand one we can see the brake handle with 'HAND BRAKE' just below it. All the lettering and borders of the plates were white. The two holders for spare lamps situated between the fire iron tunnel and coal space doors were equipped with a hinged protective shield above them. It should be noted that the use of left and right-hand side can be confusing but in railway terms the hand was determined by looking forward.

AUTHORS' COLLECTION

classic 'Stanier' tender shape emerged. The frames and running gear were the same as the first two tenders with plain-bearing axleboxes and the tank was the same capacity as before, still being made with snap-head rivets. The rear fender, however, was moved back so that it was at the front of the water dome and the sloping tank top plate was extended rearwards to meet it. The side plates were deepened and curved over and the alterations combined to give better self-trimming characteristics. There were other alterations as well. The design of the water scoop screw and stops were altered slightly to reduce the chance of jamming and only one locker was provided to the left of the coal space door.[*]Instead of fire iron supports on top of the front plate and intermediate support, a tunnel was built into the coal space against the right-hand side plate just above the hand brake handle. Because the ends of the fire irons couldn't be seen when they were stowed away, each of the handles was differently shaped so that they could be recognised.

Nos. 6200 and 6201 received tenders 9065 and 9066 of the new type in April and March 1935 respectively and Nos. 6203 *et seq* had them when built, their numbers being 9124–9133. Although the WCML was well provided with water troughs, making 4,000 gallons an adequate water capacity, nine tons of coal was sometimes barely sufficient for the distances over which many Stanier engines were required to work without taking on more. Consequently, new, higher-capacity tenders were built only a short time after the last 'Lizzie' was completed. In the new design, the side plates were continued upwards as far as the loading gauge would permit and the sloping bunker floor was extended back further over the water dome, which increased the nominal capacity to ten tons. Once again, the frames and running gear were virtually the same as the original straight-sided version and snap-head rivets were used in construction of the tanks. Re-equipping of all the 'Princesses' occurred between May 1936 and January 1937, tender numbers being in the 93XX series as shown in the table.

One of the 10-ton tenders was somewhat different from the rest. No. 9359, which was attached to 6206 in October 1936, had a steam-operated coal pusher. Although it would seem likely that this was a trial of the system for the 'Coronations' that appeared 8 months later, we have no

*Left when facing forward.

direct evidence of it. The pusher consisted of a 10½ in cylinder mounted in the rear of the coal space, its piston having two wide, wedge-shaped rams attached to it one behind the other. The rams slid down the floor plate and pushed coal forwards. Steam was taken from the manifold above the firebox backplate, through a flexible pipe to a control valve on the tender rear fender adjacent to the pusher cylinder. The

valve was operated by a handle in front of the fire-iron tunnel. From the valve, pipes led to the rear of the pusher cylinder, the connections being protected by a sheet steel cover. Originally, the exhaust from the pusher cylinder was directed into the tank but this was later changed simply to escape from pipes through the top of the cover. Since 6206 was the only engine fitted with the necessary steam supply, it

retained the pusher-fitted tender nearly all the time from its first allocation in October 1936 almost to withdrawal. From 20th November 1946 to 17th October 1947 it was recorded as having one of the ordinary 10-ton tenders and just before withdrawal, in October 1962, it exchanged tenders with 'Princess Coronation' Class No. 46221. It is doubtful whether it ever ran with the welded ex-'Coronation' tender,

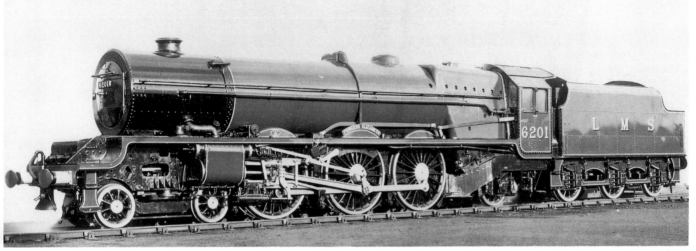

In March 1935, No. 6201 was allocated a 9-ton curved-sided tender. The following October it went into Crewe Works for a heavy repair and re-entered traffic on 3rd December with boiler 6048, which had been fitted with a dome-mounted regulator and 32-element, 4-row superheater. It was photographed at Crewe following repair and shows the quite different appearance of the new ensemble. Note the support bracket on the right-hand side of the smokebox door, a feature first seen on 6203 when built and then added to 6200 and 6201, and the fact that gravity sanding was still fitted. The picture gives an excellent reference for the pre-1936 paint scheme as applied to these engines. AUTHORS' COLLECTION

This study of 6205 Princess Victoria provides a good viewpoint for details of the cab and 10-ton tender of a 'Lizzie'. The gangway door is seen partly open, showing the rubber skirt below it. The extended tender sides and rearward positioning of the rear fender are apparent, as is the fill-in plate shaped to fit around the water dome and riveted into the fender. Steam sanding had been fitted and both locomotive and tender had vermilion shaded characters. This is the only picture we have seen of an engine in LMS crimson livery without the sighting plugs on its valve chests, indicating that it had received replacement outside cylinders. AUTHORS' COLLECTION

the exchange having been made simply because the 'Princess Royal' tender was in better condition than 46221's own.

Modifications to the 10-ton tenders included the following.

Job No. 5035 of November 1937 – reducing the size of the brake cylinder to prevent over-braking due to the 250 psi locomotive boiler pressure.

Job No. 5073 of May 1938 – fitting new standard spring links.

Job No. 5123 of March 1939 – independent lubricating pipe to brake cylinder.

Job No. 5403 of February 1945 – fitting of deflector plate to right-hand side of tender below front footstep to prevent water and steam from exhaust injector blowing back onto wheel and axlebox causing fouling of oil.

Job No. 5472 of December 1946 – fitting external water strainer to left-hand frame between leading and intermediate axleboxes so that blockages caused by foreign matter could be removed simply

by cleaning a sieve inside the strainer. Previously, it was sometimes necessary to enter the tank to clear such blockages. Subsequently, strainers were fitted to both sides. The exposed position, however, meant that they were prone to freezing in the winter.

Job No. 5357 of November 1943 – fitting clips in place of split pins on brake hanger top pins, as was done to the engines.

The following table shows the recorded tender allocations to 'Princess Royals'

Engine	Tenders
6200	9000[1], 9065[2] in May 35, 9066[2] in Jun 36, 9372 in Nov 36, 9376 in Aug 55
6201	9001[1], 9066[2] in Mar 35, 9065[2] in Jun 36, 9373 in Nov 36
6203	9124[2], 9374 in Jan 37
6204	9125[2], 9375 in Dec 36
6205	9126[2], 9344 in May 36, 9353 in Jul 36, 9344 in Mar 37
6206	9127[2], 9359[3] in Oct 36, 9353 in Nov 46, 9359[3] in Oct 47, 9816[4] in Oct 62
6207	9128[2], 9376 in Dec 36, 9353 in Dec 39, 9359[3] in Nov 46, 9353 in Oct 47
6208	9129[2], 9344 in Jul 36, 9353 in Mar 37, 9360 in Jun 39
6209	9130[2], 9361 in Oct 36, 9354 in Sep 46
6210	9131[2], 9360 in Sep 36, 9353 in Jun 39, 9376 in Dec 39, 9372 in Aug 55
6211	9132[2], 9345 in Jul 36, 9354 in Dec 44, 9361 in Sep 46
6212	9133[2], 9354 in Jul 36, 9345 in Dec 44

Notes:
1. Nine tons, straight sided.
2. Nine tons, curved sided.
3. Fitted with steam-powered coal pusher.
4. Ex-'Coronation' 10 tons, curved sided, non-streamlined with coal pusher.
All other tenders were 10 tons, curved sided examples.

Uniquely among the 'Princess Royals', No. 6206 had the wherewithal to utilise a tender with a steam-operated coal pusher. It was coupled to such a tender, 9359, constantly from October 1936 to October 1962, apart from an eleven-month period starting in November 1946 when, for some reason, it exchanged tenders with 6207. This view shows the steam pipes leading to the rear of the pusher cylinder and the sheet steel cover for the connections on the rear fender. Originally, the exhaust from the pusher cylinder was directed into the tank but this was later changed simply to escape to atmosphere via pipes through the top of the cover as seen here. The photograph was taken at Crewe and shows 46206 in Brunswick green livery not long after receiving its first domed boiler, No. 9100, in late March 1955.

D IBBOTSON

THE ENGINES IN SERVICE

Until the arrival of the 'Coronation' Class Pacifics, the 'Princess Royals' held sway on the WCML Scottish expresses. Camden-based No. 6200, showing its white enamel '1' shed code plate, was pictured at Dillicar troughs on a wet day in 1934 in charge of the down 'Royal Scot', a duty for which the class was specifically designed. It would have changed crews at Carlisle, taken the train on to Glasgow and then, after a few hours while it was disposed, turned and prepared, headed south with the return 'Night Scot'. It can be seen that the tender was still piled high with coal at the rear, even though several tons would have been consumed. This was one of the drawbacks of the straight-sided 9-ton capacity tenders as it wouldn't shake forward properly, which was the main reason for development of the curved-sided tenders with sloping rear coal plate and ultimately, of course, the steam coal pusher.
D. F. TEE COLLECTION

As already stated, the 'Lizzies' were designed for long non-stop runs and to take trains from London to Glasgow without the need to change engines. Soon after entering service, therefore, 6200 and 6201 were put to work on the 'Royal Scot', displacing the eponymous 4–6–0s, as well as the mid-day and night 'Scots'. On all these services, the engines worked the return journey within a few hours of arrival. At first they were allocated to Camden but 6201 moved almost immediately to Polmadie. The first two of the 1935 engines, Nos. 6203 and 6204, also went to Polmadie with the rest being sent to Camden and 6200 transferred to Kingmoor. The latter move was so that the engine could work a daily Carlisle–Euston express passenger train and return, which was the longest daily locomotive diagram attempted up to that time.

In November 1935, a series of dynamometer car tests was undertaken with No. 6203, having a 24-element super-heater, and 6209, which had 32 elements. Where practicable, the engines were worked on a full regulator and at about 17–20% cut-off on the level and easier gradients. The overall result can be summarised as showing a 4.8% saving in coal and 5.7% saving in water consumption for the 32-element superheater. One interesting aside in the report was that the only occasions on which steam was not maintained satisfactorily occurred south of the border with Camden or Carlisle men in charge. Polmadie crews achieved better results, the report stating:

> '… it would appear that the unsatisfactory steaming of the engines was largely due to mismanagement, as the recovery effected in the steaming of each engine by the Scotch (sic) crews was most marked.'

On 16th and 17th November 1936, No. 6201 *Princess Elizabeth* achieved what was claimed to be a world record for sustained high-speed performance over long distances with steam traction. The runs were from London to Glasgow and return and were to test the practicability of accelerating the WCML schedules. The trial was blazoned in a press release as an outstanding success and paved the way for the more conservative accelerations undertaken with the 'Coronation' Class. The press release is reproduced in full at Appendix E.

In addition to the Anglo–Scottish trains, the 'Princesses' were rostered to London–Liverpool trains such as the Merseyside Express, which ran non-stop for just under 190 miles between Euston and Mossley Hill with a load of over 500 tons. After the introduction of the 'Coronations' in 1937, some of the more prestigious duties were taken away from the earlier Pacifics but they still worked between London and Liverpool or Glasgow and from the latter to Perth and Aberdeen. The main depots to have them allocated were then Crewe North and Edge Hill. In 1939, Nos. 6201, 6206 and 6209 were stationed for a while at Longsight and used on London–Manchester trains but were restricted to working via Crewe as they were banned from the platform curves through Stoke-on-Trent. For a while in 1940, Nos. 6203, 6204 and 6205 worked the Irish Mail from London to Holyhead, where they were stationed.

The last of the 'Lizzies' to be built, No. 6212, was fitted when new with a smokebox door having eleven dogs around the rim rather than a central dart fastening. The altered appearance was quite striking, as this photograph of it leaving Euston in late 1935 or early 1936 shows. Note that the engine still had trickle sanding. The difference in cleanliness of locomotive and tender is also notable, although we cannot offer any explanation for it. No. 6212 received a 10-ton tender in July 1936, which was probably quite shortly after the picture was taken.
AUTHORS' COLLECTION

In this picture, Princess Margaret Rose *is seen leaving Rugby with an express sometime after being fitted with Hasler speed recording equipment in early 1937. The vacuum train pipe stands out well behind the left-hand end of the buffer beam, with the water trap projecting down ahead of the front bogie wheel. A close examination reveals that both engine and 10-ton tender had vermilion shaded insignia.*
REAL PHOTOGRAPHS/NRM

By nationalisation, the whole class was stationed at Crewe North but soon afterwards they started returning to Edge Hill and, in 1951, Polmadie, where Nos. 46200 and 46203 were stationed for working Birmingham–Glasgow expresses. In addition to express passenger trains, they were employed less frequently on the west coast 'postals', parcels, milk and fish traffic, especially in Scotland. They also appeared on Glasgow–Edinburgh and Crewe–Manchester stopping trains. Early in 1956, problems with the bogies of GWR 'Kings' led to four LMS Pacifics, including 6207 and 6210, being loaned to the Western Region for a few weeks. They were stationed at Old Oak Common and worked initially on Wolverhampton and Birkenhead trains. Problems with turning them at Wolverhampton, however, resulted in them being transferred after a few days to the Bristol road. Prior to withdrawal, 'Lizzies' were also stationed for a time at Carnforth, Rugby, Kingmoor and Willesden. Detailed dates of these and the other shed allocations for the Class are at Appendix D.

Availability and reliability of the 'Lizzies' were, fairly unsurprisingly, not as good as the later 'Coronations' although they were about average for comparable engines from other railways. Whilst they never achieved the goals set by the LMS for annual mileage, what they did was again as good or better than most of their counterparts. Unlike some contemporary locomotives, the 'Princess Royals' didn't suffer any

marked general deterioration as inspection time approached, usually remaining steady performers throughout unless stopped for some defect or other. Their main weaknesses were loose cylinders, until the major front end alterations already described, and fractured, leaking exhaust channels before the advent of cast-steel inside cylinders. They were seldom stopped for hot axleboxes but suffered from damaged big-end bearings and, early on, overheating crossheads. Cracked superheater headers and firebox expansion diaphragms also gave trouble. As with the majority of LMS locomotives, one of their weak spots was springs, few of those on the coupled wheels lasting over a year and even less for bogies and pony trucks.

Performance was equal to all the tasks set them, even before the early steaming problems of the type 1 boiler had been overcome. After high-degree superheat was fitted, they were considered the equal of the later 'Coronation' Class and worked the most demanding expresses on the LMS system. They were fast runners and were regularly timed in the high 80s or low 90s. One of the fastest runs on record was when 6203 took a relatively light train of 366 tons from Crewe to Euston in May 1936 and reached a measured speed of 102½ mph just south of Leighton Buzzard. A more impressive feat of haulage, however, was put up by 6200 the previous June when she took a 461 ton train from a dead stand at Lancaster to Shap Summit in under 42 minutes with a minimum speed

of 35 mph on the bank. The equivalent drawbar horsepower as the summit was reached must have been approaching 1,900.

From conversations we have had with footplatemen who worked on them, the 'Lizzies' seem to have been well liked, if sometimes a handful for the fireman. Ride quality was described as good unless the engine was very run-down, as sometimes happened in the war years and near to withdrawal, and forward visibility was good; lookout was also helped by the side screens. Demands on the fireman could be high; as John Poole put it, 'At full regulator and 30% cut-off you wouldn't put the shovel down very often.' Firing a Stanier Pacific was a different proposition from other LMS locomotives, Stanier 4–6–0s included, but once the fireman had the knack it was straightforward if tiring. The first thing to do, according to two ex-firemen with whom we have spoken, was to fill the rear corners, otherwise cold air coming in could spoil the steaming. Then the trick was to fire down the sides and particularly under the door, just putting enough on the front to fill any holes that the sloping grate and vibration missed. Some firemen apparently developed the technique of filling the rear corners and then piling coal into the firebox just ahead of the door until the heap obscured the view of the brick arch and all but blocked the firehole – a practice that would be disastrous with some engines but was seemingly tolerated by a 'Lizzie', even though it wouldn't get the best out of her. They were also reckoned to be reasonably tolerant of the various types of coal that were supplied at the various depots, although some of the briquettes and poor quality coal that were used during the austerity years did cause trouble. At least they had large ashpans.

Whilst the exhaust injectors seem to have been more reliable than they were on some LMS locomotives, they could still be troublesome from time to time. According to John Poole and others, the technique for using the injectors was to set the exhaust one as soon as the engine was under way and then fire against it, which was not difficult to achieve as the evaporation rate was generally high. From time to time, the live steam injector would have to be used as well.

The tender had a good shovelling plate and there was plenty of room on the platform but even the later tenders weren't very good at shaking the coal forward. Hence, once 3 tons or so had been used, the fireman would have to go back into the tender at frequent intervals in order to bring coal forward.

As previously stated, their power classification in LMS days was 7P but after nationalisation the system was revised. There were actually two systems used on British Railways – 'statistical', used by the Motive Power Department, and 'loading' used by the Operating Dept. to indicate the loading that could be applied to an engine on various types of train. The latter took into account braking power as well as haulage capacity. Power classifications carried by the locomotives were 'statistical' on all regions except the Southern, where loading classification was displayed. The highest passenger power classification on the LMR became 8P, which included the 'Lizzies', and was introduced in 1951.

Although the class was used on less demanding duties to some extent from the 1950s, as witnessed by their use on some ordinary passenger trains as described earlier, they continued to be used on top-link duties right up to withdrawal. English Electric type 4 diesels gradually took over most of the top-link duties starting in 1958 but there were problems with the new types and quite frequently the Pacifics had to deputise for them. In March 1961, the replacement was supposedly complete and all the 'Princess Royals' were stored out of use. However, there were still failures and more general faults with the diesels that resulted in members of the class being pressed into traffic from time to time. This situation persisted, albeit with 'Lizzies' gradually being withdrawn, until only 46200, 46201, 46203 and 46206 were left. In October 1962 Nos. 46201 and 46203 were withdrawn and the last two went the following month.

Waiting for the end, Nos. 46204 and 46208, both crimson, were placed into store at Edge Hill in May 1961. Their buffers, couplings and other bare metal parts were thickly greased, chimneys covered with bags to prevent the ingress of detritus and they sat idle for two months, during which time this photograph was taken. In July that year, however, they were put back into service to substitute for failed and ailing diesels before being stored again in late August. For 46204 that really was the end and she was withdrawn the following October. No. 46208, however, was reprieved for a while and saw service again from January to October of 1962 before she, too, was withdrawn for good. One of the authors recalls as a teenager seeing these engines on 'death row' at Edge Hill and thinking what a shame it was.

AUTHORS' COLLECTION

LIVERY

The 'Princess Royals' were at various times painted in LMS crimson lake, LMS lined black, and BR black, blue, green and maroon. Of all those schemes, however, the only two that were worn by the whole class were LMS crimson and BR green. Which of the other paint schemes were carried by which locomotives and when is in some cases a matter of conjecture as, apart from photographic and anecdotal evidence, there is little in the way of detailed information available. As stated in the introduction, some of what we have used comes from our good friend David Jenkinson, who has studied such matters for many years. However, even he admits that there are major areas of uncertainty. The quoted dates of changes are one example of this as it is clear that repaints (or, at least, changes of insignia style) took place quite often and were not confined to heavy repairs – had they been, the task would be relatively easy as the pertinent dates are known. Thus, whilst we have done our best to be accurate in what we have written, we can't pretend to have found all the answers and would welcome any additions or corrections from readers. A table of known and likely dates for livery changes, mainly prepared for us by David Jenkinson, accompanies this section.

LMS CRIMSON LAKE

All locomotives were painted in the 1928 lined crimson lake scheme when built.[27] The lining first applied to 6200 and 6201 was a pale straw colour, similar to that used by the Midland Railway, and often described as being the closest shade to gold leaf obtainable with non-metallic paint. At about the time when the main production batch was being painted, however, the painting schedules were altered to include a darker shade, generally known as middle chrome yellow. Although it is possible that the new colour would have been used on the 1935 Pacifics, we can't be certain. Hence, in the panel we have merely described the lining colour as 'yellow'. For further details of the 1935 painting specification and the actual paints used, see *LMS Locomotive Profile No.2 – The Horwich Moguls*.

LMS crimson lake paint scheme

Frames	Inside faces vermilion. Outside faces, motion brackets, valve spindle guides and brackets, life guards, injectors, pipework, brake and sanding gear black.
Axles	Vermilion, ends polished metal.
Wheels	Black, bosses and tyres polished metal.
Cylinders and motion	Cylinder wrappers crimson lake, front and rear clothing black. End covers polished metal. Clothing bands black, fine lined yellow on inside edges. Cylinder relief valves and drain cocks black, drain pipes copper. Motion and reversing rod bare metal.
Platform	Black. Platform angles crimson lake, lower edges black, fine lined yellow above. Footsteps black; supports crimson lake, edged black and fine lined yellow inside except on upper edges and either side of upper step. Grab handles polished metal. Mechanical lubricators black. Front fall plates, cylinder and tail rod covers black. Splasher tops black, sides crimson lake edged black, fine lined yellow inside. Name plates black, raised borders and letters polished brass.
Bogie	Frames black outside, possibly vermilion inside top bars and equalising beams as far as bogie cradle, otherwise black. Equalising beams outside, guard irons and bolsters black Axles vermilion, ends polished metal. Wheels black, bosses and tyres polished metal.
Pony truck	Frames, springs & axleboxes black. Wheels black, tyres polished metal.
Buffer beam	Vermilion, edged black and fine lined yellow inside. Vacuum stand pipe vermilion, black and yellow to match adjacent colour. Vacuum hose black. Buffer housings vermilion; casting beads black, fine lined yellow on inside. Buffers and coupling hooks bare metal.
Boiler, firebox & smokebox	Boiler and firebox clothing, top feed cover, dome cover (where applicable) crimson lake. Clothing band next to smokebox black, fine lined yellow at rear. Other clothing bands plain crimson lake. Angle between cab front and firebox clothing black, fine lined yellow on front edge. Smokebox, smokebox saddle, steam pipes, anti-vacuum valves and chimney black. Smokebox number plates black with polished characters. Shed code plates either enamelled white with dark blue or black characters, or black with polished, raised characters. Handrails, ejector and ejector pipework crimson lake or black to match adjacent colour. Safety valves and whistle brass.
Cab, outside	Sides and front crimson lake. Sides edged black, fine lined yellow inside except along top edge. Window frames black. Running number in 12in gold, shaded black transfers. Horizontal centreline of numbers 22in above platform and total width 44in. Power classification in 2in gilt shaded black transfers immediately below gap between windows. Roof crimson up to rainstrips, black between. Handrails and grab handles bare metal. Cab roof black all over after fitting of rain gutters.
Cab, inside	Below waist level crimson lake. Above waist level grained oak finish. Firebox backplate black, roof white (rapidly becoming cream).
Tender frames	Outside faces crimson lake edged black, fine lined yellow inside including cut-outs but excluding top edges. Inside faces black. Springs, hangers, axleboxes, life guards, brake and water pick-up gear black.
Tender platform	Black. Footsteps and supports as for locomotive.
Tender axles	Black.
Tender wheels	Black, tyres polished metal.
Tender sides & rear – 9000 & 9001	Crimson lake edged black, fine lined yellow inside. Horizontal black line 2¼in wide, fine lined yellow both sides along row of rivets at tank top. Vertical black line 2¼in wide, fine lined yellow both sides along row of rivets at tank front. Handrails and grab handles bare metal. LMS in 14in gold, shaded black transfers halfway between platform and tank top rivets. Letter M vertically above intermediate wheel. Centre of L to centre of M 5ft, centre of M to centre of S 4ft 9in. Number, capacity and makers plates black with polished characters.
Tender sides and rear – other types with 1928 style transfers (see text for details of 1936 style)	Crimson lake, edged black and fine lined yellow inside. Bottom edge of transfers 2ft 6in above platform. Transfer spacing, handrails, grab rails, number plate & capacity plate as 9000 & 9001.
Tender front and top	Black.
Tender buffer beam	Vermilion edged black, fine lined yellow inside on sides and lower edge. Buffers, housings, coupling and vacuum pipe as for locomotive. Carriage warming pipe black.

Note: Sizes given for letters and numbers discount shading.

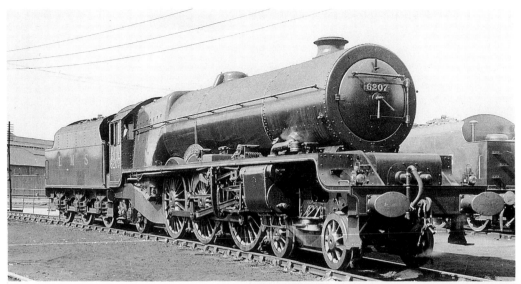

This picture of No. 6207 Princess Arthur of Connaught *shows the original LMS crimson livery with the scroll-and-serif insignia executed in gold with black shading. The locomotive is seen coupled to a 9-ton tender; the later 10-ton tender is shown below with No. 6203.*
AUTHORS' COLLECTION

The final tenders allocated to the 'Lizzies' were 4,000-gallon, 10-ton ones, the extended sides of which are quite apparent in this photograph of No. 6203 coupled to tender 9374 that it acquired in January 1937. The picture was taken at Edge Hill in about 1939 and shows 6203 in its second livery with gold or yellow, shaded vermilion insignia. The engine was transferred to Edge Hill from Camden in October 1939 but we don't know to which it was allocated when this picture was taken. As well as the other differences already noted between the first two engines and 6203 et seq when built, the two mechanical lubricators on the right-hand side of the later examples can be seen at the fronts of leading and intermediate splashers.
N. FIELDS

Several 'Princess Royals' received the shortlived 1936 sans serif livery. One such was 6204 Princess Louise, *which probably had it applied when first coupled to its 10-ton tender in December 1936. In our opinion, the style and positioning of the cabside numerals adopted for this livery didn't suit the engines and they looked much better with scroll and serif insignia. Note that steam sanding had been fitted by the time this picture was taken.*
REAL PHOTOGRAPHS/NRM

When 6200 was built, its makers' plates were fixed to the sides of the smokebox. By the time it entered traffic, however, they had been moved to the leading splashers. Those on 6201 were mounted on the leading splashers from new but 6203 *et seq* had them on the front frames above the platform. Both the first two engines actually entered traffic without name plates but a month later 6200 was seen carrying ones with the wording *Princess Royal*. A few days later it had new ones reading *The Princess Royal* and 6201 carried *Princess Elizabeth*. The name plates were affixed to the intermediate splashers on all the engines, although the drawing schedule indicates that those on 6203–6209 were originally to have been on the leading ones. Running numbers were in scroll and serif characters similar to those used by the Midland but not, in our view, quite as attractive. As indicated in the panel, shed code plates affixed at Camden were initially enamelled white with dark blue or black characters. These were later altered to the more familiar cast plates painted black with raised characters that were polished. Known dimensions of the edging and lining were as follows:

- Yellow lining on front clothing band – ⅜in.
- Black line on cab front angle 2in wide, yellow line ⅜ in.
- Edging and lining on platform angle – 1in black, ⅜ in yellow.
- Cab side black edging 2¼ in wide, yellow lining ⅜ in.
- Splashers edging 1in black, ⅜ in yellow.
- Tender side & rear edging 2¼ in black, ½ in yellow.
- Tender frame and footstep support edging 1in black, ½ in yellow.

The change to 10 ton tenders coincided with the introduction of the short-lived 1936 sans serif style of markings in gold leaf with vermilion shading, 10in high numerals, 2⅛ in high power classification figures and 14in letters, which was applied to a few of the class. From our own research plus David Jenkinson's notes and Bob Meanley's observations, we think that the following were the only ones treated, although we can't be certain:

- 6201 – confirmed photographically, probably when first coupled to a 10 ton tender in November 1936, but certainly in 1937.
- 6204 – confirmed photographically; probably when first coupled to a 10 ton tender in December 1936, but certainly during most of 1937.
- 6205 – confirmed photographically. When first given a 10 ton tender in May 1936, it is confirmed that serif 1928 style insignia were carried, so sans serif style must have been applied sometime later. It has been suggested that this occurred when the engine was fitted with derived inside motion but, as this wasn't until 1938, it seems unlikely.
- 6206 – confirmed photographically – probably when first coupled to a 10 ton tender in October 1936, but certainly during most of 1937.
- 6209 – confirmed photographically – probably when first coupled to a 10 ton tender in October 1936, but certainly in 1937.
- 6210 – reportedly with a 9 ton tender in 1936 – probably when first coupled to a 10 ton tender in September that year although not confirmed, but certainly in 1937.
- 6212 – reportedly so in 1936 – probably when first coupled to a 10 ton tender in July that year but not confirmed.

Although the smokebox door number plates were supposed to be replaced with new ones having sans serif characters, this wasn't, as far as we know, done with any of the 'Lizzies'. In late 1937, the sans serif pattern transfers were abandoned and the style reverted to the scroll and serif form, albeit with vermilion shading rather than black. There is, however, uncertainty about the ground colour of the characters on the Pacifics, even though it is known (and confirmed) to have been changed *officially* from gold to chrome yellow for all other LMS types at the time. The problem stems from the fact that the non-streamlined 'Coronations' came out in 1938 with the vermilion shaded scroll and serif insignia rendered in gold rather than yellow. Since most of the 'Lizzies' did not receive vermilion shaded transfers until the same year it is at least feasible that, being top-link motive power, they too may have had gold ones. David Jenkinson tends to favour the yellow option but, even after much research with one of the authors, has been frustrated by the matter for many years and it remains unresolved. What can be stated with certainty is that all the 'Princess Royals' were running with red shaded insignia of the scroll and serif type by the end of 1938.

The 'Princess Royals' were the only LMS engines to retain the crimson lake livery as a complete class throughout the war years. Although they were never repainted during that time, their transfers were either replaced or 'freshened' with paint, both of which would certainly have been yellow rather than gold. Since the photographic record became somewhat sparse during the war, it is hard to discover exactly what went on. One thing that is clear, however, is that many, or perhaps all, of the class had their numerals placed in a new and noticeably higher position on the cab side with the power classification below. These numerals were undoubtedly yellow and some may have been unshaded but we cannot give any further details. Can any reader help? It is also certain that two of the engines, 46204 and 46212, were taken over by BR still in crimson livery and received their new numbers in sans serif, 10in deep cream numerals in the LMS 1946 style without the maroon detail, which were set high up on the cab sides.

LMS LINED BLACK

In mid-1946, the LMS introduced an overall glossy black express passenger paint scheme with maroon and straw lining. The straw coloured letters and numbers were sans serif with inset edging lines in maroon, although some observers recorded that there were instances of fine maroon lining outside the straw. This would be virtually impossible to see in monochromatic photographs and so we are unable to give specific instances. The reason for the apparent inconsistency, we believe, was that the characters were hand painted rather than being transfers. This was the first time that the word 'maroon' had been used to describe a colour on the LMS and it was indeed a darker shade than the earlier crimson. The entire locomotive was black except for the following:

- Insides of frames, stretchers, inside weighshaft and axles possibly vermilion or red oxide.
- Buffer beams, buffer casings and parts of vacuum stand pipes adjacent to the buffer beam vermilion. Casting beads on buffer casings black.
- Motion, buffers, coupling hooks, safety valves and whistle bare metal.
- Inside of cab roof white, rapidly becoming cream and then brown.
- Locomotive number plate, shed code plate, engine and tender makers plates, tender number plate and capacity plate black with raised characters and borders picked out in white.
- Name plates maroon with borders and letters picked out in straw.
- Boiler clothing bands adjacent to smokebox and firebox maroon, edged ⅜ in pale straw both sides.
- Forward land of angle-iron between firebox clothing and cab maroon, edged ⅜ in pale straw front and rear.
- Front, bottom and rear edges of cab sides edged 2½ in maroon, fine lined ⅜ in pale straw inside. Running number in 12in sans serif pale straw characters with maroon edging, fine lined pale straw outside (for dimensioned drawings of 1946 characters see page 201 of *An Illustrated History of LMS Locomotives Vol. 1* by Bob Essery and David Jenkinson, published by Oxford Publishing Co.). Total width of numbers 4ft 2in,

In April 1946, financial authority was given to fit extra washout plugs at the front of the first ring near the top of the boiler barrel. No. 6211 was photographed at Crewe in February 1947 just four days after leaving the Works fitted with boiler 9103, which had been modified with the extra plugs since being taken off 6204 the previous September. It had also received new outside cylinders, as shown by the lack of sighting plugs on the valve chest. This is the earliest dated photograph we have of an engine with replacement cylinders, although 6205 may have received them earlier, as discussed in the text. Note also the oblong access hole and cover in the cylinder clothing, which was a fairly recent modification when the photograph was taken, although we can't date it exactly. The engine and tender had also been newly painted in lined black livery during their repair and the picture provides a good reference for the scheme as applied to a 'Princess Royal'.

D. F. TEE COLLECTION

All but two of the class were painted in the lined black LMS livery introduced in 1946. No. 6210 was photographed wearing it at Crewe North in May 1948. The engine had been fitted with replacement outside cylinders, as it has no sighting plugs on its valve chest. Note also the larger, oblong access holes and covers in the cylinder clothing that were introduced in the 1940s and the altered sandbox filler lid with recessed top and cast-in handle just behind the outside steam pipe.

W. L. GOOD

distance of bottom edges of numbers to platform 2ft 6in. Power classification about 3in below numbers.

- Platform angle, except below cab, maroon, edged ⅜ in pale straw top and bottom. Front and rear extremities not lined.
- Cylinder clothing bands maroon, edged ⅜ in pale straw front and rear.
- Tender sides edged 2½ in maroon, fine lined ⅜ in straw inside. Sans serif 'LMS', style as cab side numbers, in 14in letters spaced at 5ft 3in and 5ft with 'M' above intermediate axle. Bottom edge of letters 2ft 6in above platform.

By the end of 1947, all except 6204, 6206 and 6212 had been repainted in the 1946 LMS livery. No. 6206 received it after nationalisation and was turned out in March 1948 with the short-lived 'M' prefix, although it looked like a suffix on the cab sides as it was below the number. The smokebox door number plate had a cast extension riveted to the left-hand end with the M on it.

At least two of the Class, 6203 and 6210, had their 462XX BR numbers applied while still wearing LMS lined black. They appeared thus attired in about March 1948 with just the numbers repainted, their tenders still having 'LMS' on the sides. The new smokebox door number plates had scroll and serif LMS characters but sometime in 1949 or 1950 this was altered to BR Gill Sans style.

Princess Margaret Rose was one of two engines to have its BR number applied while still wearing LMS lined black livery in about March 1948. Only the cabside and smokebox door numbers were changed, the tender still having 'LMS' on the sides as seen in this picture of 6203 passing Ashton on 26th April 1948. The new smokebox door plates had scroll and serif LMS characters but sometime in 1949 or 1950 this was altered to BR Gill Sans style. By the time the photograph was taken, oblong access holes had been cut in the cylinder clothing and there were two extra washout plugs near the top of the boiler barrel at the front of the first ring. Its sandbox filler lids had also been changed to the recess and cast-in handle type.
L. HANSON

One of the class was painted in the 1946 LMS lined black livery after nationalisation. Princess Marie Louise was turned out in March 1948 as M6206, the only one of the class to wear the 'M' prefix. It is seen in this photograph just after repainting at Crewe North, still carrying its LMS smokebox door numberplate but with an extension for the 'M' riveted to the side. The cabside number was applied in sans serif straw and maroon characters with a matching 'M' below and 'BRITISH RAILWAYS', also in matching letters, on the tender. Its pony truck had originally been fitted to either 6200 or 6201, as the axlebox end covers show. Note the new style of sandbox filler lid just visible behind the outside-cylinder steam pipe.
D. F. TEE COLLECTION

BR BLACK

The scheme BR decided on in 1948 for mixed traffic and lesser passenger locomotives was based on the pre-Grouping L&NWR passenger livery. However, several express engines, including some of the 'Lizzies', were painted in that style at Crewe, no doubt with the approval, if not actual connivance, of Robert Riddles, the new CME and an ex-Crewe L&NWR apprentice. Locomotives we know to have received this livery were 46201, 46205, 46207, 46209, 46211 and 46212, estimated dates for repainting being in the table.

Apart from the following items, the entire engine was black inside and out:

> Insides of frames, stretchers, motion plate, inside weighshaft and axles possibly red oxide.
> Buffer beams, buffer casings and parts of vacuum standpipes adjacent to the buffer beam – signal red.
> Inside of cab roof – white when first painted.
> Motion – bare metal.
> Buffers – bare metal.
> Couplings and hooks – bare metal.
> Cylinder drain pipes – bare metal.
> Name plates – black with polished brass borders and lettering.
> Number, shed, makers' and capacity plates – black with white borders and characters.

A single panel of multi-coloured lining was inset from the edges of each cab side, the shape on the majority being asymmetric with three corners having an outside radius of 4in whilst that of the front lower corner was larger so that it more closely matched the shape of the cab side. Going from the outside, the lining was ⅝in pale grey, ⅛in cream, 1⅝in black and ¼in red. Whilst that was the official specification, on some locomotives the black line between cream and grey was narrower than specified. On the platform angles, the lower edges were grey with cream above and the red lines were halfway up the angle. Boiler and cylinder clothing bands were edged with ¼in red lines. Tender sides had multi-coloured lining inset from the bottom edge by about 5in and front and rear edges somewhat more with 4in outside radius lower corners. On the majority, the top of the panel was just below the bend in the tender side and followed the shapes of front and rear cutaways down to the verticals. The running number was displayed on a cast smokebox door plate in raised white numerals, generally Gill Sans, and on the cab sides in 8in cream Gill Sans characters with the power classification just below them. Ownership was shown on the tender sides by the legend 'BRITISH RAIL-

No. 46207 was one of six 'Princess Royals' to be painted in the mixed traffic livery based upon the pre-grouping L&NWR passenger engine livery, with 'BRITISH RAILWAYS' in full on the tender side.   AUTHORS' COLLECTION

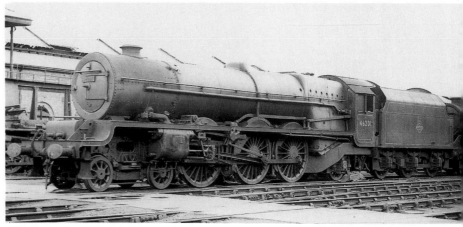

We know of only two engines that received the first BR crest while painted in what was supposed to be the mixed traffic and lesser passenger engine lined black. One of them was 46201, seen here with boiler 6050 sometime between December 1948 and December 1951. At some stage it had inherited a pony truck with flat axlebox end covers from one of the 6203-6207 series. Note that although its bogie axles had been bored out, the coupled axles were still solid. Its sandbox filler lids were the later type.   AUTHORS' COLLECTION

WAYS', again in 8in cream Gill Sans and in line with the cab side numerals. At least two engines, 46201 and 46211, later had the first BR crest with a lion astride a wheel applied to their tender sides whilst still wearing lined BR black livery.

When first repainted, 46205 had different arrangements of lining panels both on its cab and tender sides. The cab side panels were symmetrical, with all four corners having an outside radius of about 4in. The panels on the tender sides were rectangles with their top edges in line with the top pillars of the forward handrails, all corners again having an outside radius of about 4in. It also had a smokebox door

number plate with characters in a style peculiar to Derby and Bow Works. Whether these features indicate that it was, in fact, repainted at one of these places we don't know, although it was never recorded as being repaired anywhere other than Crewe. Later, however, it was altered whilst still painted black to have lining panels in the same style as its brethren and a smokebox door plate with Gill Sans numerals. It was very unusual to see any engine receive a new plate unless its original one was damaged and we can't offer any explanation as to why 46205's was changed.

Four of the class were painted in the lined blue livery that became the official scheme for top-link express passenger engines in 1950. One of them, 46208, was photographed at Crewe in September of that year the day after returning to traffic following a heavy repair and repainting. It remained blue only until November 1952. It was the first of the main production batch engines to carry one of the early boilers without a combustion chamber and ran in the condition shown, first with boiler 6049 and then 6050, until April 1957. The diamond-shaped holes on the front frames just above the leading bogie wheel were for the flanges of the inside cylinder bypass valves, which were never actually fitted. Their presence indicates that 46208 still had its original front frames when this picture was taken.
COLLECTION J. BRAITHWAITE

BR BLUE

In 1950, the approved scheme for express passenger engines became lined blue, the colour supposedly being based on the old Caledonian Perth blue although several commentators of the time cast doubt on its authenticity. It was found after a short time to fade rather badly and so its use was discontinued in 1951 after only four of the class — 46203, 46206, 46208 and 46210 — had received it. Details of the scheme as far as we know them are in the panel and suggested dates of repainting in the table.

Much of the lining was more complicated than it first appears in photographs as there was often a blue line between the black and white. Known dimensions of the edging and lining were as follows:

White lines on clothing bands – ¼ in
Edging and lining on platform angle – ½ in black on lower edge, ½ in blue above and ⅛ in white above that.
White edging on cylinder clothing bands – probably ⅛ in.
Splashers – edging ½ in black with ½ in blue and ⅛ in white lines inside.
Lining panels on cab and tender sides – 1in black flanked by ½ in blue and ⅛ in white lines each side.

The outside edges of the cab side lining panels were inset 5in from the sides and platform and 4in from the bottom of the window frames. Outside radius of all except the front lower corner was 4in. The front lower corner basically followed the curve of the platform.

The outer edges of the tender lining panels were set 5in from the platform, 1ft 5in from the front, 1ft 4in from the back and 3in below the start of the top curve. Outside radius of the lower corners was 4in and the upper corners basically followed the curves of the tender sides.

BR blue paint scheme

Frames, axles, wheels, brakes, sanding gear, injectors, motion brackets, bogie and pony truck, including all stretchers, axleboxes and pipework below the platform except as otherwise specified	Black. Insides of frames, stretchers, weighshaft and axles possibly red oxide.
Cylinders and motion	Cylinder clothing and end covers black. Clothing bands black, fine lined white on edges. Cylinder relief valves and drain cocks black, drain pipes copper. Motion and reversing rod bare metal.
Platform	Black. Platform angles blue, lower edges black, fine lined blue and white above. No lining on extremities. Footsteps and supports, grab handles, mechanical lubricators, front fall plates, cylinder and tail rod covers black. Splasher tops black, sides blue edged black, fine lined white and blue inside. Name plates black, raised borders and letters polished brass. Makers' plates probably black with white borders and letters.
Buffer beam	Beam, buffer casings and parts of vacuum standpipe adjacent to beam signal red. Rest of standpipe and vacuum hose black. Buffers and coupling hooks bare metal.
Boiler, firebox & smokebox	Boiler and firebox clothing, top feed cover, dome cover (where applicable) blue. Clothing band next to smokebox black, fine lined white at rear. Other boiler clothing bands black, fine lined white front and rear. Firebox clothing bands and angle blue. Smokebox, steam pipes, anti-vacuum valves, smokebox saddle and chimney black. Smokebox number and shed plates black with white characters. Handrails, ejector and ejector pipework black. Safety valves and whistle brass.
Cab, outside	Front and sides, including window frames, blue. Inset lining panels on sides as detailed in text. Running number in 8in cream Gill Sans numerals with tops 10½ in below window frames. Power classification in 2in cream Gill Sans characters midway between top of number and inner edge of bottom of lining panel. Roof black. Handrails and grab handles black.
Cab, inside	Sides possibly blue but not confirmed. Firebox backplate black, roof white (rapidly becoming cream).
Tender frames, axles, wheels, axleboxes, brakes, water pick-up gear, all associated linkages and pipework, platform, footsteps and supports	Black
Tender sides & rear	Blue. Inset lining panels on sides as detailed in text. Handrails and grab handles black. BR lion astride wheel crest facing forwards on each side, oblong panel with BRITISH RAILWAYS lettering placed such that its lower edge was 2ft 6½ in from platform and rear edge 11ft 2in from back of tank. Number, makers' and capacity plates black with white characters.
Tender front and top	Black.
Tender buffer beam	Beam, buffer casings and parts of vacuum standpipe adjacent to beam signal red. Carriage warming pipe black. Buffers and couplings bare metal.

BR GREEN

Starting in September 1951, all the 'Princess Royals' were painted in BR lined Brunswick green with orange and black lining, which was basically the postwar Great Western scheme. The lining colour was described in some official documents issued when it was introduced in 1949 as 'yellow' but was, in fact, more of a tangerine hue. In 1954 the shade of green changed very slightly and would have appeared a little darker if held next to the original colour. This would probably not have been apparent, however, as green is a very fugitive colour and changes with exposure to sunlight and sulphur salts, so freshly painted engines probably always looked slightly darker than those more than a few weeks on the road.

Painting details were closely similar to the BR blue livery, merely substituting Brunswick green for blue. The lining was also more complex than first appearances would suggest, not simply being black and orange but having green lines between those colours. Lining details, as far as we know them, were as follows:

Boiler clothing bands – 1 in black centre flanked by ½ in green lines and ¼ in orange edging.

Splashers – ¾ in black edging, fine lined ³⁄₁₆ in orange inside with no green line separating the two.

Platform angle – ¾ in black lower edging with ½ in green and ¼ in orange lines above.

Cylinder clothing bands – black, edged orange – probably ¼ in wide.

Lining panels on cab and tender sides – 1 in black line with ½ in green and ¼ in orange lines outside.

Lettering and numbering, as well as other details, were as described for the blue livery. Name plates were painted signal red with the letters and borders polished. The early type of 'monocycling lion' BR emblem was applied when the engines were first painted green with the lions facing forwards on each side. Those locomotives that remained green after 1958

A typical middle '50s West Coast express is illustrated by Brunswick green 46211 in charge of a rake of carmine and cream coaches emerging from Primrose Hill tunnel with the 7.50 a.m. Crewe–Euston on 7th July 1954. The engine was carrying a domed combustion chamber boiler, No. 9235, and still had a roller bearing pony truck. At the time of the photograph it was stationed at Crewe North.   BRITISH RAILWAYS

As far as we are aware, only two of the class didn't receive AWS. One of them was 46210, seen here at Polmadie less crosshead and connecting rod. It was painted in the Brunswick green livery it had worn since 1953 and was carrying one of the early boilers without a combustion chamber, which it did from January 1956 until withdrawal. It was allocated to Polmadie in July 1958 and remained there until March 1961 when it was moved to Kingmoor, where it stayed until it was withdrawn in October of that year. The engine had acquired a plain bearing pony truck originally fitted to one of the 6203-6207 series, as shown by the flat end covers, and the lack of diamond holes indicates that its front frames had been renewed.
AUTHORS' COLLECTION

received the later 'ferret and dartboard' coat-of-arms and all, as far as we are aware, had the heraldically correct left-facing lions on both sides. We have anecdotal evidence that at least some LMR Brunswick green passenger locomotives had green cab side interiors and the insides of the window frames painted brick red; whether any were 'Princess Royals' though, we cannot say. Otherwise the cab sides were black inside and all had white roof interiors, which rapidly darkened to deepening shades of cream. From 1960, overhead electrification warning flashes were applied to the outsides of the forward frames above the platform, on the boiler clothing just forward of the top feed shoulders, on the firebox clothing just above the washout plugs, and on the tender rear towards each side.

This picture of No. 46205 was taken at Crewe on 6th August 1960 and shows the non-standard valve gear fitted to this locomotive. The final livery style to be carried was the British Railways Brunswick green with the 'ferret and dartboard' coat-of-arms.   W. POTTER

BR MAROON

In 1958, as part of a move towards regional livery differentiation that also brought back SR green and GWR chocolate and cream on many carriages, twenty LMS Pacifics were selected for repainting in what amounted to a revival of LMS crimson livery. Although the colour was described in official documents at the time as maroon, it was stated to be the same shade as that worn by LMS engines before the war. Why only twenty were chosen we don't know; other than their being based in the London, Midland region rather than in Scotland, where the ex-LMS Pacifics remained green, they seem simply to have been the first to go through the paint shops after the decision was taken.

Four 'Lizzies' — 46200, 46204, 46207 and 46208 — were painted maroon/crimson. The first two, Nos. 46200 and 46207, received LMS-style yellow and black edge lining, whereas the other two had BR-type orange and black inset lining panels. Whether this was for comparison we don't know but the following year 46204 and 46208 also received LMS-pattern edge lining. David Jenkinson saw some painted panels at Euston House shortly thereafter that seemed to suggest the intention from the start had been to use the LMS style.

Numbering, lettering and smokebox door plates were as described for the blue and green liveries and the cab roof was black overall. The BR coat-of-arms with left-facing lions was applied to both sides of the tender in the same position as that

This photograph, taken at Shrewsbury, shows 46208 in maroon livery with inset lining panels shortly after repainting in September 1958. Two engines were turned out in this style, the other being 46204, but only a year later they were repainted with LMS-style edge lining. The picture also proves that 46208 received new front frames — note the absence of a diamond-shaped hole above the leading bogie wheel. It had also been fitted with steam-operated cylinder cocks as witnessed by the pipework at the rear of the platform and less obvious drain pipes on the cylinders. The boiler configuration with combustion chamber and dome was applicable to 46208 from April 1957 until its withdrawal in October 1962.   AUTHORS' COLLECTION

noted for the green livery. The insides of the frames, stretchers, weighshaft and axles were probably red oxide rather than bright red. Apart from those details, the scheme was to all intents and purposes the same as the 1928 LMS arrangement with the power classification immediately below the gap between the window frames. Makers' plates, shed code plates, and tender number, capacity and makers' plates supposedly reverted to having polished bare metal borders and characters, although we have photographs that seem to show at least some engines with white-painted

ones. Known details of the lining were as follows:

Front boiler clothing band – black with ½ in yellow line on rear edge.

Angle between cab and firebox clothing – 1½ in wide black line with ½ in yellow edging on front.

Splashers – 1 in wide black edging, lined ½ in yellow inside.

Platform angle – bottom edged 1in black, lined ½ in yellow above.

Footstep supports – sides edged 1⅛ in black, lined ⅜ in yellow inside. Lower edge black to ¼ in above lower step angle, lined ⅜ in yellow above.

Cylinder clothing bands – black, edged ⅜ in yellow inside.

Buffer beams – edged 1in black, lined ⅜ in yellow inside (not upper edge of tender beam). Buffer casing casting beads black, edged ⅜ in yellow inside touching front edge of casing footstep.
Cab and tender sides – except for top of cab side, edged all round 2½ in black, lined 2½ in yellow inside.

Tender frames – front edge, rear edge, lower edge and slots edged 1⅛ in Black, lined ⅜ in yellow inside.

The only later additions to the maroon livery, as far as we are aware, were overhead electrification warning flashes in late 1960. Flashes were applied to the firebox clothing, front frames and tender rears but not, it would seem, to the boiler clothing.

Nearing the end of its working life, 46200 was photographed by the wires at Crewe in late 1960. Its paint scheme had come almost full circle and it was again in crimson with yellow and black lining, albeit with BR insignia and warning flashes. Much else, however, had changed since it was built. Its boiler had a dome and a combustion chamber as well as a slightly different chimney from its first one. Changes apparent in this picture include a draught screen on the fireman's side of the cab, steam sanding, sandbox filler lids with recessed tops and cast-in handles, steam-operated cylinder cocks, a pony truck originally fitted to one of the 6203-6212 batch, new front frames, AWS, and its axles had been bored out. The covers on its firebox washout doors were missing. It was, however, still a fine locomotive and employed on the tasks it had been designed for nearly thirty years before.
AUTHORS' COLLECTION

SUMMARY OF 'PRINCESS ROYAL' LIVERY CHANGES

Much of the information in the following table was given to us by David Jenkinson. In it, a dash means that a particular livery was definitely not carried, a question mark means that the livery was carried but the date is slightly speculative and a blank means that the livery is very unlikely to have been carried, although we can't state categorically that it wasn't. All engines were painted in LMS crimson with gold, shaded black scroll & serif characters when built. Other livery codes are as follows:

A – LMS crimson with gold, shaded red sans serif characters.
B – LMS crimson with yellow, possibly gold, shaded red scroll & serif characters.
C – LMS lined black with 1946 style lining and sans serif characters.
D – BR black with L&NWR style lining and BRITISH RAILWAYS on tender. An asterisk indicates that the first type of crest is known to have been carried from 1949.
E – BR blue.
F – BR Brunswick green.
G – BR maroon with orange and black inset lining.
H – BR maroon with LMS style yellow and black edge lining.

Engine	A	B	C	D	E	F	G	H
6200	–	1938	Sep 47	–	–	Apr 52	–	May 58
6201	–	1938	Aug 47	Feb 48*	–	Apr 52	–	–
6203	–	1938/9	Dec 47	–	May 51	Mar 52	–	–
6204	Dec 36?	1938	–	–	–	May 52	Aug 58	1959
6205	1937?	1938	1947?	Nov 48	–	Sep 52	–	–
6206	Oct 36?	1938	Feb 48	–	Nov 50	Aug 53	–	–
6207	–	1938	1946?	May 49	–	Dec 51	–	May 58
6208	–	1938	Feb 47?	–	Sep 50	Nov 52	Sep 58	1959
6209	Oct 36?	1938	Oct 46?	May 48	–	Sep 51	–	–
6210	Sep 36?	1938	Aug 47	–	May 50	Mar 53	–	–
6211	–	1938	Feb 47	Jun 49*	–	Dec 52	–	–
6212	Jul 36?	1938	–	Apr 49	–	Nov 52	–	–

POSTSCRIPT

Fortunately, two of these magnificent engines were saved from the breaker's torch and have since been restored to operating condition. It is doubly fortunate that the preserved engines represent the first ones as well as the main production batch, being as they are 6201 *Princess Elizabeth* and 46203 *Princess Margaret Rose*. We would add a word of caution for modellers and artists if referring to these engines as neither is in exactly the condition suggested by its paint scheme. No. 6201, in LMS crimson lake, has a domed boiler with combustion chamber – a type with which she was never fitted in LMS days and didn't actually carry until 1954 – and 46203 is painted in BR crimson, which is a livery she never carried in service. Several details have been changed and air pumps fitted to allow the engines to haul air-braked stock. Their tenders have also had some modification to give greater water capacity and there are other detail alterations. Along with the preserved 'Coronation' Class Pacifics, however, they represent the epitome of LMS passenger motive power and from personal experience we can state that the sight of one in almost full cry over the Settle–Carlisle is something to be treasured.

NOTES IN TEXT

1. The requirements for standard locomotive designs were complicated by the differences in loading gauges and, more importantly, bridge stress limitations on the various divisions of the LMS. The latter seems to have been most acute on the Midland Division and was probably instrumental in the decisions to adopt the Midland Class 4 goods 0–6–0 as a standard design and to buy the 2–6–0+0–6–2 Garratts.

2. There was also at this time a proposal to electrify the West Coast Main Line between Crewe and Carlisle. Some preliminary work, including diagrams of possible locomotives, had been prepared but there was no Board approval and the whole scheme was abandoned in 1924.

3. That the majority of the fault with these engines lay simply with their valves doesn't seem to have been appreciated until much later. Horwich staff had experimented with the lead and lap of the valves and later engines had increased lap. However, the single, stiff Schmidt piston valve rings that were to give so much trouble on the 'Royal Scots', together with the Hughes ball relief valves in the valve heads, allowed a ruinous amount of steam leakage. Even when the extremely successful mogul was being designed at Horwich with multiple, thin rings, for some reason the same thinking wasn't applied to the 4–6–0s. When some of them were eventually altered in the 1930s, it became apparent that they were capable of good, economical performances but it was too late to save what was then a non-standard group of engines. There were also problems with air leaking into their built-up smokeboxes (*shades of the 'Royal Scots' again – see LMS Locomotive Profiles No. 1 – the Rebuilt Royal Scots*), which spoilt their draughting, and difficulties with axlebox lubrication on long journeys. It is probable, however, that the latter two faults could have been rectified had their performance and economy been acceptable.

4. The inclusion of the 3,500 gallon tender, which could only carry a notional 5½ tons of coal, was in order to introduce a measure of standardisation across new locomotive construction. It was this aim that led to the Horwich moguls having the same type of tender. Whether it would have been a good idea for a Pacific meant for long express runs, however, is doubtful. Had the engines been built, it would probably not have been long before they received the 9 ton tenders intended for the 2–8–2s.

5. Earlier, in 1924, C. B. Collett of the Great Western presented a report at the World Power Conference in which he claimed that a 'Castle' had been recorded with a coal consumption of less than 3 lb per drawbar horsepower. When the Compounds were only achieving something like 3½ lb per DHP in normal service, this was an amazing figure. The reaction at Horwich, according to E. S. Cox, was, 'As we could think of no earthly reason as to how this could have been achieved we simply preferred not to believe it'.

6. It has often been stated, apparently due to anecdotal evidence, that work actually started at Crewe on producing boilers for the Fowler Pacifics with a foundation ring and some flanging blocks being made. Whilst Derby issued O/6619 on 23rd February 1926 for work in connection with the construction of five engines, we have been unable to locate documentary evidence to show that anything was actually produced. There is no evidence that Horwich Works, where the frames were to have been made, started any work on them. The situation as regards five 2–8–2s, for which Derby issued O/6618 on the same day, is the same.

7. Stanier had experienced virtually the same situation on the Great Western prior to the introduction of the 'Kings'. It is interesting to speculate whether, as a result, he had insisted on greater rights to question other senior officers than Fowler apparently had as part of his terms of employment with the LMS.

8. According to Eric Langridge, the actual weight of No. 6200 was 111 tons 18 cwt and 6201 was 108 tons 'after thinning down castings' but we have been unable to establish from where he obtained the figures. Other figures to do with weight saving in later engines are included with the same caveat. The measures taken to reduce the weight of 6201 could explain the time lapse between completion of the first and second engines. No. 6201 is still around 107 tons.

9. E. A. Langridge was a draughtsman in Derby Drawing Office. Trained at Eastleigh, he went to the Midland Railway in 1919 and remained at Derby until 1959. In the 1950s he was in charge of the development section and was known to one of the authors. Much of what we report from Langridge comes from correspondence between him and three others: one of the authors; David Tee, who helped us with much material before his death in 2001; and Arthur Cook, who wrote two RCTS publications on LMS locomotives. We have also quoted from correspondence between Arthur Cook, the authors, and David Tee, which the latter made available to us.

10. The idea of having taper boilers with parallel front rings was introduced to the Great Western by G. J. Churchward so that they could easily be tailored to suit different existing engines as well as new designs. All that was needed to create boilers of different lengths was to alter the size of the parallel ring, which was a relatively simple job compared with developing and rolling different coned sections. When Stanier arrived on the LMS, studies were undertaken for re-boilering several existing locomotive classes and it is possible that the form of the No.3 boiler had the Churchward design philosophy behind it.

11. Sling stays were supposed to give more flexibility at the top and front of the firebox where movement was greatest as it heated and cooled. Instead of being attached directly to both inner and outer fireboxes, they were attached by hinge pins at the top to brackets fixed to the outer shell, which allowed some movement. For an illustration of sling and palm stays see the boiler and firebox drawings in *LMS Locomotive Profile No. 2 – The Horwich Moguls*.

12. For a description of standard Derby practice, as on the 'Royal Scots' and parallel-boiler 2–6–4Ts, see *LMS Locomotive Profile No. 3 – The Parallel Boiler 2–6–4 Tank Engines*.

13. A description of the principles and operation of an exhaust steam injector was included in an article in *LMS Journal No. 3*.

14. This method of construction was common to several Stanier classes at the time, the parallel mid-section being more pronounced on taller chimneys. Sometimes the edges of the steel ring could clearly be seen and gave the impression of a chimney built up from separate castings. Occasionally, an engine would have the ring removed, probably due to failure of welding, and the waisted mid-section of the casting would be revealed.

15. In response to experimental results in America, Stanier also gave Langridge the job of scheming a 350psi water-tube boiler for the 'Princess Royals'. Design proceeded throughout 1936 and into 1937 but reported maintenance problems, construction costs and the fact that the weight would have been greater than a conventional fire-tube boiler counted against it and the idea was dropped.

16. The subject of boiler dimensions, ratios and superheating is complex and really outside the scope of this book, so explanations given are of necessity sketchy. For a more detailed discussion of boiler design and development we recommend *Raising Steam on the LMS – The Evolution of LMS Locomotive Boilers* by A. F. Cook published by the RCTS.

17. A meeting of the Traffic Committee in July 1935 minuted that, 'In order to obtain reduced maintenance costs, 167 new 'Princess Royal', 'Jubilee' and Mixed traffic locos were built with a reduced degree of superheating but working experience has shown that this went too far and a higher

degree of superheating will result in an increased operating economy which will more than meet the additional maintenance costs of improved superheating. The chief factor in this is a reduction in coal consumption of about 5 lb per engine mile.'

18. Stanier seems to have enjoyed a fairly close liaison with German and French locomotive engineers, as did Gresley. The adoption of six-ring piston valves and development of triple elements such as those used in boiler 9236 are generally credited to Wagner.
19. The LMS experienced problems with firebox stays throughout the 1930s. Prior to the introduction of the 'Royal Scots', all stays had been copper but after that time copper, cupro-nickel, steel and monel metal were all used in various combinations. Monel is a proprietary brand name for a copper/nickel alloy marketed originally by Henry Wiggin. Some boilers gave severe problems with broken stays and there was a general drift towards using monel metal. For a detailed discussion of stays and their development, we again recommend *Raising Steam on the LMS*.
20. An official LMS photograph exists, purportedly showing 6212 with a central dart locking door when first built and several commentators have suggested that the engine was modified to have the dog ring door after entering traffic. The photograph in question, however, is actually part of a series showing 6203 wearing the names and numbers of all the different main production batch of locomotives.
21. Although tests conducted in late 1935 showed a slight saving of coal and water for the 32-element superheater (see 'engines in service' section), they were not considered conclusive. It wasn't until the 1937 trials that the combination of larger superheater and larger tubes showed a convincing improvement. According to E. S. Cox, it hadn't been realised that the resistance to gas flow as well as the number of elements affected superheater temperature.
22. The use of softened water was intended to reduce the frequency of boiler washout, which it achieved by increasing the mileage between them from 2,500 to 5,000 miles. The drawback was that the salts used to soften the water could cause priming. It was found that if a small amount of water was continuously withdrawn from the boiler when the engine was working, the concentration of these salts could be maintained just below the level at which priming would occur. In 1935 a continuous blowdown valve was developed and fitted to 80 locomotives for a six-month trial, which proved extremely successful. It was therefore decided to equip all engines in England and Wales and financial authority was granted under NWO 3098 in February 1936 for some 5,700 to be modified.
23. It is somewhat ironic that No. 6200 was stopped on her first public outing by an overheated axlebox.
24. Some sources state that 46208 and 46209 were not given new front frames. Photographs of the engines in the 1950s and 1960s, however, show quite clearly that they did not have the diamond-shaped holes in the front frames and that they had, therefore been rebuilt.
25. Other evidence for the intention to fit ATC to LMS engines on a widespread scale is shown in a drawing schedule dated 1938 that has survived for the installation of the equipment to 'Coronation' Class Pacifics.
26. The hand brake and water scoop handles on 9002 were arranged in the old Derby style whilst it was attached to 'Royal Scot'. When it was rebuilt and allocated to a Class 5 engine, the arrangement was altered to the bevel geared variety.
27. Some LMS documents refer to the colour of crimson lake engines as 'Derby Red' or 'Midland Red' right up to 1939. For a detailed discussion of the colour of LMS locomotives, see *An Illustrated History of LMS Locomotives Volume 1* by Essery and Jenkinson published by Oxford Publishing Co.

APPENDICES

APPENDIX A – ENGINE DIAGRAMS

The 'Princess Royals' were allocated to several engine diagrams, details of which were as follows:

ED 175	Nos. 620 & 6201 as built with 16-element superheaters and original tenders.
ED 175/1	Nos. 6200 & 6201 when fitted with boiler 6050 having 32-element superheater and 2⅛ in tubes and coupled to 4,000 gallon, 9 ton tenders.
ED 175A	Issued for Nos. 6203–6212 but replaced before any engines built.
ED 175A/1	Nos. 6203–6206 with 24-element superheaters, 2¼ in tubes and 9 ton tenders.
ED 175A/2	As ED 175A/1 but with 2⅜ in tubes and 10 ton tenders.
ED 175B	Nos. 6207–6212 with 32-element superheaters, 2¼ in tubes and 9 ton tenders.
ED 175B/1	As ED 175B with 10 ton tender.
ED 175B/2	As ED 175B/1 with 2⅜ in tubes.
ED 175B/3	No. 6206 with coal pusher tender.
ED 175C	Nos. 6203–6212 with domed boiler and 112 tubes of 2¼ in.
ED 175D	As ED 175C with 2⅜ in tubes.
ED 175E	As ED 175D with 123 tubes
ED 175F	As ED 175E with welded tender.
ED 175G	Boiler fitted with standard 1¼ in superheater elements.
ED 175H	Power classification altered to 8P.
ED 175J	Boiler with 1½ in superheater elements.
ED 257	Nos. 6200 & 6201 when fitted with original boilers modified with 32-element superheater, 2⅜ in tubes and domes and coupled to 9 ton tenders.
ED 257A	As ED 257 with weight altered.
ED 257B	As ED 257A with boiler 6050 after fitting with dome and 110 tubes of 2⅜ in.
ED 257C	As ED 257A with 10 ton tender.
ED 257D	As ED 257B with 10 ton tender.

APPENDIX B – BOILER DETAILS

The aim of this appendix is twofold. Firstly, it is to consolidate some of the information given in the text. Secondly, since boilers went through several visual alterations depending on when they were built and modified, the appearance of an individual locomotive at any particular time was dependent on which boiler it had. We hope, therefore, that this will assist modellers and artists to decide the appropriate style of boiler for their chosen engine at a particular date.

The first three boilers built were numbered 6048–6050. The main production batch was 9100–9109 and the spare for the reciprocating engines was 9235. The 40-element boiler made for No. 6202 was 9236. Their heating surfaces varied during their lives, not just because of design factors and alterations to superheater details, but also when sizes and thicknesses of tubes and flues were changed, the following being representative figures:

Boilers 6048 and 6049: As built with 170 tubes @ 2¼ in and 16-element, 11 swg superheaters – firebox 190 sq ft, tubes 2,523 sq ft, superheater 370 sq ft. When two tubes removed in 1934, tube heating surface reduced to 2,499 sq ft. When rebuilt in 1935/6 with 119 tubes @ 2⅜ in and 32-element, 11 swg superheaters, tube heating surface reduced to 2,425 sq ft and superheater increased to 623 sq ft. Superheater Co. elements reduced heating surface to 598 sq ft from 1946 and BR 9 swg elements further reduced it to 586 sq ft from 1952.

Boiler 6050: As built with 110 tubes @ 2¼ in and 32-element, 11 swg superheater – firebox 190 sq ft, tubes 2,240 sq ft, superheater 623 sq ft. Number of tubes increased to 112 and diameter to 2⅜ in increased tube surface to 2,310 sq ft in 1940. Superheater Co. elements reduced heating surface to 598 sq ft from 1946 and 9 swg BR elements further reduced it to 586 sq ft from 1952.

Boiler 9100: As built with combustion chamber, 112 tubes @ 2¼ in and 32-element, 13 swg superheater – firebox 217 sq ft, tubes 2,097 sq ft, superheater 653 sq ft. Enlargement of tubes to 2⅜ in diameter in 1939 increased tube heating surface to 2,167 sq ft. Thickness of elements to 11 swg decreased superheater surface to 623 sq ft in 1935, Superheater Co. elements reduced it to 598 sq ft from 1946 and 9 swg BR elements further reduced it to 586 sq ft from 1952.

Boiler 9105: As built with combustion chamber, 112 tubes @ 2¼ in and 32-element, 11 swg superheater – firebox 217 sq ft, tubes 2,097 sq ft, superheater 623 sq ft. Enlargement of tubes to 2⅜ in diameter in 1937 increased tube heating surface to 2,167 sq ft. Superheater Co. elements reduced superheater surface to 598 sq ft from 1946 and 9 swg BR elements further reduced it to 586 sq ft from 1952.

Boilers 9106–9109 and 9235: As built with combustion chambers, 112 tubes @ 2¼ in and 32-element, 11 swg superheater – firebox 217 sq ft, tubes 2,097 sq ft, superheater 623 sq ft. Enlargement of tubes to 2⅜ in diameter from 1938 increased tube heating surface to 2,167 sq ft and increase to 123 tubes @ 2⅜ in brought it to 2,299 sq ft from 1944. Superheater Co. elements reduced superheater surface to 598 sq ft from 1946 and 9 swg BR elements further reduced it to 586 sq ft from 1952.

Boilers 9101–9104: As built with combustion chambers, 141 tubes @ 2¼ in and 24 element, 11 swg superheater – firebox 217 sq ft, tubes 2,218 sq ft and superheater 467 sq ft. Enlargement of tubes to 2⅜ in increased tube surface to 2,307 sq ft from 1937. Alteration to 123 tubes @ 2⅜ in and 32 element Superheater Co. elements from 1943–1951 gave 2,299 sq ft tube area and 598 sq ft superheater. BR 9 swg elements reduced superheater surface to 586 sq ft from 1952.

Boiler 9236: As built with combustion chamber, 81 tubes @ 2¼ in and 40-element, 11 swg superheater – firebox 217 sq ft, tubes 1,951 sq ft, superheater 577 sq ft. Trifurcated elements fitted in 1938 raised superheater surface to 832 sq ft. Alteration to Superheater Co. elements in 1946 reduced it to 540 sq ft. Rebuilding in 1952 with 101 tubes @ 2⅜ in and 9 swg trifurcated elements gave tube surface of 2,232 sq ft and superheater surface of 720 sq ft.

The only boiler to be fitted with a dome from new was No. 9236. The others were modified with domes and new regulators as follows:

6048 – October 1935
6049 – June 1936
6050 – November 1952
9100 – December 1952
9101 – June 1955
9102 – December 1955
9103 – March 1953
9104 – February 1956
9105 – January 1952
9106 – December 1956
9107 – December 1952
9108 – December 1955
9109 – January 1955
9235 – September 1952

Boilers 6048, 6049 and 6050 had the water pipes to the top feeds outside the clothing. Based purely on photographic evidence compared with rebuilding dates, 6049 had its feed pipes moved inside the clothing prior to being fitted to locomotive 46208 in September 1950. The others were altered in 1952 prior to 6048 being fitted to 46204 in June and 6050 being fitted to 46208 in December.

The following table gives details of the boilers fitted to individual locomotives and the resulting visual characteristics. The first date in column 2, annotated B, is the date an engine first entered traffic. The last date in column 3, annotated W, is the end date of the week in which it was withdrawn. Note that the date a boiler was officially fitted to a locomotive was usually towards the end of its time in the works for repair. The last date on which it was in traffic with its old boiler was often several weeks earlier and it may not have re-entered traffic until some time later. We have tried to indicate this by putting the date the engine entered the works in column 3 and the date it re-entered traffic in column 2. Similarly, there are gaps between the dates in column 4, indicating the time spent in the works. Thus, our dates will probably disagree with previously published data.

Engine	From	To	Boiler(s) fitted	Visual characteristics
6200	B 27 Jun 33	30 Apr 37	6048 to 9 Mar 35, 6050 from 9 May 35	No combustion chamber, domeless
	10 Jun 37	21 Apr 42	6049 to 8 Aug 39, 6048 from 9 Sep 39	No combustion chamber, dome
	23 Jun 42	19 Oct 44	6050	No combustion chamber, domeless
	17 Nov 44	21 Jul 47	6048	No combustion chamber, dome
	16 Sep 47	12 Jul 48	6050	No combustion chamber, domeless
	14 Aug 48	21 Nov 51	6048	No combustion chamber, dome
	7 Apr 52	25 Sep 56	9106	Combustion chamber, domeless
	8 Nov 56	17 Nov 62 W	9103 to 14 Dec 59, then 9107 from 30 Jan 60	Combustion chamber, dome

Note – up to November 1951, top feed pipes were outside the clothing

Engine	From	To	Boiler(s) fitted	Visual characteristics
6201	B 3 Nov 33	10 Oct 35	6049	No combustion chamber, domeless
	3 Dec 35	4 Sep 37	6048	No combustion chamber, dome
	29 Oct 37	7 Feb 40	6050	No combustion chamber, domeless
	19 Mar 40	31 Oct 45	6049 to 5 Sep 42, then 6048 from 3 Oct 42 to 13 Jun 44 and 6049 from 28 Jul 44	No combustion chamber, dome
	8 Dec 45	27 Jun 46	6050	No combustion chamber, domeless
	7 Aug 46	23 Oct 48	6049	No combustion chamber, dome
	16 Dec 48	15 Dec 51	6050	No combustion chamber, domeless
	26 Apr 52	16 Jul 54	9109	Combustion chamber, domeless
	17 Sep 54	20 Oct 62 W	9103 to 28 Mar 56, 9235 from 19 May 56 to 18 Feb 60 and 9101 from 4 Jun 60	Combustion chamber, dome

Note – up to December 1951, top feed pipes were outside the clothing

Engine	From	To	Boiler(s) fitted	Visual characteristics
6203	B 1 Jul 35	19 Aug 55	9101 to 30 Nov 36, 9100 from 19 Jan 37 to 28 Oct 38, 9101 from 10 Jan 39 to 15 Nov 41, 9106 from 20 Dec 41 to 11 Jun 44, 9102 from 26 Jul 44 to 18 Sep 47, 9106 from 8 Dec 47 to 17 Apr 51, then 9108 from 13 Nov 51	Combustion chamber, domeless
	19 Oct 55	20 Oct 62 W	9101 to 13 Jun 58, then 9100 from 14 Aug 58	Combustion chamber, dome
6204	B 19 Jul 35	15 Apr 50	9102 to 28 Sep 37, 9105 from 15 Nov 37 to 2 Sep 40, 9109 from 9 Oct 40 to 13 May 44, 9103 from 10 June 44 to 5 Sep 46 and 9108 from 11 Oct 46	Combustion chamber, domeless
	13 Sep 50	28 Feb 52	9236	Combustion chamber, dome
	26 Jun 52	7 Oct 61 W	6048 to 20 May 55, then 6049 from 7 Jul 55	No combustion chamber, dome
6205	B 24 Jul 35	6 May 52	9103 to 1 Jan 41, 9108 from 14 Feb 41 to 3 Oct 42, 9104 from 25 Nov 42 to 24 Jan 45, 9109 from 17 Feb 45 to 24 Sep 48 and 9235 from 5 Nov 48	Combustion chamber, domeless
	9 Sep 52	25 Nov 61 W	9105 to 9 Nov 55, 9107 from 4 Feb 56 to 14 Aug 58 and 9109 from 2 Oct 58	Combustion chamber, dome
6206	B 1 Aug 35	11 Feb 55	9104 to 22 Jun 37, 9235 from 29 Jul 37 to 20 Jun 39, 9100 from 29 Jul 39 to 15 Oct 42, 9108 from 9 Jan 43 to 5 Aug 43, 9235 from 2 Sep 43 to 6 Jul 45, 9104 from 7 Aug 45 to 11 Dec 47, 9102 from 4 Mar 48 to 28 Sep 50, then 9101 from 24 Nov 50	Combustion chamber, domeless
	2 Apr 55	3 Nov 62 W	9100 to 21 Jan 58, then 9105 from 7 Mar 58	Combustion chamber, dome

Engine	From	To	Boiler(s) fitted	Visual characteristics
6207	B 9 Aug 35	26 Oct 55	9105 to 23 Aug 37, 9104 from 6 Oct 37 to 1 Jan 40, 9102 from 3 Feb 40 to 19 Nov 41, 9101 from 24 Jan 42 to 6 Nov 43, 9108 from 31 Dec 43 to 17 May 46, 9100 from 17 Jun 46 to 24 Nov 48, 9105 from 10 May 49 to 23 Sep 51, then 9102 from 22 Dec 51	Combustion chamber, domeless
	9 Dec 55	25 Nov 61 W	9109 to 8 Mar 58, then 9106 from 9 May 58	Combustion chamber, dome
6208	B 16 Aug 35	31 Mar 50	9106 to 18 Mar 38, 9109 from 2 May 38 to 28 Mar 40, 9104 from 3 May 40 to 10 Sep 42, 9107 from 3 Oct 42 to 12 Jul 45, 9235 from 13 Oct 45 to 17 Mar 48 and 9104 from 18 May 48	Combustion chamber, domeless
	22 Sep 50	20 Feb 57	6049 to 23 Jul 52 and 6050 from 6 Nov 52	No combustion chamber, dome
	3 Apr 57	20 Oct 62 W	9104 to 12 Nov 59, then 9236 from 13 Jan 60	Combustion chamber, dome
6209	B 23 Aug 35	28 Nov 55	9107 to 11 Feb 37, 9101 from 2 Mar 37 to 15 Oct 38, 9106 from 21 Nov 38 to 21 Jul 41, 9103 from 16 Aug 41 to 27 Sep 43, 9105 from 4 Dec 43 to 1 Oct 45, 9107 from 21 Dec 45 to 16 Oct 48, 9109 from 18 Jan 49 to 15 Aug 51, 9104 from 8 Oct 51	Combustion chamber, domeless
	18 Feb 56	29 Sep 62 W	9108 to 8 Oct 58, then 9102 from 10 Dec 58	Combustion chamber, dome
6210	B 6 Sep 35	4 Sep 43	9108 to 7 Nov 40, then 9105 from 14 Dec 40	Combustion chamber, domeless
	21 Oct 43	15 Aug 44	9236	Combustion chamber, dome
	9 Sep 44	29 Dec 52	9106 to 4 Jul 47, 9101 from 28 Aug 47 to 27 Mar 50, then 9103 from 26 May 50	Combustion chamber, domeless
	7 Mar 53	3 Nov 55	9107	Combustion chamber, dome
	6 Jan 56	7 Oct 61 W	6048 to 13 Feb 58, then 6050 from 29 Mar 58	No combustion chamber, dome
6211	B 18 Sep 35	13 Oct 52	9109 to 14 Feb 38, 9102 from 24 Feb 38 to 6 Nov 39, 9107 from 23 Dec 39 to 20 Jul 42, 9102 from 11 Aug 42 to 19 Apr 44, 9101 from 18 May 44 to 12 Dec 46, 9103 from 18 Feb 47 to 25 Apr 49, then 9100 from 16 Jun 49	Combustion chamber, domeless
	24 Dec 52	5 Jul 58	9235 to 20 Dec 55, then 9102 from 20 Mar 56	Combustion chamber, dome
	12 Sep 58	7 Oct 61 W	6048	No combustion chamber, dome
6212	B 21 Oct 35	25 Sep 52	9235 to 24 May 37, 9107 from 3 Jul 37 to 24 Jul 39, 9235 from 30 Aug 39 to 4 Jun 43, 9100 from 13 Jul 43 to 18 Oct 45, 9105 from 17 Jan 46 to 8 Nov 48 and 9107 from 20 Apr 49	Combustion chamber, domeless
	26 Nov 52	1 Jan 54	6049	No combustion chamber, dome
	25 Feb 54	7 Oct 61 W	9236 to 1 Sep 58, 9101 from 12 Nov 58 to 12 Nov 59 and 9108 from 19 Jan 60	Combustion chamber, dome

APPENDIX C – BUILDING, REBUILDING, RENUMBERING AND WITHDRAWAL DATES

Building and rebuilding dates are calendar dates the locomotives officially entered or re-entered traffic. Withdrawal dates are week endings. Dates for the fitting of new front frames are conjectural and based on interpretation of the history cards as described in the text.

Engine	Built	New front frames	New inside cylinders	BR No. applied	Stored out of use	Withdrawn
6200	27 Jun 33	7 Apr 52	16 May 53	14 Mar 48	26 Mar – 16 Jun 61, 3 Sep 61 – 19 Jan 62 and 5 – 11 Nov 62	17 Nov 62
6201	3 Nov 33	26 Apr 52	19 Oct 54	7 Aug 48		20 Oct 62
6203	1 Jul 35	17 Mar 52	4 Dec 53	8 May 48	5 Mar – 9 Jul 61, 1 Sep 61–24 Jan 62 and 9 Sep – 15 Oct 62	20 Oct 62
6204	19 Jul 35	26 Jun 52	23 Dec 55	22 May 48	12 May – 7 Jul and 20 Aug – 1 Oct 61	7 Oct 61
6205	24 Jul 35	9 Sep 52	3 Apr 54	22 May 48	23 Mar – 7 Jul and 20 Aug – 1 Oct 61	25 Nov 61
6206	1 Aug 35	4 Aug 53	4 Aug 53	27 May 48	12 Mar – 2 Jul 61, 10 Sep 61 – 21 Jan 62 and 13 Sep – 29 Oct 62	3 Dec 62
6207	9 Aug 35	1 Jan 54	1 Jan 54	5 Jun 48	12 Mar – 6 Jul and 17 Sep – 25 Nov 61	25 Nov 61
6208	16 Aug 35	6 Nov 52	10 Dec 55	22 May 48	5 Mar – 9 Jul 61 and 30 Aug 61 – 22 Jan 62	20 Oct 62
6209	23 Aug 35	19 Jan 56	23 Jan 54	22 Jan 49	11 Sep – 2 Oct 39, 12 Mar – 16 Jun 61, 5 Sep 61 – 25 Jan 62 and 13–24 Sep 62	29 Sep 62
6210	6 Sep 35	7 Mar 53	6 Jan 56	5 Jun 48		7 Oct 61
6211	18 Sep 35	24 Dec 52	20 Mar 56	5 Jun 48	12 Mar – 9 Jul and 21 Aug – 1 Oct 61	7 Oct 61
6212	21 Oct 35	—	1 Jul 54	10 Apr 48	6 Mar – 1 Oct 61	7 Oct 61

APPENDIX D – SHED ALLOCATIONS

Dates are taken from the engine history cards.

Engine   Allocation

6200   30 Sep 33 Camden, 6 Apr 40 Edge Hill – on loan to Camden 21 Mar–16 May 42 and 17 Oct 42–3 Apr 43, 22 May 43 Crewe, 20 May 44 Edge Hill – on loan to Camden 18 Oct 47–17 Jan 48, 13 Mar 48 Crewe N, 11 Dec 48 Edge Hill, 22 Sep 51 Polmadie, 16 May 53 Edge Hill, 28 May 53 Crewe N, 19 Sep 53 Edge Hill, 12 Jun 54 Upperby, 26 Jun 54 Crewe N, 18 Sep 54 Edge Hill, 25 Jun 55 Crewe N, 15 Sep 56 Edge Hill, 22 Jun 57 Crewe N, 21 Sep 57 Edge Hill, 20 Jun 59 Crewe N, 2 Sep 61 Carnforth, 27 Jan 62 Upperby, 7 Apr 62 Kingmoor

6201   4 Nov 33 Camden, 6 Jan 34 Polmadie, 24 Aug 35 Camden, 15 Jul 39 Longsight, 16 Sep 39 Camden, 5 Oct 40 Crewe N, 20 May 44 Edge Hill, 24 Mar 45 Crewe N, 11 Dec 48 Edge Hill, 13 Jun 53 Crewe N, 5 Jul 58 Polmadie, 11 Mar 61 Kingmoor

6203   6 Jul 35 Camden, 24 Aug 35 Polmadie, 29 Feb 36 Camden, 21 Oct 39 Edge Hill 6 Apr 40 Holyhead, 28 Sep 40 Crewe N, 2 Nov 40 Holyhead, 9 Nov 40 Edge Hill, 26 Dec 42 Camden – on loan to Crewe 9 Oct 43–26 Nov 43, 27 Nov 43 Crewe, 20 May 44 Edge Hill, – on loan to Crewe N 18 Oct 47–13 Feb 48, 14 Feb 48 Edge Hill – on loan to Polmadie 22 Sep 51–15 May 55, 23 May 55 Crewe N, 23 Sep 58 Edge Hill, 20 Aug 60 Camden, 10 Sep 60 Edge Hill, 11 Mar 61 Carnforth, 15 Jul 61 Crewe N, 9 Sep 61 Carnforth, 27 Jan 62 Upperby, 7 Apr 62 Kingmoor

6204   20 Jul 35 Camden, 24 Dec 35 Polmadie, 29 Feb 36 Camden, 16 Sep 39 Crewe N, 21 Oct 39 Edge Hill, 6 Apr 40 Holyhead, 9 Nov 40 Edge Hill – on loan to Camden 21 Mar 42 – 16 May 42, and 17 Oct 42–21 May 43, 22 May 43 Crewe N, 20 Mar 44 Edge Hill, 24 Mar 45 Crewe N, 11 Dec 48 Edge Hill, 28 May 49 Crewe N, 1 Oct 49 Edge Hill, 10 Jun 50 Crewe N, 30 Sep 50 Edge Hill, 22 Jun 57 Crewe N, 21 Sep 57 Edge Hill, 14 Oct 58 Crewe N, 5 Jul 58 Edge Hill

6205   27 Jul 35 Camden, 3 Aug 35 Polmadie, 28 Sep 35 Camden, 21 Oct 39 Edge Hill – on loan to Polmadie 9 Dec 39–20 May 44 and to Upperby 12 Jul 47–17 Oct 47 and to Crewe N 18 Oct 47–21 Feb 48, 11 Dec 48 Crewe N, 1 Oct 49 Edge Hill, 7 Jul 51 Crewe N, 13 Sep 51 Edge Hill, 10 Nov 51 Crewe N, 20 Sep 52 Edge Hill, 22 Jun 57 Crewe N, 11 Mar 61 Willesden, 15 Jul 61 Camden, 9 Sep 61 Willesden

6206   10 Aug 35 Crewe N, 24 Aug 35 Camden, 15 Jul 39 Longsight, 2 Dec 39 Edge Hill, 6 Apr 40 Camden, 2 May 42 Crewe, 22 May 49 Camden, 16 Oct 43 Crewe N – on loan to Camden 23 Jun 51–21 Jul 51, 22 Sep 54 Edge Hill, 23 Oct 54 Crewe N, 11 Mar 61 Rugby, 8 Jul 61 Crewe N, 9 Sep 61 Rugby, 27 Jan 62 Camden

6207   10 Aug 35 Crewe, 31 Aug 35 Camden, 6 Aug 38 Crewe, 27 Aug 38 Camden, 16 Sep 39 Rugby, 21 Oct 39 Longsight, 21 Dec 39 Camden, 1 Jun 40 Edge Hill, 10 Aug 40 Crewe N, 22 Sep 51 Edge Hill – on loan to Old Oak Common 14–25 Feb 56, 3 Oct 59 Camden, 11 Mar 61 Willesden, 15 Jul 61 Camden, 9 Sep 61 Willesden

6208   17 Aug 35 Crewe, 31 Aug 35 Camden – on loan to Crewe 16 Jul 38 – 16 Aug 38, 21 Oct 39 Longsight, 2 Dec 39 Camden, 8 Jun 40 Edge Hill, 10 Aug 40 Crewe N, 22 Sep 51 Edge Hill

6209   24 Aug 35 Crewe, 7 Sep 35 Camden, 12 Feb 38 Crewe, 16 Sep 39 Longsight, 2 Dec 39 Camden, 2 May 42 Crewe N, 6 Sep 58 Edge Hill, 20 Jun 59 Crewe N, 13 Aug 60 Upperby, 3 Sep 60 Crewe N, 27 Jan 62 Camden

6210   9 Nov 35 Camden, 22 May 43 Crewe – on loan to Old Oak Common 14–18 Feb 56, 15 Sep 56 Edge Hill, 5 Jul 58 Polmadie, 11 Mar 61 Kingmoor

6211   9 Nov 35 Camden – on loan to Crewe 22 Jan – 26 Feb 38, 22 May 43 Crewe N, 1 Oct 55 Edge Hill, 9 Jun 56 Crewe N, 16 Jun 56 Edge Hill, 7 Jul 56 Crewe N, 29 Nov 58 Edge Hill, 7 Nov 59 Crewe N, 21 Nov 59 Edge Hill, 11 Mar 61 Carnforth, 15 Jul 61 Crewe N,

6212   22 Oct 35 Crewe, 26 Oct 35 Camden, 16 Sep 39 Crewe, 21 Oct 39 Camden, 22 May 43 Crewe, 28 Jan 56 Edge Hill, 10 Mar 56 Crewe N

APPENDIX E — PRESS RELEASE FOLLOWING RECORD-BREAKING RUNS

LONDON MIDLAND AND SCOTTISH RAILWAY

A WORLD'S RECORD ON THE L.M.S.
802¾ MILES AT 69 M.P.H.AVERAGE
HIGH-SPEED TEST RUNS BETWEEN
LONDON AND GLASGOW

A world's record for sustained high speed performance over long distances with steam traction was achieved by the London Midland and Scottish Railway in the course of experimental high-speed test journeys of a special train from London (Euston) to Glasgow (Central) and back on Monday and Tuesday, November 16th and 17th.

During these trials, which were carried out to determine the potentialities of developing high-speed long-distance express services when using standard locomotive and coaching-stock equipment, a total distance of 802.8 miles was covered, with an average load of 240 tons tare, at a mean average speed of 69 m.p.h. Apart from the world's record so involved, and the hitherto unprecedented standards of performance set up over the famous West Coast Route to Scotland, the L.M.S. are confident that extremely valuable technical data has been secured.

For the purpose of the trials an experimental schedule of six hours was laid down for the 401.4 miles from Euston to Glasgow and vice-versa, non-stop in each direction and involving a booked average speed of 66.87 m.p.h. In actual performance, notwithstanding the severe character of the gradients between Carnforth and Glasgow, and the fact that a total of some 50 speed restrictions were imposed in each direction, the test train considerably improved upon this experimental schedule.

On the Down run on Monday, November 16th, the train reached Glasgow 6½ minutes ahead of time in 353

- 2 -

minutes 38 seconds for the 401.4 miles (68.1 m.p.h.), while on the return journey the following day, despite the addition of an extra coach (making the tare tonnage 255 instead of 225) and unfavourable weather conditions, the overall time from Glasgow (Central) to Euston was 344 minutes 15 seconds. Thus on the return journey the experimental schedule was improved upon by nearly 16 minutes and the previous day's performance by over 9 minutes, the overall average speed being 70 m.p.h. Bearing in mind the nature of the route north of Carnforth, these standards of performance are claimed to be unprecedented with steam traction.

THE LOCOMOTIVE.

The locomotive employed throughout the test was No.6201 "Princess Elizabeth", a standard 4-6-2 (Class 7) engine built at Crewe Works in 1933 to the designs of Mr. W.A.Stanier, Chief Mechanical Engineer. Except for the addition of a speed-recorder no special fittings were made to the engine for the tests; Grimesthorpe coal was burned throughout. This type of engine, which has a working steam pressure of 250 lbs per sq. in., is designed to be driven with a fully-opened regulator in conjunction with an early cut-off; at no stage on the trial runs did the steam pressure fall below 220 lbs., and was repeatedly at blowing-off point. The maximum cut-off used in the ascent of the Shap incline was 37 per cent going north, and 35 per cent coming south; otherwise the locomotive was worked on an average cut-off of 15-18 per cent.

The engine crew comprised Driver T.J.Clarke and Fireman C.Fleet, of Crewe, with Passed Fireman A.Shaw, also of Crewe, as reserve engineman on the footplate. They were

- 3 -

accompanied by Mr. R.A.Riddles, Principal Assistant to the Chief Mechanical Engineer, who rode on the engine throughout.

The coal consumption in the Down direction was 46.8 lbs per mile, and on the return trip 44.8 lbs per mile.

THE TRAIN.

The coaching-stock used was of the latest standard L.M.S. design, the train being marshalled from the engine in the following order: Dynamometer Car, Composite Brake, Corridor First, Vestibule First, Kitchen Car, Vestibule Third, Third Brake; for the return journey, an additional Vestibule Third was added next to the Dynamometer Car, raising the load from 225 to 255 tare tons.

Accompanying the train were Messrs. E.J.H.Lemon and W.V.Wood (Vice-Presidents), W.K.Wallace (Chief Civil Engineer), S.J.Symes (Chief Stores Supt. and Acting Chief Mechanical Engineer), S.H.Fisher (Assistant Chief Operating Manager), D.C.Urie (Supt. of Motive Power), J.Purves (Carriage & Wagon Assistant to C.M.E.) and other officials.

Since the object of the experimental runs was to investigate the possibility of high average speeds rather than high maximum speeds, the schedule incorporated a general restriction of speed to 90 m.p.h. although in one or two short stretches this was slightly exceeded. Owing to the very high average speeds, it was considered desirable to impose additional speed restrictions of between 60 and 75 m.p.h. at a number of points where speed is not normally restricted. These special restrictions, in addition to the normal service slacks for junctions and curves, and temporary slacks for engineering operations, bridge reconstructions, colliery subsidences, etc., brought the total number of speed restrictions applied up to approximately 50 in each direction.

- 4 -

It is interesting to note that the average booked speed of 66.87 m.p.h. for the non-stop test journeys compares with an overall average (including stops) of 51.8 m.p.h. by the Down Royal Scot, and of 54.1 m.p.h. by the Up Royal Scot; the fastest regular journey time at present in force in either direction between London and Glasgow is at present 7 hours 25 minutes, compared with the 6 hours schedule of the experimental journeys.

As will be seen from the detailed particulars of the running, the outstanding features of the performance of the test train were, firstly, the high average speed and the exceptionally high speeds on the rising gradients, in conjunction with relatively low downhill maxima, and, secondly, the extremely rapid acceleration from the various speed restrictions.

THE DOWN JOURNEY.

Favourable weather prevailed for the northbound journey of the test train on Monday, November 16th. After being severely slowed by two permanent way restrictions between Willesden Junction and Wembley, the train accelerated with such rapidity that it breasted the 7¼ miles rising at 1 in 339 from Wembley to Hatch End at 73.5 m.p.h. The 14.3 miles ascent from Watford to Tring, culminating in 7 miles at 1 in 335, yielded no greater fall in speed than from 80.4 m.p.h. to 77 m.p.h.; on the corresponding descent to Leighton Buzzard speed was sustained for a mile at 95.7 m.p.h. before being reduced by brakes. Bletchley, 46.7 miles from the start, was thus passed in 40¼ minutes, and Roade (59.9 miles) in slightly under 51 minutes, with a minimum speed of 77.6 m.p.h. on the 7 miles rise, mostly at 1 in 330, to this point. The climb from Weedon to the south end of the Kilsby Tunnel also yielded a similar

- 5 -

minimum, and Rugby (82½ miles) was passed in 68 minutes 33 seconds. The ensuing 75.5 miles from passing Rugby to passing Crewe (at greatly reduced speed in both cases, with two severe and several minor intermediate restrictions of speed) occupied 64 minutes 19 seconds only, with maxima of 90 m.p.h. before Nuneaton, 90 near Armitage, and 93.7 before slowing for Crewe. The 158.1 miles from Euston to passing Crewe were covered in 132 minutes 52 seconds, at an average speed of 71.4 m.p.h. On the favourable gradients between Crewe and Weaver Junction 95 m.p.h. was again reached, but between Weaver Junction and Preston the running was necessarily somewhat restrained in view of the number of speed restrictions; the chief feature of note on this section was a minimum speed of 54 m.p.h. on the climb of nearly two miles at 1 in 104 from Wigan (passed at 50 m.p.h.) to Boar's Head.

Preston, 209 miles from Euston, was passed at 20 m.p.h. in 179¼ minutes from the start, and over the generally level stretch from Oxheys to Lancaster the engine ran with such freedom as to average 83 m.p.h. for 12 miles over practically level track.

HIGH SPEED UP SHAP.

Carnforth, 236.3 miles from the start, was passed in 201¼ minutes (3½ minutes ahead of schedule), and the famous Shap ascent now began in earnest. Over this section of 31.4 miles from Carnforth to Shap Summit the line rises practically from sea level to an altitude of 916 ft., the almost continuous ascent (broken by five miles of falling or level track from Grayrigg to Tebay) culminating in the 5½ miles of the Shap "bank" itself, four miles of which are rising at 1 in 75. Touching 85½ m.p.h. through Burton & Holme, the train passed Oxenholme at 68 m.p.h. (reduced to 60 through the station) and did not fall below 65 m.p.h. on

- 6 -

the steepest part of the next five miles, starting at 1 in 104, continuing at 1 in 124 and 1 in 131 and finishing at 1 in 106, to Grayrigg. Approaching Tebay at a maximum of 78.5 m.p.h., the train then ascended the final 5.5 miles to Shap Summit in 5 minutes 7 seconds (63.5 m.p.h. average), with a minimum speed of 57.5 m.p.h. at the Summit.

The 31.4 miles Carnforth to Shap Summit were thus covered in 26 minutes 44 seconds, at an average speed of 70.5 m.p.h., the times and speeds being undoubtedly a record for this famous ascent.

On the descent from Shap Summit into Carlisle there was a momentary maximum of 88 m.p.h., but speed was repeatedly reduced by brake applications over the numerous curves. Carlisle, 299.1 miles from Euston, was passed in 255 minutes 24 seconds (4½ minutes before time), the average speed to this point being 70.3 m.p.h.

ASCENT OF BEATTOCK.

Further remarkable climbing was achieved in the ascent of Beattock Summit, 1,014 ft. above sea level. In the initial easy stretch from Carlisle to Floriston, 6 miles, there was an acceleration from 20 to 85½ m.p.h., and, after slacking through Gretna Junction, there was a further acceleration to 70 m.p.h. up 7 miles rising at 1 in 200 to Cove Quarry, with a minimum of 75 m.p.h. on the four miles climb at the same gradient to Castlemilk Siding. On through Lockerbie the gradients are mainly in favour of the engine, the 17 miles from Castlemilk to Beattock being run in 12 minutes 20 seconds with a maximum of 90 m.p.h.

This fast running enabled a good impetus to be obtained for the 10 miles of the Beattock Bank proper from Beattock Station to the Summit; this 10 miles, on which the average gradient is 1 in 75, took only 9 minutes 31 seconds, with a minimum of 56 m.p.h. The 49.7 miles from Carlisle to

- 7 -

the Summit were thus run in 41 minutes 42 seconds, at the remarkable average speed of 71.5 m.p.h.

The final 52½ miles from Beattock Summit into Glasgow took 56½ minutes, the running being somewhat hampered by the severe slowing over the Clyde Viaduct in course of reconstruction at Lamington, and the numerous speed restrictions through the colliery area from Law Junction to Glasgow.

The 401.4 miles of the throughout journey were thus completed in 353 minutes 38 seconds, at an average speed of 68.1 m.p.h., the gain on the experimental schedule amounting to 6½ minutes.

THE RETURN JOURNEY.

For the return journey on Tuesday, November 17th, the load was increased to 8 vehicles, 255 tons tare, and as already stated the weather was showery from Glasgow, with squalls of wind and rain on the exposed mountain sections, and heavy rain and strong winds on the final stage of the journey. In view of this bad weather the performance is all the more exceptional.

Owing to permanent way slacks, the initial 28.8 miles from Glasgow to Carstairs required 1½ minutes more than schedule, but this was more than recouped by an astonishingly rapid climb to Beattock Summit, after which the train began steadily to gain time. The 13.5 miles from Lamington to Summit took only 11 minutes 3 seconds, the minimum of 72½ m.p.h. on the 1 in 142-152 ascent from Crawford to Elvanfoot being followed by an acceleration to 80 m.p.h. on the 1½ miles level past Elvanfoot, while the final two miles rising at 1 in 99 to the Summit produced a minimum of 66.5 m.p.h. From Beattock Summit to Gretna, the 41.1 miles were run at an average of 77.5 m.p.h. with a maximum of 89 m.p.h.,

- 8 -

Carlisle (102.3 miles from Glasgow) being passed in 93 minutes 20 seconds at an average of 65.8 m.p.h.

Although the southward ascent of Shap Summit is easier than when coming north, the running in this direction was also extremely fine. From 20 m.p.h. through Carlisle the train accelerated steadily to 65 m.p.h. on 1 in 131-184 to Wreay, to 78 at Calthwaite with a fall to 74 on the mile rising at 1 in 114 beyond, and to 83.3 on the level at Plumpton. The two miles rising at 1 in 186 after Plumpton brought the speed down to 80, rising to 85 before slacking through Penrith and Eamont Junction. Seven miles rising at 1 in 125 past Thrimby Grange yielded a sustained speed of 64 m.p.h., with a final minimum at Shap Summit (after three miles at 1 in 142, 106, 130, with ¾-mile of level intervening) of 66 m.p.h. From Carlisle to Shap Summit the 31.4 miles were run in exactly 28½ minutes, at an average speed of 66.1 m.p.h.

From Shap Summit to Preston, 58.7 miles were run in 47 minutes 5 seconds (average 74.8 m.p.h.) with maxima of 82 before and 88 after Oxenholme, 86.6 before Carnforth, and 87 before Preston; the 50.9 miles from Preston to Crewe occupied 44 minutes 22 seconds (including numerous service slacks), while for a distance of 6 miles, from Winsford Junction to Coppenhall Junction, the average speed was 90 m.p.h. with a maximum of 95. This last feat was one of the most notable of the whole test, since the gradients on this stretch are either dead level or slightly against the engine.

Passing Crewe (243.3 miles) in 213 minutes 17 seconds from the start (average 68.1 m.p.h.), the train covered the 10.5 miles steady ascent to Whitmore, of which three miles rise at 1 in 177, in 9 minutes 36 seconds, the minimum speed on the 1 in 177 being 74 recovering to 77 m.p.h. Averaging 72 m.p.h. over the 75.5 miles from passing Crewe to passing

- 9 -

Rugby, the train passed Rugby, 318.8 miles from the start, in 276 minutes 5 seconds, and was now 13 minutes before time. Across the Trent Valley the maximum speed had been 90 m.p.h. between Lichfield and Tamworth, but a noteworthy effort was the acceleration from 30 m.p.h. over the colliery subsidence at Polesworth to 79 m.p.h. at Atherstone, in 4.2 miles of slightly adverse grades.

From Welton, on the south side of Kilsby Tunnel, the 67.2 miles of generally favourable line to passing Wembley were run in 49 minutes 36 seconds, at an average speed of 81.3 m.p.h., with sustained speeds of 90 m.p.h. near Castle-thorpe and again near Hemel Hempsted; the 15 miles Bletchley to Tring, involving the ascent of the Chiltern Hills with 6 miles rising at 1 in 333, were covered in 11 minutes 3 seconds (average 81.7 m.p.h.) with a minimum of 77.6 m.p.h. at the summit. On this section of the journey weather conditions were extremely bad.

With a permanent way slack at Willesden, the final section of the journey into Euston was run cautiously, and the terminus was reached 16 minutes early in a gross time of 344 minutes 15 seconds from Glasgow - start-to-stop average, 70 m.p.h.

On arrival at Euston the train was met by Sir Josiah Stamp, Chairman of the L.M.S. Railway, Sir Harold Hartley (Vice-President), Mr. C.R.Byrom, Chief Operating Manager and Mr.Ashton Davies, Chief Commercial Manager, who congratulated the train crew on their remarkable dual performance.

LONDON MIDLAND AND SCOTTISH RAILWAY.

Experimental Dynamometer Car Test, LONDON-GLASGOW
Monday, 16th November, 1936.

Train Load (Vehicles) 7   Axles: 28   Tons (Tare) 225

Locomotive, 4-6-2 (Class 7) 6201 "Princess Elizabeth"

Driver T. Clarke
Fireman T.Fleet } Crewe
Passed Fireman A.Shaw
Guard F.W.C.Howes (Euston)

Weather Conditions: Dull from Euston,
Fine from Preston, Dull from Carlisle.

Miles		Booked Time (Mins.)	Actual Time Mins. Secs.	Speeds M.P.H.
0.0	EUSTON	Depart 0	00 00	-
1.0	Mile Post 1 pass	-	2 23	32
3.0	Kilburn "	-	5 05	57
5.4	WILLESDEN "	8	7 24	66
-	2 P.W.Slacks "	-	P.W.S. -	40, 35 *
8.1	Wembley "	-	10 38	-
13.3	Hatch End "	-	15 42	73½
17.4	WATFORD JCT. "	18	18 55	80¼
24.5	Hemel Hempsted "	-	24 20	78½
31.7	TRING "	30	29 55	77 Minimum
36.1	Cheddington "	-	32 56	95.7 Maximum
40.2	Leighton Buzzard "	-	35 49	76 *
46.7	BLETCHLEY "	41	40 32	85-79 *
52.4	Wolverton "	-	44 53	85½-70 *
59.9	ROADE "	51	50 53	79-77½
62.8	Blisworth "	53½	53 02	87-73 *
69.7	Weedon "	-	58 19	82-68 *
75.3	Welton "	-	62 46	77½ Minimum
80.3	Hillmorton "	-	66 25	86½ *
82.6	RUGBY "	70	68 33	35
88.1	Brinklow "	-	74 17	77½-68 *
91.4	Shilton "	-	76 58	76 *

2.

Miles		Booked Time (Mins.)	Actual Time Mins. Secs.	Speeds M.P.H.
97.1	NUNEATON pass	82	81 08	90-83 *
102.3	Atherstone "	-	84 56	86-64 *
106.5	Polesworth "	-	88 22	82 before
-	Colliery Subsidance "	-	P.W.S. -	30 *
110.0	TAMWORTH "	95	92 53	67-85 *
116.3	Lichfield "	100	97 38	82-74 *
124.3	RUGELEY "	106	103 36	90-71 *
127.2	Colwich "	-	105 58	75-62 *
129.5	Milford "	-	107 58	78½ Maximum
133.6	STAFFORD "	114	111 52	30 *
138.9	Norton Bridge "	119	116 50	75-60 *
147.6	Whitmore "	127	123 47	82-60 *
153.3	Botley Road "	-	128 15	93.7 Maximum
156.1	CREWE (Station) "	136	132 52	20 *
160.8	Coppenhall Jct. "	-	136 24	72 *
165.5	Winsford "	-	139 53	88 *
169.9	Hartford "	-	142 44	93.7 *
172.5	Acton Bridge "	-	144 27	90 *
174.3	WEAVER JCT. "	149	146 00	50 *
179.3	Moore "	-	150 30	82-65 *
182.1	WARRINGTON "	156	153 30	45-50 *
185.6	Winwick Jct. "	160	157 03	55 *
187.9	Golborne Jct. "	-	159 27	51 *
191.3	Bamfurlong "	-	162 33	75 *
193.9	WIGAN "	168	164 55	50 *
196.1	Boar's Head "	-	167 23	56½-54 *
197.2	Standish Junction "	171½	168 30	66 *
203.6	Euxton Jct. "	177	173 36	90-60 *
206.7	Farington "	-	176 25	80-61 *
209-0	PRESTON (Station) "	183	179 15	20 *

109

Miles			Booked Time (Mins.)	Actual Time Mins. Secs.	Speeds M.P.H.	
210.3	OXHEYS	pass	185	181 34	50	
213.8	Berton	"	-	184 29	75	
218.5	Garstang	"	191½	188 05	88-85	
225.7	Galgate	"	-	193 08	86½	
230.0	LANCASTER	"	200	196 35	57	*
233.1	Hest Bank	"	-	199 10	82	
236.3	CARNFORTH	"	205	201 28	80-83.3	
238.5	Yealand Box	"	-	203 10	74	
240.8	Burton & Holme	"	-	204 47	85½	
243.6	Milnthorpe	"	-	206 45	83.3	
245.5	Hincaster Junction	"	-	208 18	62	
249.1	OXENHOLME	"	215	211 38	68-60	
252.6	Hay Fell	"	-	214 51	65-66	
254.3	Lambrigg Crossing	"	-	216 22	67-68	
256.2	Grayrigg	"	-	218 04	66	
257.9	Low Gill	"	-	219 34	65	
262.2	TEBAY	"	227	223 05	78½	Maximum
266.0	Mile Post 36	"	-	226 28	61	
267.0	Mile Post 37	"	-	227 29	59	
267.7	SHAP SUMMIT	"	233	228 12	57	
269.7	Shap Station	"	-	229 58	82	
277.0	Clifton & Lowther	"	-	236 12	75-65	
280.1	Eamont Junction	"	-	238 55	79-53	
281.2	PENRITH	"	245	240 05	*	
286.0	Plumpton	"	249	243 45	89	Maximum
288.3	Calthwaite	"	-	245 25	75	
291.7	Southwaite	"	-	247 58	85½	
294.2	Wreay	"	-	250 00	60 * - 81	
299.1	CARLISLE (Citadel)	"	260	255 24	20	
301.1	Kingmoor	"	-	258 15	63½	

Miles			Booked Time (Mins.)	Actual Time Mins. Secs.	Speeds M.P.H.	
305.2	Florieton	pass	-	261 35	85½	
307.7	GRETNA	"	268	263 27	58	*
312.1	Kirkpatrick	"	-	267 39	70½	Minimum
315.8	Kirtlebridge	"	-	270 38	82	
321.8	Castlemilk Siding	"	-	275 15	75	Minimum
324.9	LOCKERBIE	"	282	277 40	80	
327.8	Nethercleugh	"	-	279 50	85½	
330.8	Dinwoodie	"	-	282 00	82	
333.6	Wamphray	"	-	283 58	90	Maximum
338.8	BEATTOCK	"	293	287 35	80	
341.4	Auchencastle	"	-	289 34	68	
344.5	Greskine Siding	"	-	292 30	57½	
346.9	Harthope	"	-	294 59	56-57	
348.8	BEATTOCK SUMMIT	"	306	297 06	56	
354.4	Crawford	"	-	301 40	81	
356.9	Abington	"	-	303 49	65* - 83½	
-	Clyde Viaduct	"	-	P.W.S.	20	
362.3	Lamington	"	-	309 25		
366.0	Symington	"	-	313 15	69	
369.1	Leggatfoot Box	"	-	316 05	66-77½	
372.5	CARSTAIRS	"	328	319 30	35	
375.4	Cleghorn	"	-	322 47	64	
377.6	Braidshill Box	"	-	324 44	75	
383.4	LAW JUNCTION	"	338	329 38	79-40	
-	A.W.S.	"	-	P.W.S.		
388.5	HOLYTOWN	"	344	336 34	30	
391.9	Uddingston	"	-	339 50	68	
				- P.W.S.		
397.4	Rutherglen Jct.	"	-	347 08	20	
400.4	Eglinton Street	"	-	351 06	-	
401.4	GLASGOW CENTRAL	arrive	360	353 38	-	

Booked Average speed, start-to-stop, Euston-Glasgow (C) - 66.87 m.p.h.
Actual " " " " - 68.1 m.p.h.
* indicates speed reduced by brakes to figure shown.

LONDON MIDLAND AND SCOTTISH RAILWAY.

Experimental Dynamometer Car Test, GLASGOW-LONDON

Tuesday, 17th November, 1936.

Train Load (Vehicles) 8   Axles: 32   Tons (Taro): 255

Locomotive 4-6-2 (Class 7) 6201   "Princess Elizabeth"

Driver / Fireman / Guard : As on Down Journey

Weather Conditions: Considerable rain, side winds.

Miles	Station		Booked Time (Mins.)	Actual Time Mins.	Secs.	Speeds m.p.h.
0.0	GLASGOW (Central)	Depart	0	00	00	-
1.0	Eglington Street	pass	-	2	28	-
4.0	Rutherglen Junction	"	-	6	21	62½
6.6	Newton	"	-	9	05	50 M
-	P.W.S.	"	-	- P.W.S. -		25 M
8.4	Uddingston	"	-	11	37	-
9.5	Fallside	"	-	12	58	51-55
12.9	MOTHERWELL	"	16	16	50	M
-	P.W.S.	"	-	- P.W.S. -		-
15.9	Wishaw South	"	-	21	24	43-48½
-	P.W.S.	"	-	- P.W.S. -		40
18.3	LAW JUNCTION	"	22	24	30	48
21.6	Braidwood	"	-	28	10	58½
23.8	Craigenhill Siding	"	-	30	16	64-62½
26.0	Cleghorn	"	-	32	03	83.3
28.8	CARSTAIRS	"	33	34	30	45 M
32.3	Leggatfoot Box	pass	-	38	01	64
35.4	Symington	"	-	40	35	77½-71½
39.1	Lamington	"	-	43	17	86½-65 M
44.5	Abington	"	-	47	49	74
47.0	Crawford	pass	-	49	49	77½-76
49.7	Elvanfoot	"	-	51	57	72½-80
52.6	BEATTOCK SUMMIT	"	57	54	20	66½ Min.

Miles	Station		Booked Time (Mins.)	Actual Time Mins.	Secs.	Speeds m.p.h.
62.6	BEATTOCK	pass	66	62	29	-
67.8	Wamphray	"	-	66	20	88-77½
70.6	Dinwoodie	"	-	68	24	89
73.6	Nethercleugh	"	-	70	33	75 M
76.5	LOCKERBIE	"	77	72	49	77½
79.6	Castlemilk Siding	"	-	75	13	72½
86.6	Kirtlebridge	"	-	79	55	86½-75 M
93.7	GRETNA	"	90	86	10	86½-75 M
98.2	Rockcliffe	"	-	89	26	85-79
100.3	Kingmoor	"	-	90	55	86
102.3	CARLISLE (Citadel)	"	97	93	20	20 M
103.7	Carlisle No.13	"	-	95	31	51
107.2	Wreay	"	-	99	12	65
109.7	Southwaite	"	-	101	18	71½
113.1	Calthwaite	"	-	103	57	78-74
115.4	Plumpton	"	-	105	45	83.3-80
120.2	PENRITH	"	114	109	15	85-75 M
124.4	Clifton & Lowther	"	-	113	00	55
128.5	Thrimby Grange	"	-	117	05	64
131.7	Shap Station	"	-	120	03	67
133.7	SHAP SUMMIT	"	127	121	50	66
139.2	TEBAY	"	132	126	15	82-68 M
143.5	Low Gill	"	-	129	45	76-65 M
152.3	OXENHOLME	"	143	137	18	80-65 M
155.9	Hincaster Junction	"	-	140	15	84-65 M
157.8	Milnthorpe	"	-	141	45	88
162.8	Yealand Box	"	-	145	25	72½
166.1	CARNFORTH	"	153	147	12	86½-65 M
171.4	LANCASTER	"	158	152	07	80-66 M
175.8	Galgate	"	-	155	46	79
182.9	Garstang	"	167	161	00	87-84